Student Solutions Manual

STATISTICS FOR BUSINESS AND ECONOMICS

Student Solutions Manual

STATISTICS FOR BUSINESS AND ECONOMICS

Fifth Edition

Paul Newbold
William L. Carlson
Betty Thorne

Steven C. Huchendorf

Senior Lecturer, Department of Operations Management and Sciences
Carlson School of Management, University of Minnesota

Upper Saddle River, New Jersey 07458

Acquisitions editor: Tom Tucker
Assistant editor: Erika Rusnak
Production editor: Carol Zaino
Manufacturer: Technical Communication Services

ISBN 0-13-067252-1

10 9 8 7 6 5 4

Contents

Chapter 1: Why Study Statistics?

1-2   Web sites that contain government or business data include: www.bea.doc.gov - National Income & Product Accounts – GDP, Consumption, Investment, GDP deflator, etc. www.bls.gov - Bureau of Labor Statistics – employment & unemployment, CPI, productivity. www.federalreserve.gov - Federal Reserve – monetary & banking data. www.conferenceboard.org - consumer confidence measures. www.nber.org - National Bureau of Economic Research – U.S. business cycle data.

1-4   Various answers.

1-6   Variation is encountered in all data. Even in a simple production process of stamping out a piece of sheet metal, the size of the metal will vary slightly from piece to piece. Too much variability and the sheet metal may very well be scrap. Variability can arise due to a variety of sources including people – encountering the same situation can still result in slightly different outcomes.

1-8   Various answers.

Chapter 2: Describing Data

2-2   a. Categorical data. The measurements levels are qualitative - ordinal.
     b. Categorical data. The measurement levels are are qualitative - nominal.
     c. Numerical data. Discrete.

2-4   a. This is yes-no categorical data. The measurement level is based on a nominal scale
     b. This is yes-no categorical data. The measurement level is based on a nominal scale
     c. This is numerical data. The measurement level is by a quantitative measurement = dollars

2-6   Answers will vary. One possibility is to use five classes with width of 10.

     a.   If the first class is 50 less than 60, the following results:

Classes	Frequency
50 < 60	4
60 < 70	7
70 < 80	10
80 < 90	11
90<100	8

     b.   The cumulative frequency distribution is:

Scores	Cumulative Frequency
< 60	4 or 10.00%
< 70	11 or 27.50%
< 80	21 or 52.50%
< 90	32 or 80.00%
<100	40 or100.00%

c.

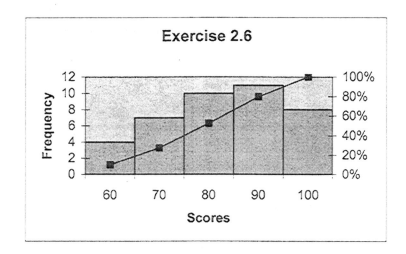

Exercise 2.6

d.

Stem unit: 10

5	4 6 6 9
6	0 2 2 6 7 8 8
7	0 0 3 3 3 5 7 8 9 9
8	1 1 2 3 3 5 6 6 8 9 9
9	0 0 1 3 3 4 5 8

2-8   a.

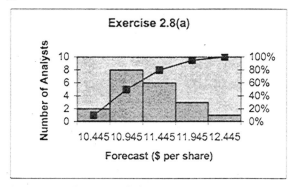

Exercise 2.8(a)

Answer to b., c. and d. are:

	(b) Relative Freq.	(c) Cumulative Freq.	(d) Cumulative %
2	0.1	2	10.00%
8	0.4	10	50.00%
6	0.3	16	80.00%
3	0.15	19	95.00%
1	0.05	20	100.00%

d. See the cumulative relative frequencies in the last column of the table above. These numbers indicate the percent of analysts who forecast that level of earnings per share and all previous classes, up to and including the current class. The third bin of 80% indicates that 80% of the analysts have forecasted up to and including that level of earnings per share.

2-10   a. Pie Chart

Pie Chart of BusinessTrip

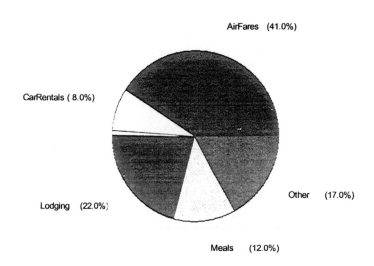

b. Bar Chart

Ex 2-10 U.S. business trip expenditures by category

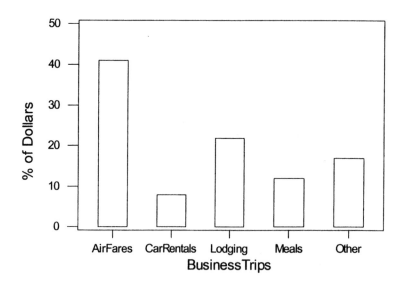

2-12   a. Pie chart

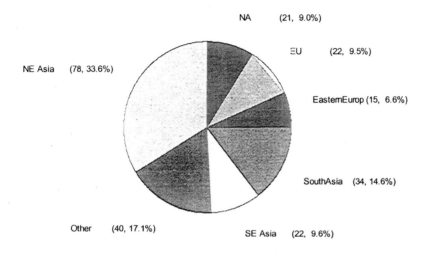

Pie Chart of Workforce

NA   (21, 9.0%)

EU   (22, 9.5%)

NE Asia   (78, 33.6%)

EasternEurop (15, 6.6%)

SouthAsia   (34, 14.6%)

Other   (40, 17.1%)

SE Asia   (22, 9.6%)

b.   Bar chart

Ex 2-12 Global workforce location -1998

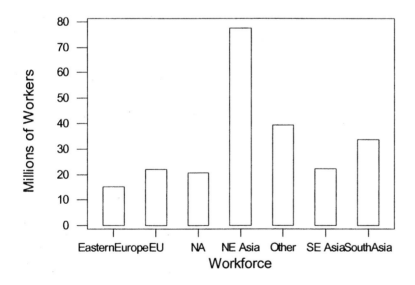

2-14

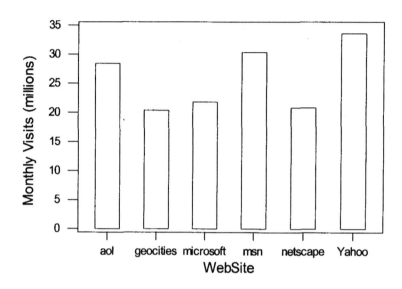

Ex 2-14 Monthly internet visitors - Top six sites - October 1999

2-16   Time series plot – number of first-time freshmen and transfers

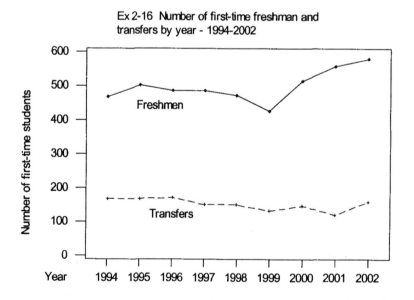

Ex 2-16 Number of first-time freshman and transfers by year - 1994-2002

Enrollment is increasing in 2002, strongest with incoming freshmen. The University may wish to restrict entry if space and capacity conditions warrant smaller classes.

2-18   Tennis errors – Pareto diagram

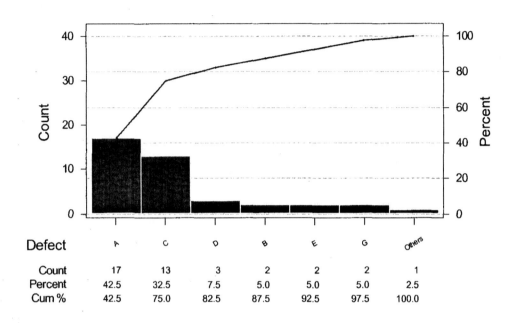

Pareto Chart for ErrorType

Defect	A	C	D	B	E	G	Others
Count	17	13	3	2	2	2	1
Percent	42.5	32.5	7.5	5.0	5.0	5.0	2.5
Cum %	42.5	75.0	82.5	87.5	92.5	97.5	100.0

2-20 Number of complaints per week
   a. Mean = 11.4 complaints per week
   b. Median = 12.00

Minitab Output:

Descriptive Statistics: NumComplaints

Variable	N	Mean	Median	TrMean	StDev	SE Mean
NumCompl	10	11.40	12.00	11.25	5.68	1.80

Variable	Minimum	Maximum	Q1	Q3
NumCompl	3.00	21.00	7.00	15.25

2-22 a. Mean CPI percent growth prediction = 3.35%
   b. Median CPI percent growth prediction = 3.40%

Minitab Output:

Descriptive Statistics: CPI

Variable	N	Mean	Median	TrMean	StDev	SE Mean
CPI	22	3.350	3.400	3.350	0.477	0.102

Variable	Minimum	Maximum	Q1	Q3
CPI	2.500	4.200	2.975	3.725

PHStat Output:

Statistics	
Sample Size	22
Mean	3.35
Median	3.4
Std. Deviation	0.476845
Minimum	2.5
Maximum	4.2

2-24 a. Median % of total compensation from bonus payments = 17.55%
  b. Mean % = 19.91%

Minitab Output:

Descriptive Statistics: Comp%

Variable	N	Mean	Median	TrMean	StDev	SE Mean
Comp%	12	19.91	17.55	19.69	8.44	2.44

Variable	Minimum	Maximum	Q1	Q3
Comp%	7.30	34.70	13.58	27.63

PHStat Output:

Statistics	
Sample Size	12
Mean	19.90833
Median	17.55
Std. Deviation	8.440429
Minimum	7.3
Maximum	34.7

2-26 a. Use the geometric mean to calculate the mean growth rate over the five year
  period: $[(4.3)(6.0)(3.5)(8.2)(7.0)]^{1/5}$ = 5.53248
    b. Number of years to double at this growth rate: Solve the following equation
      for x:
      $(1.0553248)^X = 2.0$. Take the log of both sides of the equation:
      $X \log(1.0553248) = \log (2.0)$. Simplify:
      $X = .301029996/.023386144$
      $X = 12.87$ years

2-28 Minitab Output:

Descriptive Statistics: Water

Variable	N	Mean	Median	TrMean	StDev	SE Mean
Water	75	3.8079	3.7900	3.8054	0.1024	0.0118

Variable	Minimum	Maximum	Q1	Q3
Water	3.5700	4.1100	3.7400	3.8700

PHStat Output:

Statistics	
Sample Size	75
Mean	3.807867
Median	3.79
Std. Deviation	0.102407
Minimum	3.57
Maximum	4.11

a. range = 4.11 – 3.57 = .54, standard deviation = .1024, variance = .010486
b. Five number summary:

Min	Q1	Median	Q3	Max
3.57	3.74	3.79	3.87	4.11

c. IQR = Q3 – Q1 = 3.87 – 3.74 = .13. This tells that the range of the middle 50% of the distribution is .13
d. Coefficient of variation = $s / \bar{X}$ = .1024 / 3.8079 = .02689 or 2.689%
e. Box and whiskers plot – Minitab:

Boxplot of Water

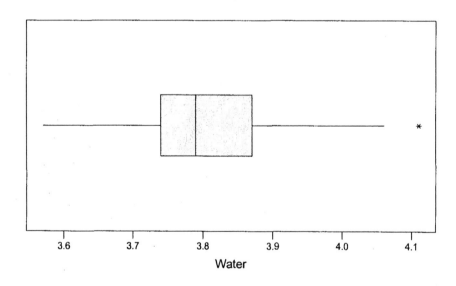

f. The report should include a discussion of all of the measures of location as well as the measures of variability.

2-30   Standard deviation (s) of the assessment rates:

$$ s = \sqrt{\frac{\sum x_i^2 - \frac{\left(\sum x_i\right)^2}{n}}{n-1}} = \sqrt{\frac{32563 - \frac{(1131)^2}{40}}{39}} = 3.86959 $$

2-32   Estimate the sample mean and standard deviation
    a.   Sample mean = 234/25 = 9.36
    b.   Sample variance = $[2692 - 25(9.36)^2]/24 = 20.9067$
       Sample standard deviation = 4.572

Study time				
x	m	f	fm	fm^2
0 < 4	2	3	6	12
4 < 8	6	7	42	252
8 < 12	10	8	80	800
12 < 16	14	5	70	980
16 < 20	18	2	36	648
		25	234	2692

2-34   a. Pie chart of gender percentages

Pie Chart of Internet usage: Males

Do Not Use Internet (58.0%)

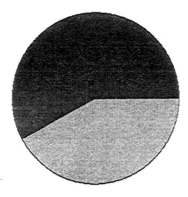

InternetUser (42.0%)

Pie Chart of Internet usage: Females

Do Not Use Internet (65.0%)

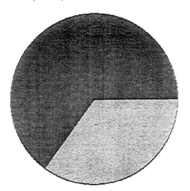

InternetUser (35.0%)

b. Bar chart for Internet Usage by Income Percentages:

Ex 2-34 Internet Usage by Income %

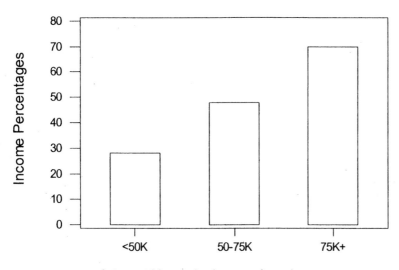

2-36   Tourism by country

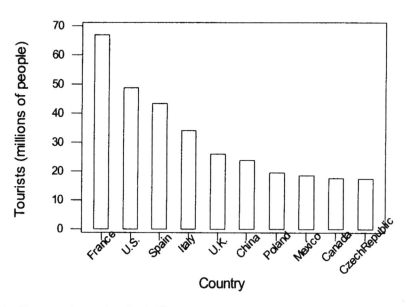

2-38   County Appraiser's Office – Data Entry Process
   a.   Pareto diagram

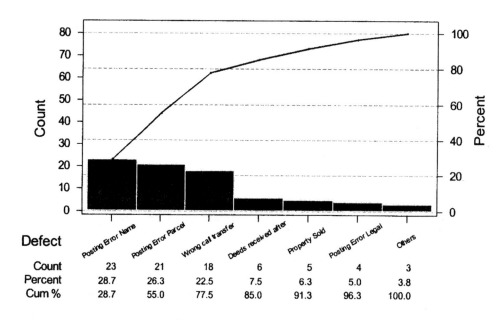

Defect	Posting Error Name	Posting Error Parcel	Wrong cat transfer	Deeds received after	Property Sold	Posting Error Legal	Others
Count	23	21	18	6	5	4	3
Percent	28.7	26.3	22.5	7.5	6.3	5.0	3.8
Cum %	28.7	55.0	77.5	85.0	91.3	96.3	100.0

   b.   Recommendations should include a discussion of the data entry process. The data entry was being made by individuals with no knowledge of the data. Training of the data entry personnel should be a major recommendation. Increasing the size of the monitors used by the data entry staff would also reduce the number of errors.

Chapter 3: Summarizing Descriptive Relationships

3-2   Scatterplot – Bishop's Supermarket

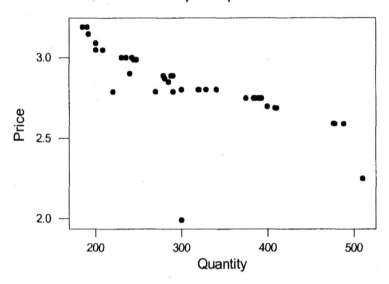

The scatterplot shows the expected negative relationship between price and quantity demanded per unit of time. This is what economic theory suggests for a typical demand curve.

3-4   a. Scatter plot

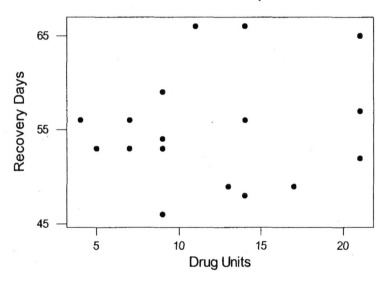

b. Very weak positive association between the two. Because higher dosages of the drug does not appear to reduce the number of recovery days, recommend low or no dosages of the drug.

3-6   a. Cov(X,Y) = 0.00008527
       b. r (X,Y) = 0.147

3-8   a. Cov (X,Y) = 1069.333
       b. r (X,Y) = 0.989
       c. Strong positive association between the number of workers and the number of tables produced per day.

3-10   a. Cov (X,Y) = - 5.5
       b. r (X,Y) = -.776
       c. Higher prices are associated with faster delivery time.

3-12   a. $\hat{Y}$ =53.7 + 0.134 Drug Units
       b. 54.40, 55.71
       c. Because there is a weak positive association between recovery time and drug units; recommend low or no drug unit dosage.

3-14   Due to the differences in product demand by neighborhood, the marketing department should emphasize tools in their advertising campaign in the east residential neighborhood. Paint should be emphasized in the north residential neighborhood and both tools & lumber in the west neighborhood. The column marginal totals indicate that demand for tools will be the highest across all three residential neighborhoods followed by the demand for paint. Lumber will have the lowest total demand for all three residential locations.

3-16   a. scatter plot

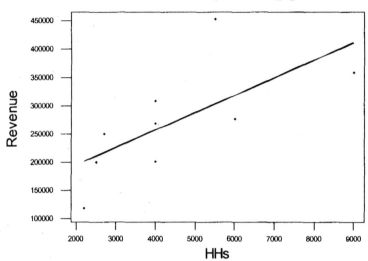

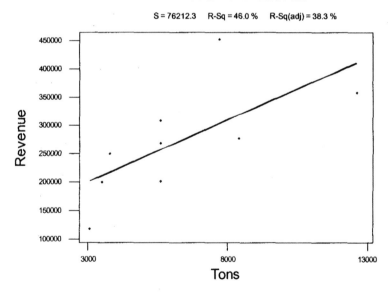

b.   0.678, 0.678
        Revenue = 134517 + 30.7119 households
        Revenue = 134517 + 21.9371 tons
        c. 2,900 households   revenue = $223,582
              12,600 tons   revenue = $410,924
        d. M.R = 21.9 per ton

3-18   His forecast provides direction for investing based on temperature and the correlation
        coefficient is reasonable given the observation.

3-20   a. Quantity = 268.696 – 18.2174 Price
        b. 177.61(5); 141.17(7); 122.96(8)   e = 3.48; -31.17; -2.96
        c. In addition to the general (negative) relationship between price and quantity demanded
        we now have estimated a specific mathematical relationship between the two variables.

3-22   a. scatter plot

Weight training program vs. Batting Average Improvement

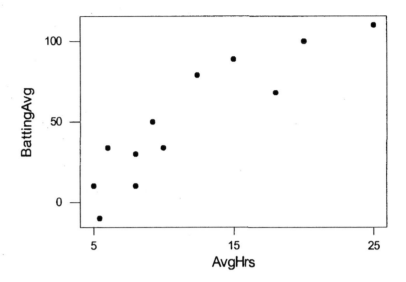

The data shows a positive relationship between the average number of hours spent in the weight training program vs. the increment to their batting average. It appears that the weight training program has been effective.

b. $\hat{Y} = -14.4 + 5.47\ X$. Each additional hour of weight training program yields an expected improvement in batting average of 5.47 points.

3-24   a. scatter plot

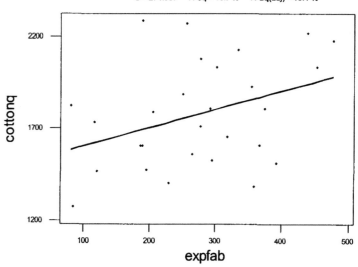

Regression Plot

cottonq = 1506.12 + 0.998643 expfab

S = 274.957   R-Sq = 13.7 %   R-Sq(adj) = 10.4 %

b. $\hat{Y}$ = 1506 + .999 export
     marginal value = 0.999

3-26   a. r (X,Y) = 0.408
        b. pounds of grits = 14851 + 0.0506 production
        c. 0.0506 pounds of grits for each additional pound of cereal produced

3-28   a. scatter plots, and b. regression equations and regression lines are shown below:

Per capita health care expenditures vs. per capita personal income

Helexp82 = -37.6481 + 0.0990188 Perinc84

S = 220.927   R-Sq = 41.2 %   R-Sq(adj) = 40.0 %

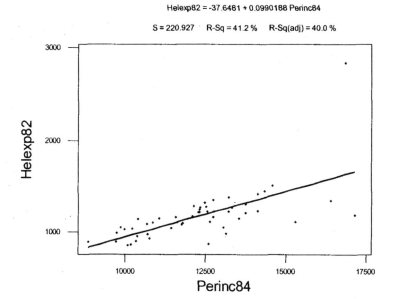

Per capita retail sales vs. per capita personal income

Retsal84 = 2127.13 + 0.277669 Perinc84

S = 635.000   R-Sq = 40.1 %   R-Sq(adj) = 38.8 %

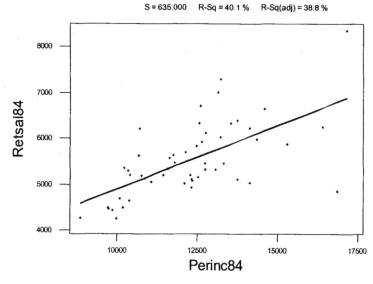

Per capita energy consumption vs. per capita personal income

Peren84 = 92.1544 + 0.0261803 Perinc84

S = 642.830   R-Sq = 0.6 %   R-Sq(adj) = 0.0 %

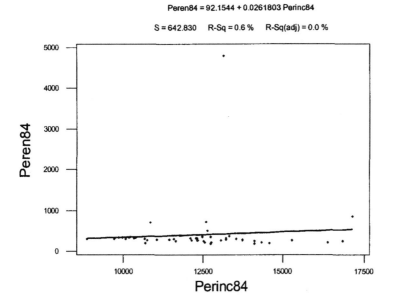

c. The more affluent a state (as measured by per capital personal income), we would expect to observe greater per capita spending on retail sales, health care expenditures and energy consumption.

3-30   a. scatter plot

GDP Growth vs. Defense/GDP (%)

GDP Growth = 5.18314 + 0.0259053 Defense/GDP(

S = 2.49122   R-Sq = 1.9 %   R-Sq(adj) = 0.0 %

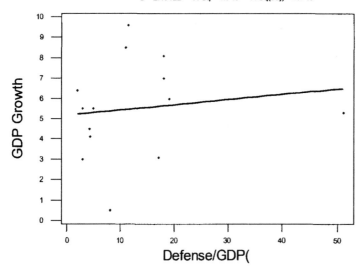

b. $r(X,Y) = 0.137$
c. GDP growth = 5.18 + 0.0259 defense/GDP (%)
d. very little if any effect

e. defense expenditures reduce GDP growth

f. not substantially

3-32   a. and b. scatter plots

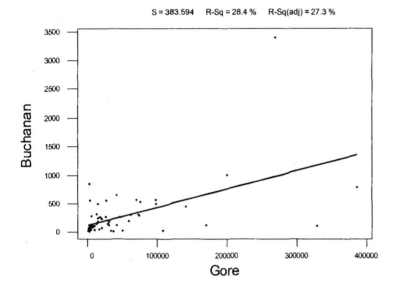

Regression Plot

Buchanan = 121.540 + 0.0032016 Gore

S = 383.594   R-Sq = 28.4 %   R-Sq(adj) = 27.3 %

We would expect that the higher the Gore vote, the lower the total for Buchanan. One county (Palm Beach) represents a much higher than predicted vote total for Buchanan, given the high level of Gore votes.

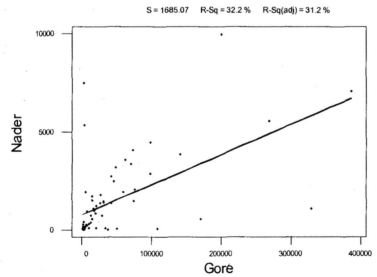

Regression Plot

Nader = 784.595 + 0.0153789 Gore

S = 1685.07   R-Sq = 32.2 %   R-Sq(adj) = 31.2 %

Regression Plot

Buchanan = 120.564 + 0.0032230 Bush

S = 413.711   R-Sq = 16.8 %   R-Sq(adj) = 15.5 %

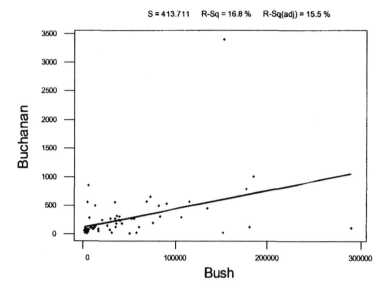

Regression Plot

Nader = 697.274 + 0.0173837 Bush

S = 1784.98   R-Sq = 23.9 %   R-Sq(adj) = 22.8 %

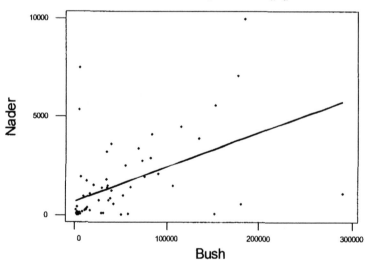

The scatterplots above show several 'outliers' which would indicate that in some counties there were substantially more votes cast for one of the minor candidates than we would predict from the regression equation.

The first scatter plot shows the relation between Gore votes and Buchanan votes. We would expect that counties with higher Gore votes would be associated with lower Buchanan votes. And yet one county (Palm Beach) has a substantially higher vote total for Buchanan than we would predict. Based on the following regression equation:

Buchanan = 121.54 + .0032016 Gore

Then, in Palm Beach county with 268,945 Gore votes, we would estimated (based on the regression equation) that Buchanan votes would be 983 votes. They were actually 3,407 votes, a difference of 2,424 votes. A plausible explanation for the 'outliers' would be voter confusion regarding the ballots.

Chapter 4: Probability

4-2   a. (A∩B) is the event that the Dow-Jones average rises on both days which is O_1.
      ($\overline{A}$∩B) is the event the Dow-Jones average does not rise on the first day but it
      rises on the second day which is O_3. The union between these two will be the
      events O_1 O_3 which by definition is event B: the Dow-Jones average rises on the
      second day.
      b. Since ($\overline{A}$∩B) is the event the Dow-Jones average does not rise on the first day
      but rises on the second day which is O_3 and because A is the event that the Dow-
      Jones average rises on the first day, then the union will be the event that either the
      Dow-Jones average does not rise on the first day but rises on the second day or the
      Dow-Jones average rises on the first day or both. This is the definition of A∪B.

4-4   a. P(A) = P(5 days ∪ 6 days ∪ 7 days) = .41 + .20 + .07 = .68
      b. P(B) = P(3 days ∪ 4 days ∪ 5 days) = .08 + .24 + .41 = .73
      c. P($\overline{A}$) = P(3 days, 4 days) = .08 + .24 = .32
      d. P(A∩B) = P(5 days) = .41
      e. P(A∪B) = P(A) + P(B) - P(A∩B) = .68 + .73 - .41 = 1.0

4-6   a. P(A) = 4/8 = 0.5
      b. P(B) = 2/8 = 0.25
      c. P(A ∩ B) = P(B) = 0.25
      d. P(A ∪ B) = P(A) + P(B) - P(A∩B) = 0.5 + 0.25 – 0.25 = P(A) of 0.5

4-8   a. P(A) = .39 + .23 + .15 + .06 + .03 = .86
      b. P(B) = .14 + .39 + .23 + .15 = .91
      c. P($\overline{A}$) = 1 – P(A) = 1 - .86 = .14
      d. P(A ∪ B) = P(A) + P(B) - P(A∩B) = .86 + .91 - .77 = 1.00
      e. P(A ∩ B) = .39 + .23 + .15 = .77
      f. Check if P(A ∩ B) = 0. Because P(A ∩ B) = .77 ≠ 0, A and B are not
          mutually exclusive
      g. Yes, because P(A ∪ B) = 1, A and B are collectively exhaustive

4-10 The probability of the intersection between two independent events is equal to the
      product of the individual probabilities. Therefore, the probability of both Superior
      Packaging and Intense Media campaign = (1/3)(1/3) = 1/9

4-12 P_2^{50} = 50!/ 48! = 2,450

4-14 If A is the event 'no graduate student is selected', then the number of
      combinations of 3 chosen from 6 is C_3^6 = 6!/ 3!3! = 20 and the number of
      combinations of 0 objects chosen from 2 is C_0^2 = 2!/ 0!2! = 1. P(A) =1/20 =.05

4-16   a. Number of arrangements = 4! = 24

      b. $C_1^4 = 4!/1!3! = 4$. Therefore, the probability of one assignment is ¼

4-18   a. $P_2^7 = 7!/5! = 42$

      b. $P_1^6 = 6!/5! = 6$

      c. $P_1^6 = 6!/5! = 6$

      c. Probability of being chosen as the heroine = 6 chances out of 42 = 1/7. Since there are seven candidates for 1 part – a randomly chosen candidate would have a 1 in 7 chance of getting any specific part.

      d. Since being chosen as the heroine or as the best friend are mutually exclusive, then P(A ∪ B) = P(A) + P(B) - P(A∩B) = 1/7 + 1/7 – 0 = 2/7. Since there are seven candidates for 2 parts – a randomly chosen candidate would have a 2 in 7 chance of getting apart.

4-20   a. $C_2^6 = 6!/2!4! = 15$, $C_2^4 = 4!/2!2! = 6$. Because the selections are independent, there are (15)(6) = 90 diffferent sets of funds from which to choose

      b. P(no U.S. fund under performs) = $C_2^5/15 = 5!/2!3!/15 = 10/15$. P(no foreign fund under performs) = $C_2^3/6 = 3!/1!2!/6 = 3/6$, P(at least one fund under performs) = 1 – P(no fund under performs) = 1-(10/15)(3/6) = 2/3

4-22   Let A – customer asks for assistance, B – customer makes a purchase, A∩B – both. Then P(A ∪ B) = P(A) + P(B) - P(A∩B) = .3 + .2 - .15 = .35

4-24   a. Let A – Immediate donation, B-Information request, C-No interest, D-donate later. Then P(A) = .05, P(B) = .25, P(C)=.7. Then P(4 misses) = $(.95)^4 = .8145$.

      b. P(donation) = P(A) + P(B) = .05 + .25(.2) = .10

           Then P(4 misses) = $(.9)^4 = .6561$

4-26   Let A – graduating with adequate grades, B – passing the standardized test. P(A) = 1-.02 = .98, P(B) = 1-.15 = .85. Probability that the player will be eligible is (.98)(.85) = .833

4-28   Let A – inspector accepts an item, and B – item is defective, then P(A|B) = .08 and P(A∩B) = .01. Find P(B) = P(A∩B) / P(A|B) = .01 / .08 = .125

4-30   Let event A – high risk stock, B – loan in default, then P(A) = .15, P(B) = .05 and P(A|B) =.40. Find P(B|A) = P(A|B)P(B)/P(A) = [(.4)(.05)]/.15 = .1333

4-32   Let A – picking 3 high tech stocks in order, B – picking 3 airline stocks in order out of five. The number of ways of choosing three high tech stocks out of 5 or three airline stocks out of 5 in order is $P_3^5 = 5!/2! = 60$. Then P(A∪B) = 1/60 + 1/60 – 1/3600 = .0331. Therefore, the probability of getting either the high tech stocks or the airline stocks picked correctly is relatively small.

4-34   Let A – Reading class, B—math class, then P(A) = .4, P(B) = .5 and P(B|A) = .3
   a.   P(A∩B) = P(B|A)P(A) = (.3)(.4) = .12
   b.   P(A|B) = P(A ∩ B)/P(B) = .12 / .5 = .06
   c.   P(A∪B) = .4 + .5 - .12 = .78
   d.   Check if P(A∩B) = P(A)P(B). Since .12 ≠ .2 the two events are not independent events

4-36   Given that P(A ∩ B ∩ C) = .02, P(B) = .2 and P(A|B) = .8, then find the probability that P(C|(A ∩ B) = P(A ∩ B ∩ C)/[PA|B)P(B)] = .02/.16 = .125

4-38   Let PH – Predicted High, PN – Predicted Normal, PL – Predicted Low, H-High Outcome, N – Normal Outcome, L – Low Outcome
   a.   P(PH) = .3
   b.   P(H) = .38
   c.   P(PH|H) = P(PH∩H)/P(H) - .23/.38 = .6053
   d.   P(H|PH) = P(PH∩H)/P(PH) = .23/.3 = .7667
   e.   P(L|PH) = P(PH∩L) / P(PH) = .01/.3 = .0333

4-40   Let G—good part, D – defective part
   a.   P(D) = .1
   b.   P(B) = .35
   c.   P(D|B) = P(B ∩ D)/P(B) = .05/.35 = .1429
   d.   P(B|D) = P(B ∩ D)/P(D) = .05/.1 = .5
   e.   No, since P(G∩B) which is .3 ≠ P(G)P(B) which is .315
   f.   P(G|A) = .27/.29 = .931, P(G|B) = .3/.35 =.857 P(G|C) = .33/.36 = .917. Therefore, Subcontractor A is the most reliable

4-42   Let event S-- Stayed, L – Left, M—Married and S—Single
   a.   P(M) = .77
   b.   P(L) = .19
   c.   P(L|S) = P(L∩S)/P(S) = .06/.23 = .2609
   a.   P(M|S) = P(M∩S) / P(S) = .64/.81 = .7901

4-44   Let J – joined, M – Men, W—Women
   a.   P(J) = P(J|M)P(M) + P(J|W)P(W) = (.07)(.4) + (.09)(.6) = .082
   b.   P(W|J) = P(J|W)P(J) = (.09)(.6)/.082 = .6585

4-46   P(HC) = .42, P(WS) = .22, P(WS|HC) = .34
    a. P(HC ∩ WS) = P(WS|HC)P(HC) = (.42)(.34) = .1428
    b.P(HC ∪ WS) = P(HC) + P(WS) – P(HC ∩ WS) = .42 + .22 - .1428 = .4972
    c. P(HC|WS) = P(HC ∩ WS)/P(WS) = .1428 / .22 = .6491

4-48   a. P(H|F) = P(F ∩ H)/P(F) = .173 / .303 = .571
    b. P(L|U) = P(U ∩ L)/P(U) = .141/.272 = .5184
    c. P(L|N ∪ F) = P((N ∪ F) ∩ L) / P(N ∪ F) = .155/.728 = .2129
    d. P(N ∪ F|L) = P((N ∪ F) ∩ L) / P(L) = .155/.296 = .5236

4-50   P(E) = .7, P(B) = .3, P(SE|E) = .6, P(SE|B) = .25, P(SE ∩ E) = P(SE|E)P(E) = .42,
P(SE∩ B) = P(SE|B)P(B) = .075, P(SE) = P(SE∩E) + P(SE∩B) = .495
    a. P(E|SE) = P(SE∩E)/P(SE) = .42/.495 = .8485, P(3E|SE) = [P(E|SE)]3 = .8485^3 = .6109
    b. P(at least 1E|SE) = 1 – P(no E|SE) = 1 – [P(B|SE)]^3 = 1 – [.075/.495]^3 = .9965

4-52 E_1 = Stock performs much better than the market average
E_2 = Stock performs same as the market average, E_3 = Stock performs worse than
the market average, A = Stock is rated a 'Buy'
Given that P(E_1) = .25, P(E_2) = .5, P(E_3) =.25, P(A| E_1)=.4, P(A| E_2)=.2, P(A| E_3)=.1
Then, P(E_1 ∩ A) = P(A| E_1)P(E_1) = (.4)(.25) = .10
    P(E_2 ∩ A) = P(A| E_2)P(E_2) = (.2)(.5) = .40
    P(E_3 ∩ A) = P(A| E_3)P(E_3) = (.1)(.25) = .025

$$P(E_1 | A) = \frac{P(A|E_1)P(E_1)}{P(A|E_1)P(E_1) + P(A|E_2)P(E_2) + P(A|E_3)P(E_3)} =$$

$$= \frac{(.40)(.25)}{(.4)(.25) + (.2)(.5) + (.1)(.25)} = .444$$

4-54   a. True by definition
    b. False, only the sum of the probabilities of mutually exclusive events which are collectively exhaustive sum to 1.
    c. True, $C_x^n = \dfrac{n!}{x!(n-x)!} = C_{n-x}^n = \dfrac{n!}{(n-x)!(n-(n-x)!} = \dfrac{n!}{(n-x)!x!}$
    d. True, $P(A|B) = \dfrac{P(A \cap B)}{P(B)} = \dfrac{P(A \cap B)}{P(A)} = P(B|A)$ for P(A) = P(B)
    e. True, P(A) = 1 – P(A) ➔ 2P(A) = 1 ➔ P(A) = .5
    f. True, $P(\bar{A} \cap \bar{B}) = P(\bar{A}) - P(\bar{A} \cap B)$
$$= 1 - P(A) - [P(B) - P(A \cap B)]$$
$$= 1 - P(A) - P(B) + P(A \cap B)$$
$$= 1 - P(A) - P(B) + P(A)P(B)$$
$$= [1 - P(A)][1 - P(B)] = P(\bar{A})P(\bar{B})$$

g. False, $P(\bar{A} \cap \bar{B}) = P(\overline{A \cup B})$
$$= 1 - P(A \cup B)$$
$$= 1 - P(A) - P(B) \quad [P(A \cap B) = 0]$$
$$= P(\bar{A}) + P(\bar{B}) - 1$$
$$= 0 \text{ which holds if and only if } P(\bar{A}) + P(\bar{B}) = 1$$

4-56   Bayes' theorem is a summary of the relationship between a specific event that has occurred and the effect on a subsequent event. The occurrence of the specific event is the prior information or 'prior probability' that is known. This prior knowledge can be analyzed to understand the effect on the probability of a subsequent event which is the 'posterior probability'.

4-58   *Joint Probability* is the probability that two events will occur together
Marginal probability is defined as the probability of an individual event
Conditional probability is the probability of occurrence of one event given that another event has occurred.

4-60 $P(A \cup B) = P(A) + P(B) - P(A \cap B)$
$$= P(A) + P(B) - [P(A|B)P(B)]$$
$$= P(A) + P(B)[1 - P(A|B)]$$

4-62   Solve the following for P(thick) and P(thin):
$.8 = P(thick) + P(thin)[1 - P(thick/thin)] = P(thick) + .6 P(thin)$
$.8 = P(thin) + P(thick)[1 - P(thin/thick)] = P(thin) + .4 P(thick)$
Solving, P(thin) = .6316
   a. P(thick) = .8 - .6 P(thin) = .8 - (.6)(.6316) = .4211
   b. P(thin) = .6316
   c. P(thick∩thin) = P(thick|thin) P(thin) = (.4)(.6316) = .2526

4-64   Let HM – customer orders a hot meal, S – customer is a student. P(HM) = .35, P(S) = .5, P(HM|S) = .25
   a. P(HM∩S) = P(HM|S)P(S) = (.25)(.5) = .125
   b. P(S|HM) = P(HM∩S)/P(HM) = .125/.35 = .3571
   c. $P(\overline{HM} \cup \bar{S}) = 1 - P(HM \cap S) = 1 - .125 = .875$
   d. No, since P(HM∩S) which is .125 ≠ .175 which is P(HM)P(S)
   e. No, their intersection is not zero, hence the two events cannot be mutually exclusive. P(HM∩S) = .125 ≠ 0
   f. No, the probability of their union does not equal 1. P(HM∪S) = P(HM) + P(S) – P(HM ∩ S) = .35 + .5 - .125 = .725 which is less than 1.

4-66　Let M—men, F – women, G – graduate training, UG—undergraduate training, HS – High School training. P(M)=.8, P(F)=.2, P(HS|M)=.6, P(UG|M)=.3, P(G|M)=.1

   a.　P(M∩HS) = P(HS|M)P(M) = (.6)(.8) = .48

   b.　P(G) = P(M∩G) + P(F∩G) = P(G|M)P(M) + P(G|F)P(F) = (.10)(.8) + (.15)(.2) = .11

   c.　P(M|G) = P(M∩G)/P(G) = .08/.11 = .7273

   d.　No, check if P(M∩G) which is .8 ≠ .088 which is P(M)P(G)

   e.　P(F|$\overline{G}$) = P(F∩ $\overline{G}$)/P($\overline{G}$)=[P(F) – P(F∩ G)]/P($\overline{G}$)=(.2 – (.15)(.2))/.89=.191

4-68　a.　C_{12}^{16} = 16!/ 4!12! = 1,820

   b.　P(number of men ≥ 7) = [$C_5^8 + C_4^8 + C_2^8$ +8]/1820 = 162/1820 = .089

4-70　Let T – treatment , C – patient was cured. P(C) = .5, P(C|T) = .75

   a.　P(C ∩ T) = P(C|T)P(T) = (.75)(.1) = .075

   b.　P(T|C) = P(C∩T)/P(C) = .075/.525 = .1429

   c.　The probability will be 1 / [C_{10}^{100} = 1/ 100!/10!90! = 10!90!/100!

4-72　P(D|P) = P(P∩D)/P(P) = P(P|D)P(D)/[P(P|D)P(D) + P(P|$\overline{D}$)P($\overline{D}$)] = (.8)(.08)/[(.8)(.08) + (.2)(.92)] = .2581

4-74　P(Af|Am) = P(Af∩Am)/P(Am) = P(Am|Af)P(Af)/[P(Am\Af)P(Af) + P(Am|$\overline{A}$ f)P($\overline{A}$ f) = (.7)(.2)/[(.7)(.2) + (.1)(.8)] = .6364

4-76　a.　P(G∩F) = P(G|F)P(F) = (.62)(.73) = .4526

   b.　P(G) = P(G|F)P(F) + P(G|JC)P(JC) = .4526 + (.78)(.27) = .6632

   c.　P(G ∪ F) = P(G) + P(F) – P(G ∩F) = .6632 + .73 - .4526 = .9406

   d.　No, since P(G∩JC) which is (.78)(.27) = .2106 ≠ .1791 which is P(G)P(JC) = (.6632)(.27)

4-78　Let W – customer orders Wine, WD – customer is Well Dressed, MD – customer is Moderately Dressed, PD – customer is Poorly Dressed

   a.　P(W) = P(W|WD)P(WD) + P(W|MD)P(MD) + P(W|PD)P(PD) = (.7)(.5) + (.5)(.4) + (.3)(.1) = .58

   b.　P(WD|W) = P(WD∩W)/P(W) = .35/.58 = .6034

   c.　P($\overline{WD}$ |W) = P(MD∪PD|W) = [P(MD∩W) + P(PD∩W)]/P(W) = (.2 + .03)/.58 = .3966

4-80　The sample space is the number of combinations from C_5^{16} = 16!/ 5!11! = 4,368. To obtain all five F's for women: [C_5^8 = 8!/ 5!3!][C_0^8 = 8!/ 0!8!] = [56][1] = 56 . Probability = 56/4368 = .0128.

4-82   Let F – failure (from any source), D – disk error

$P(F) = (.5)(.6)+(.3)(.7)+(.2)(.4) = .59$

$P(D|F) = \dfrac{P(D \cap F)}{P(F)} = \dfrac{(.5)(.6)}{(.5)(.6)+(.3)(.7)+(.2)(.4)} = \dfrac{.3}{.59} = .5085$

Chapter 5: Discrete Random Variables and Probability Distributions

5-2   Discrete

5-4   Total sales, advertising expenditures, competitor's sales

5-6   a. $P(3 \leq x <) = .20 + .20 + .15 = 0.55$
        b. $P(x > 3) = .20 + .15 + .10 = 0.45$
        c. $P(x \leq 4) = .05 + .10 + .20 + .20 + .20 = 0.75$
        d. $P(2 < x \leq 5) = .20 + .20 + .15 = 0.55$

5-8   a. Probability function:

Probability distribution function

Proportion of new cars returned: Correction of defects

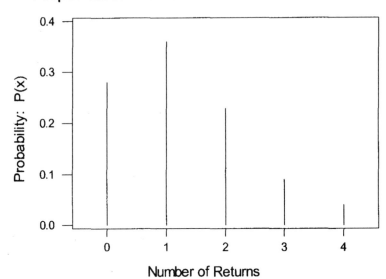

b. Cumulative probability function:

Cumulative probability function
Proportion of new cars returned: Correction of defects

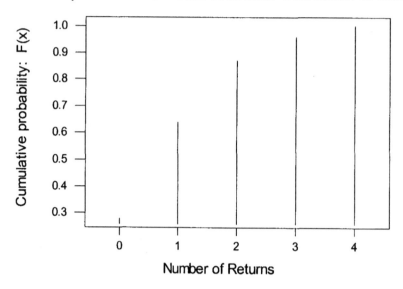

c. $\mu = 0 + .36 + 2(.23) + 3(.09) + 4(.04) = 1.25$ defects

d. $\sigma^2 = \sum x^2 Px(x) = 1.1675$ defects

e. Excel output:

Microsoft Excel - Book1

File Edit View Insert Format Tools QIC Data Window Hel

Arial

A10 =

	A	B	C	D	E
1	Returns	P(x)	F(x)	Mean	Variance
2	0	0.28	0.28	0	0.4375
3	1	0.36	0.64	0.36	0.0225
4	2	0.23	0.87	0.46	0.129375
5	3	0.09	0.96	0.27	0.275625
6	4	0.04	1.00	0.16	0.3025
7	Ex 5.8	1.00		1.25	1.1675
8					

5-10   a. Probability function

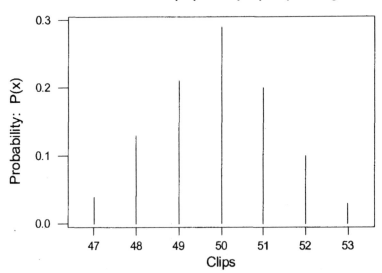

b. Cumulative probability function

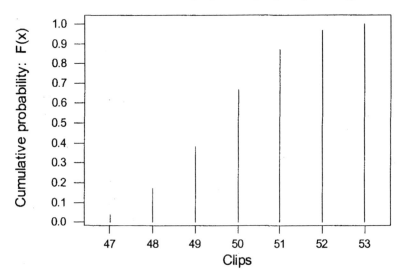

c. $P(49 \leq x \leq 51) = .70$

d. $1 - [P(x < 50)]^2 = 1 - .1444 = .8556$

e. $\mu = 47(.04) + 48(.13) + 49(.21) + 50(.29) + 51(.20) + 52(.10) + 53(.03) = 49.9$ clips

   $\sigma^2 = 1.95$ clips $\sigma = 1.3964$ clips

Excel output:

	M	N	O	P	Q	
1	Clips	P(x)	F(x)	Mean	Variance	
2	47	0.04	0.04	1.88	0.3364	
3	48	0.13	0.17	6.24	0.4693	
4	49	0.21	0.38	10.29	0.1701	
5	50	0.29	0.67	14.5	0.0029	
6	51	0.20	0.87	10.2	0.242	
7	52	0.10	0.97	5.2	0.441	
8	53	0.03	1.00	1.59	0.2883	
9		1.00		49.9	1.95	
10						

f. Mean and standard deviation of profit per package:

	S	T	U	V	W	
1	ProfitPerPackage	P(x)	F(x)	Mean	Variance	
2	0.4	0.04	0.04	0.016	0.00013456	
3	0.38	0.13	0.17	0.0494	0.00018772	
4	0.36	0.21	0.38	0.0756	0.00006804	
5	0.34	0.29	0.67	0.0986	0.00000116	
6	0.32	0.20	0.87	0.064	0.00009680	
7	0.3	0.10	0.97	0.03	0.00017640	
8	0.28	0.03	1.00	0.0084	0.00011532	
9		1.00		0.342	0.00078000	
10						

$\pi = 1.5 - (.16 + .02X)$

$\mu = E(\pi) = 1.5 - (.16 + (.02)(49.9)) = \$.342$

$\sigma_\pi = |.02|(1.3964) = \$.0279$

5-12   a. Probability function

X	0	1	2
P(x)	0.81	0.18	.01

$P_x(0) = (.90)(.90) = .81$

$P_x(1) = (.90)(.10) + (.10)(.90) = .18$

$P_x(2) = (.10)(.10) = .01$

b. $P(Y = 0) = 18/20 + 17/19 = 153/190$

$P(Y=1) = (2/20 \times 18/19) + (18/20 \times 2/19) = 36/190$

$P(Y=2) = 2/20 \times 1/19 = 1/190$

The answer in part b. is different from part a. because in part b. the probability of picking a defective part on the second draw depends upon the result of the first draw.

c. $\mu = 0(.81) + .18 + 2(.01) = 0.2$ defects

$\sigma^2_x = .22 - (.20)^2 = .18$ defects

d. $\mu = 0(153/190) + (36/190) + 2(1/190) = 39/190 = 0.2$ defects

$\sigma^2_y = 40/190 - (.20)^2 = .1705$

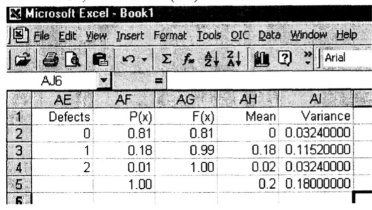

5-14   "One and one" $E(X) = 1(.75)(.25) + 2(.75)^2 = 1.3125$

"Two-shot foul" $E(X) = 1((.75)(.25) + (.25)(.75)) + 2(.75)^2 = 1.50$

The "two-shot foul" has a higher expected value

5-16 $\mu = 3.29$ $\sigma^2 = 1.3259$ $\sigma = 1.1515$

	AQ	AR	AS	AT	AU
1	Rating	P(x)	F(x)	Mean	Variance
2	1	0.07	0.07	0.07	0.367087
3	2	0.19	0.26	0.38	0.316179
4	3	0.28	0.54	0.84	0.023548
5	4	0.30	0.84	1.20	0.15123
6	5	0.16	1.00	0.80	0.467856
7	Ex 5.16	1.00		3.29	1.3259
8					

5-18   a. $\mu = 1.82$ breakdowns $\sigma^2 = 1.0276$ breakdowns $\sigma = 1.0137$ breakdowns

	BD	BE	BF	BG	BH	BI	BJ	BK	BL	BM
1	Breakdowns	P(x)	F(x)	Mean	Variance	Cost	P(x)	F(x)	Mean	Variance
2	0	0.1	0.10	0	0.33124	0	0.1	0.10	0	745290
3	1	0.26	0.36	0.26	0.174824	1500	0.26	0.36	390	393354
4	2	0.42	0.78	0.84	0.013608	3000	0.42	0.78	1260	30618
5	3	0.16	0.94	0.48	0.222784	4500	0.16	0.94	720	501264
6	4	0.06	1.00	0.24	0.285144	6000	0.06	1.00	360	641574
7		1.00		1.82	1.0276		1.00		2730	2312100
8	Ex 5.18			S.D.	1.013706	Ex 5.18			S.D.	1520.559
9										

b. Cost: $C = 1500X$

$E(C) = 1500(1.82) = \mu = \$2,730$

$\sigma = |1500|(1.0137) = \$1,520.559$

5-20

Cumulative Distribution Function

Binomial with n = 6 and p = 0.0500000

x	P(X <= x)
0.00	0.7351
1.00	0.9672
2.00	0.9978
3.00	0.9999
4.00	1.0000
5.00	1.0000

a. $Px(0) = .7351$

b. $Px(1) = P(X \le 1) - P(X \le 0) = .9672 - .7351 = .2321$

c. $P(X \ge 2) = 1 - P(X \le 1) = 1 - .7351 - .2321 = .0328$

5-22
Cumulative Distribution Function
Binomial with n = 6 and p = 0.700000

x	P(X <= x)
0.00	0.0007
1.00	0.0109
2.00	0.0705
3.00	0.2557
4.00	0.5798
5.00	0.8824
6.00	1.0000

a. $P(x \geq 2) = 1 - P(X \leq 1) = 1 - .0109 = .9891$

b. $P(x \leq 4) = .5798$

5-24
Cumulative Distribution Function
Binomial with n = 6 and p = 0.150000

x	P(X <= x)
0.00	0.3771
1.00	0.7765
2.00	0.9527
3.00	0.9941
4.00	0.9996
5.00	1.0000
6.00	1.0000

a. $Px(6) = .000011$

b. $Px(0) = .3771$

a. $P(X > 1) = 1 - P(X \leq 1) = 1 - .7765 = .2235$

5-26 $P(\text{Overbooking}) = (.1)[\binom{9}{9}(.8)^9(.2)^0] + (.05)[\binom{10}{9}(.8)^9(.2)^1] + [\binom{10}{10}(.8)^{10}(.2)^0] = .0322$

5-28   a $E(X) = 50(.15) = 7.5$, $\sigma_x = \sqrt{50(.15)(.85)} = 2.5249$

b. Let $Z = 250X$, $E(Z) = 250(7.5) = \$1,875$, $\sigma_z = |250|(2.5249) = \$631$

5-30

Microsoft Excel - CH5-DiscreteRV

File Edit View Insert Format Tools OIC Data Window Help

Arial

BZ2   = 0

	BY	BZ	CA	CB	CC	CD
1		ContractSale	P(x)	F(x)	Mean	Variance
2		0	0.07776	0.07776	0	0.31104000
3		1	0.25920	0.33696	0.2592	0.25920000
4		2	0.34560	0.68256	0.6912	0.00000000
5		3	0.23040	0.91296	0.6912	0.23040000
6		4	0.07680	0.98976	0.3072	0.30720000
7		5	0.01024	1.00000	0.0512	0.09216000
8		Example 5.7			2	1.20000000
9				S.D.		1.09544512
10						

$\mu_x = 2.0$ sales   OR $\mu_x = n\pi = 5(.4) = 2.0$ sales

5-32   a. $Px(0) + Px(1) = (.95)^{16} + 16(.05)(.95)^{15} = .8108$
        b. $Px(0) + Px(1) = (.85)^{16} + 16(.15)(.85)^{15} = .2839$
        c. $Px(0) + Px(1) = (.75)^{16} + 16(25)(.75)^{15} = .0635$

5-34 $P(\text{Supplier1}|x=1) = \dfrac{\left(\binom{20}{1}(.1)(.9)^{19}\right)(.7)}{\left(\binom{20}{1}(.1)(.9)^{19}\right)(.7) + \left(\binom{20}{1}(.2)(.8)^{19}\right)(.3)} = .916$

5-36
Cumulative Distribution Function
Hypergeometric with N = 16, X = 8, and n = 8

x	P(X <= x)
1.00	0.0051
2.00	0.0660
3.00	0.3096
4.00	0.6904
5.00	0.9340
6.00	0.9949
7.00	0.9999

$P(x = 4) = P(x \le 4) - P(x \le 3) = .6904 - .3096 = .3808$

5-38
Cumulative Distribution Function
Hypergeometric with N = 10, X = 5, and n = 6

x	P(X <= x)
0.00	0.0000
1.00	0.0238
2.00	0.2619
3.00	0.7381
4.00	0.9762
5.00	1.0000

$P(x \le 2) = .2619$

5-40   a. $P(x < 2) = P(x \le 1) = .2674$
        b. $P(x > 3) = 1 - P(x \le 3) = 1 - .7360 = .2640$
Cumulative Distribution Function
Poisson with mu = 2.60000

x	P(X <= x)
0.00	0.0743
1.00	0.2674
2.00	0.5184
3.00	0.7360
4.00	0.8774
5.00	0.9510
6.00	0.9828
7.00	0.9947
8.00	0.9985
9.00	0.9996
10.00	0.9999

5-42

Cumulative Distribution Function
```
Poisson with mu = 3.20000
      x     P( X <= x )
    0.00        0.0408
    1.00        0.1712
    2.00        0.3799
    3.00        0.6025
    4.00        0.7806
    5.00        0.8946
    6.00        0.9554
    7.00        0.9832
    8.00        0.9943
    9.00        0.9982
   10.00        0.9995
```

a. $P(x \leq 1) = .1712$

b. $P(x > 4) = 1 - P(x \leq 4) = 1 - .7806 = .2194$

5-44

Cumulative Distribution Function
```
Poisson with mu = 2.50000
      x     P( X <= x )
    0.00        0.0821
    1.00        0.2873
    2.00        0.5438
    3.00        0.7576
    4.00        0.8912
    5.00        0.9580
    6.00        0.9858
    7.00        0.9958
    8.00        0.9989
    9.00        0.9997
   10.00        0.9999
```
$P(x \leq 3) = .7576$

5-46

Cumulative Distribution Function
```
Poisson with mu = 4.50000
      x     P( X <= x )
    0.00        0.0111
    1.00        0.0611
    2.00        0.1736
    3.00        0.3423
    4.00        0.5321
    5.00        0.7029
    6.00        0.8311
    7.00        0.9134
    8.00        0.9597
    9.00        0.9829
   10.00        0.9933
```
$P(x \geq 3) = 1 - P(x \leq 2) = 1 - .1736 = .8264$

The calculations to find the exact binomial probabilities would be to use the binomial formula for each of the individual probabilities: $P(3) + P(4) + P(5) + P(6) + ...+ P(60)$. Thus, the binomial formula would need to be utilized 58 times to calculate the exact probability.

5-48   a. Joint cumulative probability function at $X = 1$, $Y = 4$:
$F_{X,Y}(1,4) = .09 + .07 + .14 + .23 = .53$

b. $P_{Y|X}(3|0) = .09/.19 = .4737$
$P_{Y|X}(4|0) = .07/.19 = .3684$
$P_{Y|X}(5|0) = .03/.19 = .1579$

c. $P_{Y|X}(0|5) = .03/.24 = .125$
$P_{Y|X}(1|5) = .10/.24 = .4167$
$P_{Y|X}(2|5) = .11/.24 = .4583$

d. $E(XY) = 0 + 1(3)(.14) + 1(4)(.23) + 1(5)(.10) + 2(3)(.07) + 2(4)(.16) + 2(5)(.11) = 4.64$

$\mu_x = 0 + .47 + 2(.34) = 1.15$

$\mu_y = 3(.3) + 4(.46) + 5(.24) = 3.94$

$Cov(X,Y) = 4.64 - (1.15)(3.94) = .109$

The covariance indicates that there is a positive association between the number of lines in the advertisement and the volume of inquiries.

e. No, because $Cov(X,Y) \neq 0$

X Return			Y Return 0	1	2	P(x)	Mean of X	Var of X	StDev of X
		3	0.09	0.14	0.07	0.3	0.9	0.26508	
		4	0.07	0.23	0.16	0.46	1.84	0.001656	
		5	0.03	0.1	0.11	0.24	1.2	0.269664	
P(y)			0.19	0.47	0.34		3.94	0.5364	0.732393
Mean of Y			0	0.47	0.68	1.15			
Var of Y			0.251275	0.010575	0.24565	0.5075			
StDev of Y						0.4956309			
xyP(x)			0	1.84	2.8	4.64			
sum xyP(x)*muxmuy		0.109							

5-50   a. $P(0,0) = .54$, $P(0,1) = .30$, $P(1,0) = .01$, $P(1,1) = .15$

b. $P_{Y|X}(y|1) = 1/16 = .0625$; $15/16 = .9375$

c. $E(XY) = .15$

$\mu_x = 0 + 1(.16) = .16$

$\mu_y = 0 + 1(.45) = .45$

$Cov(X,Y) = .15 - (.16)(.45) = .078$

The covariance indicates that there is a positive association between brand watchers of a late-night talk show and brand name recognition.

X Watch		0	1	Y Identify P(x)	Mean of X	Var of X	StDev of X
	0	0.54	0.3	0.84	0	0.021504	
	1	0.01	0.15	0.16	0.16	0.112896	
P(y)		0.55	0.45		0.16	0.1344	0.366606056
Mean of Y		0	0.45	0.45			
Var of Y		0.111375	0.136125	0.2475			
StDev of Y			0.49749372				
xyP(x)		0	0.15	0.15			
Sum xyP(x)*muxmuy		0.078					

5-52   Because of independence, the joint probabilities are the products of the marginal probabilities, so $P(0,0)=.0216$, and so on.

X Food		0	1	Y Service 2	3	P(x)	Mean of X	Var of X	StDev of X
	0	0.0216	0.0456	0.0408	0.012	0.12	0	0.322752	
	1	0.0522	0.1102	0.0986	0.029	0.29	0.29	0.118784	
	2	0.0756	0.1596	0.1428	0.042	0.42	0.84	0.054432	
	3	0.0306	0.0646	0.0578	0.017	0.17	0.51	0.314432	
P(y)		0.18	0.38	0.34	0.1	1	1.64	0.8104	0.900222
Mean of Y		0	0.38	0.68	0.3	1.36			
Var of Y		0.332928	0.049248	0.139264	0.26896	0.7904			
StDev of Y						0.889044			

5-54

X Large		0	1	Y Small 2	3	4	P(x)	Mean of X	Var of X	StDev of X
	0	0.0144	0.0208	0.0288	0.0104	0.0056	0.08	0	0.453152	
	1	0.0288	0.0416	0.0576	0.0208	0.0112	0.16	0.16	0.304704	
	2	0.0504	0.0728	0.1008	0.0364	0.0196	0.28	0.56	0.040432	
	3	0.0576	0.0832	0.1152	0.0416	0.0224	0.32	0.96	0.123008	
	4	0.018	0.026	0.036	0.013	0.007	0.1	0.4	0.26244	
	5	0.0108	0.0156	0.0216	0.0078	0.0042	0.06	0.3	0.411864	
P(y)		0.18	0.26	0.36	0.13	0.07	1	2.38	1.5956	1.263171
Mean of Y		0	0.26	0.72	0.39	0.28	1.65			
Var of Y		0.49005	0.10985	0.0441	0.23693	0.38658	1.2675			
StDev of Y							1.12583302			

$$\mu = 5\mu_x + 10\mu_y = 5(2.38) + 10(1.65) = 28.4$$

$$\sigma = \sqrt{(5)\sigma_x^2 + (10)\sigma_y^2} = \sqrt{5(1.5965) + 10(1.2675)} = 4.545$$

5-56

Days	P(x)	F(x)	Mean	Variance	
1	0.05	0.05	0.05	0.242	
2	0.2	0.25	0.4	0.288	
3	0.35	0.60	1.05	0.014	
4	0.3	0.90	1.2	0.192	
5	0.1	1.00	0.5	0.324	
Ex 5.56	1.00		3.2	1.06	
			S.D.	1.029563	

a. $P(x < 3) = .05 + .20 = .25$

b. $E(X) = 3.2$

c. $\sigma = 1.029563$

d. Cost = $20,000 + $2,000X = E(Cost) = $26,400,
standard deviation = ($2,000)(1.029563) = $2,059.13

e. The probability of a project taking at least 4 days to complete is $.30 + .10 = .4$.
Given independence of the individual projects, the probability that at least two of
three projects will take at least 4 days to complete is a binomial random variable
with n = 3, p = .4. $P(2) + P(3) = 3(.4)^2(.6) + (1)(.4)^3(1) = .352$

5-58   a. $\mu = n\pi = 9(.25) = 2.25$

b. $\sigma = \sqrt{n\pi(1-\pi)} = \sqrt{9(.25)(.75)} = 1.299$

c. (i) $E(X) = 1 + 2.23 = 3.25$, (ii) $\sigma = 1.299$

5-60   a. $P(4) = (.95)(.90)(.90)(.80) = .6156$
$P(3) = (.05)(.90)(.90)(.8) + 2(.95)(.10)(.90)(.80) + (.95)(.90)(90)(.20) = .3231$
$P(2) = 2(.95)(.90)(.10)(.2) + 2(.05)(.90)(.10)(.80) + (.05)(.90)(.90)(.2) + (.95)(.10)(.10)(.8) = .0571$
$P(1) = (.95)(.10)(.10)(.2) + 2(.05)(.90)(.10)(.20) + (.05)(.10)(.10)(.8) = .0041$
$P(0) = (.05)(.10)(.10)(.20) = .0001$

b. $E(X) = .0041 + 2(.0571) + 3(.3231) + 4(.6156) = 3.55$ vehicles

c. $\sum x^2 Px(x) = 12.99$, $\sigma_x = \sqrt{12.99 - (3.55)^2} = .6225$ vehicles

5-62   Assume that the shots are independent of each other

a. $P(x \geq 2) = 1 - P(x \leq 1) = 1 - [(\binom{6}{0}(.4)^0(.6)^6 + \binom{6}{1}(.4)(.6)^5] = 0.767$

b. $P(x=3) = \binom{6}{3}(.4)^3(.6)^3 = 0.2765$

c. $\mu = n\pi = (6)(.4) = 2.4, \quad \sigma = \sqrt{6(.4)(.6)} = 1.2$

d.   Mean of total points scored $= 3(\mu) = 3(2.4) = 7.2,$ Std dev $= 3\sigma = 3(1.2)=3.6$

5-64   a. This is a binomial probability (assuming independence) with a p=.6 and n=7. Then
the P(A wins) $= P(X \geq 4) = \binom{7}{4}.6^4.4^3 + \binom{7}{5}.6^5.4^2 + 7(.6^6).4+.6^7 = 0.71021$

b. $\binom{6}{3}.6^3.4^3 = 0.27648$

c. (i) The outcome of the first four games are known with certainty. Therefore, the
series is a best out of three games. To compute the probability that team A wins, find $P(x \geq 3) =$
$3(.6)^2(.4) + (.6)^3 = 0.648,$ (ii) $\binom{2}{1}(.6)(.4) = 0.48$

5-66   Find $P(X \geq 2) = 1 - \dfrac{C_0^4 C_4^{16} + C_1^4 C_3^{16}}{C_4^{20}} = 1 - \dfrac{1820 + 2240}{4845} = .16202$

5-68 $1 - e^{-6.5} - e^{-6.5}(6.5) - e^{-6.5}(6.5)^2/2! = 0.95696$

Chapter 6: Continuous Random Variables and Probability Distributions

6-2   a.

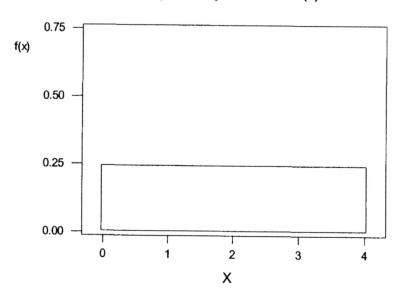

b.

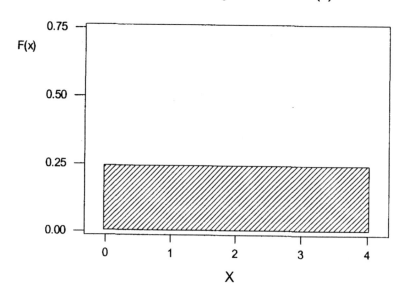

c. $P(x < 1) = .25$

d. $P(X < .5) + P(X > 3.5) = P(X < .5) + 1 - P(X < 3.5) = .25$

6-4   a. $P(380 < X < 460) = P(X < 460) - P(X < 380) = .6 - .4 = .2$
        b. $P(X < 380) < (PX < 400) < P(X < 460); \ .4 < P(X < 400) < .6$

6-6 $\mu_Z = 20 + \mu_X = 20 + 4 = \$24$ million
        Bid $= 1.1 \ \mu_z = 1.1(24) = \$26.4$ million, $\sigma_\pi = \$1$ million

6-8 $\mu_Z = 6,000 + .08 \ \mu_X = 6,000 + 48,000 = \$54,000$
        $\sigma_Z = |.08| \ \sigma_X = .08(180,000) = \$14,400$

6-10   a. Find Z_0 such that $P(Z < Z_0) = .7$, closest value of $Z_0 = .52$
        b. Find Z_0 such that $P(Z < Z_0) = .25$, closest value of $Z_0 = -.67$
        c. Find Z_0 such that $P(Z > Z_0) = .2$, closest value of $Z_0 = .84$
        d. Find Z_0 such that $P(Z > Z_0) = .6$, closest value of $Z_0 = -.25$

6-12   a. $P(Z > \dfrac{1,000 - 1,200}{100}) = P(Z > -2) = F_Z(2) = .9772$

        b. $P(\dfrac{1,100 - 1,200}{100} < Z < \dfrac{1,300 - 1,200}{100}) = P(-1 < Z < 1) = 2F_Z(1) - 1 = .6826$

        c. $P(Z > 1.28) = .1$, plug into the z-formula all of the known information and
            solve for the unknown: $1.28 = \dfrac{Xi - 1,200}{100}$. Solve algebraically for $Xi = 1,328$

6-14   a. $P(Z > \dfrac{20 - 12.2}{7.2}) = P(Z > 1.08) = 1 - F_z(1.08) = .1401$

        b. $P(Z < \dfrac{0 - 12.2}{7.2}) = P(Z < -1.69) = 1 - F_z(1.69) = .0455$

        c. $P(\dfrac{5 - 12.2}{7.2} < Z < \dfrac{15 - 12.2}{7.2}) = P(-1 < Z < .39) = F_z(.39) - [1 - F_z(1)] = .6517 -$
            $.1587 = .4930$

6-16   a. $P(\dfrac{460 - 500}{50} < Z < \dfrac{540 - 500}{50}) = P(-.8 < Z < .8) = 2 \ F_z(.8) - 1 = .5762$
        b. If $P(Z < -.84) = .2$, then plug into the z formula and solve for the Xi: the
            value of the cost of the contract. $-.84 = \dfrac{Xi - 500}{50}$. $Xi = \$458$ (thousand
            dollars)
        c. The shortest range will be the interval centered on the mean. Since the $P(Z >$
            $1.96) = .025, \ 1.96 = \dfrac{Xi - 500}{50}$. $Xi = 598$. The lower value of the interval

will be $-1.96 = \dfrac{Xi - 500}{50}$ which is Xi = \$402 (thousand dollars). Therefore,

the shortest range will be 598 – 402 = \$196 (thousand dollars).

6-18 $P(Z < -1.28) = .1,\ -1.28 = \dfrac{Xi - 18.2}{1.6}$ Xi = 16.152

6-20   a. $P(Z > \dfrac{820 - 700}{120}) = P(Z > 1) = 1 - F_z(1) = .1587$

   b. $P(\dfrac{730 - 700}{120} < Z < \dfrac{820 - 700}{120}) = P(.25 < Z < 1) = .8413 - .5987 = .2426$

   Number of students = .2426(100) = 24.26 or 24 students

   c. $P(Z < -1.645) = .05,\ -1.645 = \dfrac{Xi - 700}{120}$, Xi = 502.6

6-22   For Supplier A: $P(Z < \dfrac{5 - 4.4}{.4}) = P(Z < 1.5) = .9332$

   For Supplier B: $P(Z < \dfrac{5 - 4.2}{.6}) = P(Z < 1.33) = .9082$

   Therefore, Supplier A has a greater probability of achieving less than 5% impurity
   and is hence the better choice

6-24   a. $P(Z < \dfrac{60 - 75}{20}) = P(Z < -.75) = .2266$

   b. $P(Z > \dfrac{90 - 75}{20}) = P(Z > .75) = .2266$

   c. The graph should show that 60 minutes and 90 minutes are equidistant from
      the mean of 75 minutes. Therefore, the areas above 90 minutes and below 60
      minutes by the property of symmetry must be equal.

   d. $P(Z > 1.28) = .1,\ 1.28 = \dfrac{Xi - 75}{20}$, Xi = 100.6

6-26   a. $P(\dfrac{180 - 200}{20} < Z < 0) = .5 - [1 - F_z(1)] = .5 - .1587 = .3413$

   b. $P(Z > \dfrac{245 - 200}{20}) = 1 - F_Z(2.25) = .0122$

   c. Smaller

   d. $P(Z < -1.28) = .1,\ -1.28 = \dfrac{Xi - 200}{20}$, Xi = 174.4

6-28   a. $E[X] = \mu = 900(.2) = 180,\ \sigma = \sqrt{(900)(.2)(.8)} = 12$

$$P(Z > \frac{200-180}{12}) = P(Z > 1.67) = 1 - F_Z(1.67) = .0475$$

b. $P(Z < \frac{175-180}{12}) = P(Z < -.42) = 1 - F_Z(.42) = .3372$

6-30 $E[X] = (100)(.6) = 60,\ \sigma = \sqrt{(100)(.6)(.4)} = 4.899$

$$P(Z < \frac{50-60}{4.899}) = P(Z < -2.04) = 1 - F_Z(2.04) = 1 - .9793 = .0207$$

6-32   a. $E[X] = (45)(.25) = 11.25,\ \sigma = \sqrt{(45)(.25)(.75)} = 2.9047$

$$P(Z < \frac{9.5-11.25}{2.9047}) = P(Z < -.60) = 1 - F_Z(.60) = 1 - .7257 = .2743$$

b. $P(\frac{11.5-11.25}{2.9047} < Z < \frac{15.5-11.25}{2.9047}) = P(.09 < Z < 1.46) = F_z(1.46) - F_z(.09) =$
.9279 - .5359 = .392

6-34 $P(Z > \frac{10-12.2}{2.8}) = P(Z < -.79) = 1 - F_Z(.79) = 1 - .7852 = .2148$

$E[X] = 400(.2148) = 85.92,\ \sigma = \sqrt{(400)(.2148)(.7852)} = 8.2137$

$$P(Z > \frac{100-85.92}{8.2137}) = P(Z > 1.71) = 1 - F_Z(1.71) = 1 - .9564 = .0436$$

6-36 $P(X > 18) = e^{-(18/15)} = .3012$

6-38   a. $P(X > 3) = 1 - [1 - e^{-(3/\mu)}] = e^{-3\lambda}$ since $\lambda = 1/\mu$

b. $P(X > 6) = 1 - [1 - e^{-(6/\mu)}] = e^{-(6/\mu)} = e^{-6\lambda}$
c. $P(X>6|X>3) = P(X > 6)/P(X > 3) = e^{-6\lambda}/e^{-3\lambda}] = e^{-3\lambda}$
     The probability of an occurrence within a specified time in the future is not
     related to how much time has passed since the most recent occurrence.

6-40   Assume that costs are independent across years
       $\mu_z = 5\ \mu_x = 5(200) = 1,000$

       $\sigma_Z = \sqrt{5\sigma_x^2} = \sqrt{5(3,600)} = 134.16$

6-42   If X and Y are not independent:
       $Var(R) = \alpha^2\ Var(X) + (1,000 - \alpha)^2 Var(Y) + 2\alpha(1,000 - \alpha)Cov(X,Y)$
       $= \alpha^2\sigma^2 + (1,000,000 - 2,000\alpha + \alpha^2)\ \sigma^2 + 2\alpha(1,000 - \alpha)C$

$= (2\alpha^2 - 2{,}000\alpha + 1{,}000{,}000)\sigma^2 + 2\alpha(1{,}000 - \alpha)C$

If $\alpha = 0$, then $Var(R) = 500{,}000\ \sigma^2 + 500{,}000\ C$

If $\alpha = 0$, then $Var(R) = 1{,}000{,}000\ \sigma^2$

The former variance will be smaller than the latter if $C < \sigma^2$. Risk would be minimized as C tended toward zero, i.e., as the investments became independent, and would be even smaller if C were negative.

6-44   The calculation of the mean is correct, but the standard deviations of two random variables cannot be summed. To get the correct standard deviation, add the variances together and then take the square root. The standard deviation:

$$\sigma = \sqrt{5(16)^2} = 35.7771$$

6-46   a. The cumulative density function provides information about the probability that the variable will be less than a specific value (x)

      b. The probability density function shows the relative frequencies of a random variable for each value of the random variable

      c. The mean of a continuous random variable is a measure of location of a random variable. This is the expected value of the random variable

      d. The standard deviation shows how far on average the values in the distribution lie from the mean

      e. The covariance is a measure of how two variables vary together. It is the average of the deviation products of the two variables

6-48   a. The area under the normal curve can be found through integral calculus; however, the calculation requires approximation techniques. The tables provide a simplified method of determining the probabilities

      b. All normal probability distributions with any mean and any variance can all be converted into the 'standard normal' distribution with a mean of zero and a standard deviation of 1. Thus, only one table is necessary once the conversion is done.

      c. There are examples of variables that occur in the real world that can be approximated by the normal probability distribution, and it has properties that allow for convenient calculations of probabilities

6-50   a. $P(X < 10) = (10/12) - (8/12) = 1/6$

      b. $P(X > 12) = (20/12) - (12/12) = 8/12 = 2/3$

      c. $E[\pi] = \pi(20/12 - 12/12) = 2(2/3) = 1.333$

      d. To jointly maximize the probability of getting the contract and the profit from that contract, maximize the following function: max $E[\pi] = (B - 10)(20/12 - B/12)$. Where B is the value of the bid. To determine the value for B that maximizes the expected profit, an iterative approach can be used. The value of B is 15.

6-52   a. The probability density function f(x):

Probability density function: f(x)

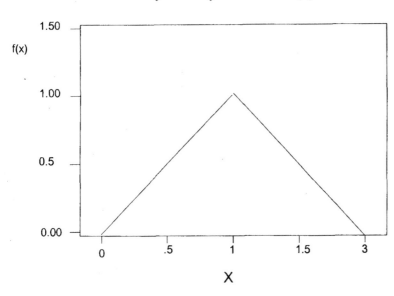

b. $F_x(x) \geq 0$ for all x. The area under $f_x(x) = 2[½(\text{base x height})] = 1$

c. $P(.5 < X < 1.5) = (.5 - \dfrac{.5^2}{2}) + (.5 - \dfrac{.5^2}{2}) = .375 + .375 = .75$

6-54   a. $\mu_R = 1.45\,\mu_x = 1.45(530) = 768.5$

   b. $\sigma_R = |1.45|\,\sigma_x = 1.45(69) = 100.05$

   c. $\pi = R - C = .5X - 100.$ $E[\pi] = .5\,\mu_x - 100 = 165.$ $\sigma_\pi = |.5|\,\sigma_x = .5(69) = 34.5$

6-56 $Cov[(X_1 + X_2), (X_1 - X_2)] = E[(X_1 + X_2)(X_1 - X_2)] - E[X_1 + X_2]\,E[X_1 - X_2] =$
   $E[X_1^2 - X_2^2] - E[(X_1) + E(X_2)][E(X_1) - E(X_2)] =$
   $E(X_1^2) - E(X_2^2) - [(E(X_1))^2 - (E(X_2)^2] = Var\ (X_1) - Var\ (X_2)$
   Which is 0 if and only if $Var\ (X_1) = Var\ (X_2)$

6-58   a. $P(Z > \dfrac{65 - 60}{10}) = P(Z > .5) = 1 - F_Z(.5) = .3085$

   b. $P(\dfrac{50 - 60}{10} < Z < \dfrac{70 - 60}{10}) = P(-1 < Z < 1) = 2\,F_z\,(1) - 1 = .6826$

   c. $P(Z > 1.96) = .025,\ 1.96 = \dfrac{Xi - 60}{10},\ Xi = 79.6$

   d. $P(Z > .675) = .025,\ .675 = $ The shortest range will be the interval centered on

   the mean. Since the $P(Z > .675) = .025,\ .675 = \dfrac{Xi - 60}{10}.$ Xi = 66.75. The

   lower value of the interval will be $-.675 = \dfrac{Xi - 60}{10}$ which is Xi = 53.25.

   Therefore, the shortest range will be $66.75 - 53.25 = 13.5.$ This is by
   definition the InterQuartile Range (IQR).

e. $P(X > 65) = .3085$ (from part a)

Use the binomial formula: $P(X = 2) = C_2^4(.3085)^2(.6915)^2 = 0.2731$

6-60   a. $P(\dfrac{15-20}{4} < Z < \dfrac{25-20}{4}) = P(-1.25 < Z < 1.25) = 2\ F_Z(1.25) - 1 = .7888$

b. $P(Z > \dfrac{30-20}{4}) = P(Z > 2.5) = 1 - F_z\ (2.5) = .0062$

c. $P(X \geq 1) = 1 - P(X = 0) = 1 - [F_Z(2.5)]^5 = .0306$

d. $P(Z > .525) = .3, .525 = \dfrac{Xi - 20}{4}$, $Xi = 22.1$ The shortest range will be the interval centered on the mean. The lower value of the interval will be $-.525 = \dfrac{Xi - 20}{4}$ which is Xi=17.9. The shortest range will be $22.1 - 17.9 = 4.2$.

e. $19 - 21$

f. $21 - 23$

6-62 $P(Z > 1.28) = .1, 1.28 = \dfrac{15 - \mu}{2.5}$, $\mu = 11.8$. $P(Z < \dfrac{10 - 11.8}{2.5}) = P(Z < -.72) = 1 - F_Z(.72) = .2358$

6-64 $E[X] = 400(.6) = 240, \sigma_x = \sqrt{(400)(.6)(.4)} = 9.798$. $P(Z > \dfrac{200 - 240}{9.798}) = P(\ Z > -4.08) \approx 1.00$

6-66   a. $P(X = 6) = \dfrac{e^{-6}6^6}{6!} = .1606$

b. 20 minutes = 1/3 hours, $P(X > 1/3) = e^{-\frac{6}{3}} = .1353$

c. 5 minutes = 1/12 hour, $P(X < 1/12) = 1 - e^{-\frac{6}{12}} = .3935$

d. 30 minutes = .5 hour, $P(X > .5) = e^{-(.5)(6)} = .0498$

6-68   a. $P(\dfrac{120 - 132}{12} < Z < \dfrac{150 - 132}{12}) = P(-1 < Z < 1.5) = F_Z\ (1.5) - [1 - F_Z(1)] = .7745$

b. $P(Z > .44) = .33, .44 = \dfrac{Xi - 132}{12}$, $Xi = 137.28$

c. $P(Z < \dfrac{120 - 132}{12}) = P(Z < -1) = 1 - F_Z(1) = .1587$

d. $E[X] = 100(.1587) = 15.87, \sigma_x = \sqrt{(100)(.1587)(.8413)} = 3.654$

$P(Z > \dfrac{25 - 15.87}{3.654}) = P(Z > 2.5) = 1 - F_Z(2.5) = .0062$

Chapter 7: Sampling and Sampling Distributions

7-2   The sampling distribution of the sample mean can be generated by listing out all possible samples of size n, calculate each possible $\bar{x}$, determine the probability of each possible $\bar{x}$ and generate the sampling distribution. Alternatively, the probabilities of each $\bar{x}$ can be generated by use of the binomial formula.

a.   When n = 5: Use the binomial formula for x = 0, x = 1, etc.:

X	P(X)	$\bar{x}$
0	.07776	0
1	.25920	.2
2	.34560	.4
3	.23040	.6
4	.07680	.8
5	.01024	1.0

$E(p_x) = np = (5)(.4) = 2.0, \ \sigma_p^2 = \dfrac{p(1-p)}{n} = = \dfrac{.4(.6)}{5} = .048, \ \sigma_p = .2191$

b. Using the result from part a:

$E(p_x) = np = (100)(.4) = 40, \ \sigma_p^2 = \dfrac{p(1-p)}{n} = = \dfrac{.4(.6)}{100} = .0024, \ \sigma_p = .04899$

7-4   a. $E(\bar{X}) = \mu_{\bar{x}} = 92.$

c. $\sigma_{\bar{x}} = \dfrac{\sigma_{\bar{x}}}{\sqrt{n}} = \dfrac{3.6}{2} = 1.8$

b. $\sigma_{\bar{x}}^2 = \dfrac{\sigma_{\bar{x}}^2}{n} = \dfrac{(3.6)^2}{4} = 3.24$

d. $P(Z > \dfrac{93-92}{1.8}) = P(Z > .56) = .2877$

7-6   a.   i) $P(Z > \dfrac{24-25}{2}) = P(Z < -.5) = .3085$

ii) $P(Z < \dfrac{24-25}{2/\sqrt{4}}) = P(Z < -1) = .1587$

iii) $P(Z < \dfrac{24-25}{2/\sqrt{16}}) = P(Z < -2) = .0228$

b.   As the sample size increases, the standard error of the sampling distribution will decrease. That is, as the sample size increases, the sampling distribution of the sample means will clump up tighter around the true population mean.

7-8   a. $\sigma_{\bar{x}} = \dfrac{60}{\sqrt{9}} = 20$

b. $P(Z < \dfrac{270-280}{20}) = P(Z < -.5) = .3085$

c. $P(Z > \dfrac{250-280}{20}) = P(Z > -1.5) = .9332$

d. If the population standard deviation is smaller, then the standard error of the sampling distribution of the means will also be smaller. The probabilities calculated for parts a and b will be smaller.

7-10   a. $\sigma_{\bar{x}} = \dfrac{.6}{\sqrt{4}} = .3$ b. $P(Z < \dfrac{19.7-20}{.3}) = P(Z < -1) = .1587$

c. $P(Z > \dfrac{20.6-20}{.3}) = P(Z > 2) = .0228$

d. $P(\dfrac{19.5-20}{.3} < Z < \dfrac{20.5-20}{.3}) = P(-1.67 < Z < 1.67) = .905$

e. $P(\dfrac{19.5-20}{.6/\sqrt{2}} < Z < \dfrac{20.5-20}{.6/\sqrt{2}}) = P(-1.18 < Z < 1.18) = .762$

7-12   a. $\sigma_{\bar{x}} = \dfrac{8}{\sqrt{4}} = 4, \quad P(Z > 2/4) = P(Z > .5) = .3085$

b. $P(Z < -3/4) = P(Z < -.75) = .2266$
c. $P(-4/4 > Z > 4/4) = P(-1 > Z > 1) = .3174$
d. Lower, lower, lower

7-14   a. $P(Z > 1.645) = .05, 1.645 = \dfrac{1}{3.8/\sqrt{n}}$, n = 39.075, take n = 40

b. larger   c. larger

7-16   a. $\sigma_{\bar{x}}^{2} = \dfrac{1}{N}\sum(X_i - \bar{X})^2 = \dfrac{\sum x_i^2 - N\bar{x}^2}{N} = \dfrac{205 - (6)(5.5)^2}{6} = \dfrac{23.5}{6} = \dfrac{47}{12}$

b.

$\sigma_{\bar{x}}^{2} = \sum(\bar{X}_i - \mu)^2 P_x(\bar{x}) = \dfrac{(4.5-5.5)^2}{15} + \dfrac{2(4.75-5.5)^2}{15} + \dfrac{2(5-5.5)^2}{15} +$

$+ \dfrac{2(5.25-5.5)^2}{15} + \dfrac{1(5.5-5.5)^2}{15} + \dfrac{3(5.75-5.5)^2}{15} + \dfrac{(6-5.5)^2}{15} +$

$+ \dfrac{2(6.25-5.5)^2}{15} + \dfrac{(6.75-5.5)^2}{15} = \dfrac{47}{120}$

c. $\sigma_{\bar{x}}^{2} = \dfrac{\sigma_{\bar{x}}^{2}}{n} \dfrac{N-n}{N-1} = \dfrac{47/12}{4} \dfrac{6-4}{6-1} = \dfrac{47}{120}$

7-18   a. $\sigma_{\bar{x}} = \dfrac{300,000}{\sqrt{100}} \sqrt{\dfrac{400}{499}} = 26,859,689$

b. $P(Z > \dfrac{825,000-800,000}{26,859.689}) = P(Z > .93) = .1762$

c. $P(Z > \dfrac{780,000-800,000}{26,859.689}) = P(Z > -.74) = .7704$

d. $P(\dfrac{790,000-800,000}{26,859.689} < Z < \dfrac{820,000-800,000}{26,859.689}) = P(-.37 < Z < .74) = .4147$

7-20 $\sigma_{\bar{x}} = \dfrac{10}{\sqrt{150}}\sqrt{\dfrac{450}{599}} = .7077$

a. $P(Z > \dfrac{31-32}{.7077}) = P(Z > -1.41) = .9207$

b. $P(Z < \dfrac{33-32}{.7077}) = P(Z < 1.41) = .9207$

d. $P(\dfrac{31-32}{.7077} < Z < \dfrac{33-32}{.7077}) = P(-1.41 < Z < 1.41) = .1586$

7-22   a. $E(p_x) = .75$

b. $\sigma_p^{\ 2} = \dfrac{(.75)(.25)}{100} = .001875$

c. $\sigma_p = .0433$

d. $P(Z > \dfrac{.8-.75}{.0433}) = P(Z > 1.15) = .1251$

7-24   a. $\sigma_p^{\ 2} = \sqrt{\dfrac{(.3)(.7)}{200}} = .0324$

b. $P(Z < \dfrac{.25-.3}{.0324}) = P(Z < -1.54) = .0618$

c. $P(Z > \dfrac{.33-.3}{.0324}) = P(Z > .93) = .1762$

d. $P(\dfrac{.27-.3}{.0324} < Z < \dfrac{.33-.3}{.0324}) = P(-.93 < Z < .93) = .6476$

7-26   a. $\sigma_p = \sqrt{\dfrac{(.42)(.58)}{300}} = .0285$

b. $P(Z > \dfrac{.5-.42}{.0285}) = P(Z > 2.81) = .0025$

c. $P(\dfrac{.4-.42}{.0285} < Z < \dfrac{.45-.42}{.0285}) = P(-.7 < Z < 1.05) = .6111$

d. .41 - .43

7-28   a. $\sigma_p = \sqrt{\dfrac{(.3)(.7)}{280}} = .02739$

b. $P(Z < \dfrac{.32-.3}{.02739}) = P(Z < .73) = .7673$

c.   .29 - .31

7-30 $P(Z > 1.96) = .025$, $.03 = 1.96\sqrt{\dfrac{(.5)(.5)}{n}}$, solving for n = 1067.11. Take a sample of size 1,068.

7-32 $\sigma_p = \sqrt{\dfrac{(.5)(.5)}{150}} = .04082$, $P(Z > \dfrac{.56 - .5}{.04082}) = P(Z > 1.47) = .0708$

7-34 $\sigma_p = \sqrt{\dfrac{(.55)(.45)}{81}}\sqrt{\dfrac{419}{499}} = .05065$

$P(Z > \dfrac{.5 - .55}{.05065}) = P(Z < -.99) = .1611$

7-36   a. $p = \dfrac{239}{438} = .5457$, $\sigma_p = \sqrt{\dfrac{(.5457)(.4543)}{80}}\sqrt{\dfrac{358}{437}} = .05038$

b. $P(Z < \dfrac{.5 - .5457}{.05038}) = P(Z < -.91) = .1814$

c. $P(\dfrac{.5 - .5457}{.05038} < Z < \dfrac{.6 - .5457}{.05038}) = P(-.91 < Z < 1.08) = .6785$

7-38 $P(\dfrac{(n-1)s^2{}_x}{\sigma^2{}_x} > \dfrac{19(3.1)}{1.75}) = P(\chi^2{}_{(19)} > 33.66) =$ between .01 and .025 (.0201 exactly)

7-40   a. $P(\dfrac{(n-1)s^2{}_x}{\sigma^2{}_x} > \dfrac{15(3,000)^2}{(2,500)^2}) = P(\chi^2{}_{(15)} > 21.6) =$ just greater than .1 (.1187 exactly)

b. $P(\dfrac{(n-1)s^2{}_x}{\sigma^2{}_x} < \dfrac{15(1,500)^2}{(2,500)^2}) = P(\chi^2{}_{(15)} < 5.4) =$ between .01 and .025 (.0118 exactly)

7-42. a. $P(\dfrac{(n-1)s^2{}_x}{\sigma^2{}_x} < \dfrac{24(75)^2}{(100)^2}) = P(\chi^2{}_{(24)} < 13.5) =$ between .025 and .05 (.0428 exactly)

b. $P(\dfrac{(n-1)s^2{}_x}{\sigma^2{}_x} > \dfrac{24(150)^2}{(100)^2}) = P(\chi^2{}_{(24)} > 54) =$ less than .005 (.0004 exactly)

7-44 $s^2_x = 1/3[(2\text{-}4.5)^2 + (4 - 4.5)^2 + 2(6 - 4.5)^2] = 3.6667$

$s^2_x = 1/3[(2\text{-}4.75)^2 + (4 - 4.75)^2 + (6 - 4.75)^2 + (7\text{-}4.75)^2] = 4.9167$

$s^2_x = 1/3[(2\text{-}5)^2 + (4 - 5)^2 + (6 - 5)^2 + (8 - 5)^2] = 6.6667$

$s^2_x = 4.9167$

$s^2_x = 6.6667$

$s^2_x = 1/3[(2\text{-}5.25)^2 + (4 - 5.25)^2 + (7 - 5.25)^2 + (8 - 5.25)^2] = 7.5833$

$s^2_x = 1/3[(2\text{-}5.25)^2 + 2(6 - 5.25)^2 + (7 - 5.25)^2] = 4.9167$

$s^2_x = 1/3[(2\text{-}5.5)^2 + 2(6 - 5.5)^2 + (8 - 5.5)^2] = 6.3333$

$s^2_x = 1/3[(2\text{-}5.75)^2 + (6 - 5.75)^2 + (7 - 5.75)^2 + (8 - 5.75)^2] = 6.9167$

$s^2_x = 6.9167$

$s^2_x = 1/3[(4 - 5.75)^2 + 2(6 - 5.75)^2 + (7 - 5.75)^2] = 1.5833$

$s^2_x = 1/3[(4 - 6)^2 + 2(0) + (8 - 6)^2] = .2.6667$

$s^2_x = 1/3[(4 - 6.25)^2 + (6 - 6.25)^2 + (7 - 6.25)^2 + (8 - 6.25)^2] = 2.9167$

$s^2_x = 2.9167$

$s^2_x = 1/3[2(6 - 6.75)^2 + (7 - 6.75)^2 + (8 - 6.75)^2] = .9167$

$$\frac{1}{15}\sum s^2_x = \frac{70.5}{15} = 4.7 \neq 3.9167 = \frac{47}{12} = \sigma^2_x$$

However, $\dfrac{N\sigma^2_x}{N-1} = 4.7$

7-46   a. $P(\chi^2_{(9)} > 14.68) = .05,\ \ 14.68 = 9(\text{Difference}),\ \text{Difference} = 1.6311\ (163.11\%)$

b. $P(\chi^2_{(9)} < 2.7) = .025,\ \ P(\chi^2_{(9)} > 19.02) = .025,$

$2.7 = 9a,\ a = .3,\ \ 19.02 = 9b,\ b = 2.1133$

The probability is .95 that the sample variance is between 30% and 211.33% of the population variance

c. The interval in part b. will be smaller

7-48   a. $P(\chi^2_{(11)} > 4.57) = .95,\ \ 4.57 = 11\text{Difference},\ \text{Difference} = .4155\ (41.55\%)$

b. $P(\chi^2_{(11)} > 5.58) = .90,\ \ 5.58 = 11\text{Difference},\ \text{Difference} = .5073\ (50.73\%)$

c. $P(\chi^2_{(11)} < 3.82) = .025,\ \ P(\chi^2_{(11)} > 21.92) = .025,$

$3.82 = 11a,\ a = .34727,\ 21.92 = 11b,\ b = 1.9927$

The probability is .95 that the sample variance is between 34.727% and 199.27% of the population variance

7-50 $P(\dfrac{(n-1)s^2_x}{\sigma^2_x} < \dfrac{24(12.2)}{15.4}) = P(\chi^2_{(24)} < 19.01) = \text{less than }.90\ (.5438\ \text{exactly})$

7-52   a. $C_2^6 = \dfrac{6!}{2!4!} = 15$ possible samples

b. (41, 39), (41, 35), (41, 35), (41, 33), (41, 38), (39, 35), (39, 35), (39, 33), (39, 38), (35, 35), (35, 33), (35, 38), (35, 33), (35, 38), (33, 38)

c. $34P_{\bar{X}}(34) = 34\dfrac{2}{15} = 4.5333$

$35P_{\bar{X}}(35) = \dfrac{35}{15} = 2.3333$

$35.5P_{\bar{X}}(35.5) = \dfrac{35.5}{15} = 2.3667$

$36P_{\bar{X}}(36) = \dfrac{36}{15} = 2.4$

$36.5P_{\bar{X}}(36.5) = 36.5\dfrac{2}{15} = 4.8667$

$37P_{\bar{X}}(37) = 37\dfrac{3}{15} = 7.4$

$38P_{\bar{X}}(38) = 38\dfrac{2}{15} = 5.0667$

$38.5P_{\bar{X}}(38.5) = \dfrac{38.5}{15} = 2.5667$

$39.5P_{\bar{X}}(39.5) = \dfrac{39.5}{15} = 2.6333$

$40P_{\bar{X}}(40) = \dfrac{40}{15} = 2.6667$

$\sum \bar{x}P_{\bar{x}}(\bar{x}) = 36.8333$

$\dfrac{1}{N}\sum x_i = 36.8333$

d. The mean of the sampling distribution of the sample mean is

$\sum \bar{x}P_{\bar{x}}(\bar{x}) = 36.8333$ which is exactly equal to the population mean: $\dfrac{1}{N}\sum x_i = 36.8333$.

This is the result expected from the Central Limit Theorem.

7-54 $P_x(0) = 3/15$, $P_x(.5) = 9/15$, $P_x(1) = 3/15$

$$p = \sum xP_x(x) = 0(\dfrac{3}{15}) + .5(\dfrac{9}{15}) + 1(\dfrac{3}{15}) = .5 = \dfrac{3}{6} = p$$

7-56   a. $P(Z > \dfrac{65-60}{10/\sqrt{4}}) = P(Z > 1) = .1587$

b. $P(Z < -1.28) = .1,\ -1.28 = \dfrac{Xi-60}{10/\sqrt{4}},\ X_i = 53.6$

c. $P(\chi^2_{(3)} > 6.25) = .1,\ 6.25 = \dfrac{3s^2_x}{(10)^2},\ s_x = 14.4337$

d. $P(\chi^2_{(3)} < .584) = .1,\ .584 = \dfrac{3s^2_x}{(10)^2},\ s_x = 4.4121$

e. $P(Z > \dfrac{65-60}{10}) = P(Z > .5) = .3085$

Use the binomial formula: $P(X > 2) = P(X = 3) + P(X = 4)$
$C^4_3(.6915)^3(.3085)^1 + C^4_4(.6915)^4(.3085)^0 = .6367$

7-58   a. $P(Z > \dfrac{1,500-1,600}{400/\sqrt{16}}) = P(Z > -1) = .8413$

b. $P(Z > 1.04) = .15,\ 1.04 = \dfrac{X_i-1,600}{400/\sqrt{16}},\ X_i = 1,704$

c. $P(\chi^2_{(15)} > 22.31) = .1,\ 22.31 = \dfrac{15s^2_x}{(400)^2},\ s_x = 487.825$

d. $p = P(Z > \dfrac{1,500-1,600}{400}) = P(Z > -.25) = .4013$

$\sigma_p = \sqrt{\dfrac{(.5987)(.4013)}{121}} = .04456$

$P(Z < \dfrac{.5-.5987}{.04456}) = P(Z < -2.21) = .0136$

7-60   a. $P(Z > \dfrac{120-100}{30/\sqrt{9}}) = P(Z > 2) = .0228$

b. $P(Z < -.843) = .20,\ -.843 = \dfrac{X_i-100}{30/\sqrt{9}},\ X_i = 91.57$

c. $P(\chi^2_{(8)} < 2.73) = .05,\ 2.73 = \dfrac{8s^2_x}{(30)^2},\ s_x = 17.525$

7-62 a. $P(\chi^2_{(15)} > 30.58) = .01, \ 30.58 = \dfrac{15 s^2_x}{(1.8)^2}, \ s_x = 2.5701$

b. $P(Z > 1.04) = .15, \ 1.04 = \dfrac{Difference}{1.8/\sqrt{16}}, \ Difference = .468$

c. $P(Z > 1.96) = .025, \ 1.96 = \dfrac{Difference}{1.8/\sqrt{16}}, \ Difference = .882$

7-64 a. $P(Z > \dfrac{.6 - .5}{\sqrt{(.5)(.5)/100}}) = P(Z > 2) = .0228$

b. $P(\dfrac{.4 - .5}{\sqrt{(.5)(.5)/100}} < Z < \dfrac{.55 - .5}{\sqrt{(.5)(.5)/100}}) = P(-1 < Z < 1) = .6826$

c. Replace 100 with 10 in parts a. and b. The answer will be larger for part a. and smaller for part b.

7-66 $P(Z < \dfrac{29.5 - 30}{1.3/\sqrt{16}}) = P(Z < -1.54) = .0618$

7-68 a. $P(Z > \dfrac{.28 - .2}{\sqrt{(.2)(.8)/300}}) = P(Z > 3.46) = .0003$

b. $P(Z < \dfrac{.28 - .4}{\sqrt{(.2)(.8)/300}}) = P(Z < -4.24) \approx .0000$

7-70 $P(\dfrac{(n-1)s^2_x}{\sigma^2_x} > \dfrac{19(2.5)^2}{(2)^2}) = P(\chi^2_{(19)} > 29.69) = $ between .05 and .1 (.0559 exactly)

Chapter 8: Estimation

8-2 a. Evidence of non-normality?

Normal Probability Plot

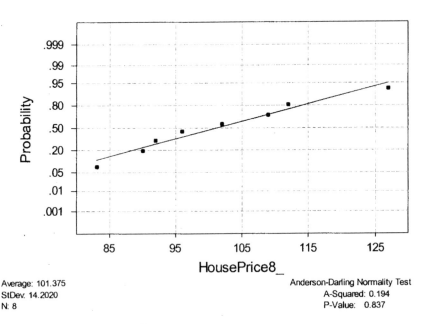

HousePrice8_

Average: 101.375
StDev. 14.2020
N: 8

Anderson-Darling Normality Test
A-Squared: 0.194
P-Value: 0.837

No evidence of non-normality.

b. The minimum variance unbiased point estimator of the population mean is the

sample mean: $\bar{X} = \dfrac{\sum X_i}{n} = 101.375$

c. The unbiased point estimate of the variance of the sample mean:

$s^2{}_x = \dfrac{\sum x_i^2 - n\bar{x}^2}{n-1} = \dfrac{83627 - 8(101.375)^2}{7} = 201.6964$

$Var(\bar{X}) = \dfrac{\sigma_{\bar{x}}^2}{n}; \quad V\hat{a}r(\bar{X}) = \dfrac{s_{\bar{x}}^2}{n} = \dfrac{201.6964}{8} = 25.2121$

d. $p_x = \dfrac{x}{n} = \dfrac{3}{8} = .375$

8-4   a. $E(\bar{X}) = \frac{1}{2}E(X_1) + \frac{1}{2}E(X_2) = \frac{\mu}{2} + \frac{\mu}{2} = \mu$

$E(Y) = \frac{1}{4}E(X_1) + \frac{3}{4}E(X_2) = \frac{\mu}{4} + \frac{3\mu}{4} = \mu$

$E(Z) = \frac{1}{3}E(X_1) + \frac{2}{3}E(X_2) = \frac{\mu}{3} + \frac{2\mu}{3} = \mu$

b. $Var(\bar{X}) = \frac{\sigma^2}{n} = \frac{1}{4}Var(X_1) + \frac{1}{4}Var(X_2) = \frac{1}{2}\frac{\sigma^2}{8} = \frac{\sigma^2}{4}$

$Var(Y) = \frac{1}{16}Var(X_1) + \frac{9}{16}Var(X_2) = \frac{5\sigma^2}{8}$

$Var(Z) = \frac{1}{9}Var(X_1) + \frac{4}{9}Var(X_2) = \frac{5\sigma^2}{9}$

$\bar{X}$ is most efficient since $Var(\bar{X}) < Var(Y) < Var(Z)$

c. Relative efficiency between Y and $\bar{X}$: $\frac{Var(Y)}{Var(\bar{X})} = \frac{5}{4} = 1.25$

Relative efficiency between Z and $\bar{X}$: $\frac{Var(Z)}{Var(\bar{X})} = \frac{10}{9} = 1.111$

8-6   a. Evidence of non-normality?

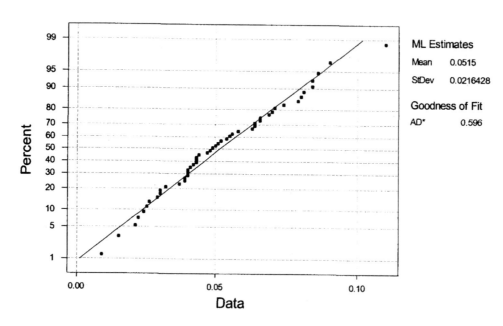

Normal Probability Plot for Leak Rates (
ML Estimates

No evidence of nonnormality exists.

b. The minimum variance unbiased point estimator of the population mean is the sample mean: $\bar{X} = \frac{\sum X_i}{n} = .0515$

b. The unbiased point estimate of the variance of the sample mean:

$s^2_x = (.0216428)^2 = .0004684$

$$Var(\bar{X}) = \frac{\sigma^2_{\bar{x}}}{n}; \quad V\hat{a}r(\bar{X}) = \frac{s^2_{\bar{x}}}{n} = \frac{.0004684}{50} = .00000937$$

8-8   a. $n = 25, \quad \bar{x} = 2.90, \quad \sigma = .45, \quad z_{.025} = 1.96$

$\bar{x} \pm z\left(\sigma / \sqrt{n}\right) = 2.90 \pm 1.96(.45/5) = 2.7236$ up to 3.0764

b. $2.99 - 2.90 = .09 = z_{\alpha/2}(.45/5), \quad z_{\alpha/2} = 1$

$\alpha = 2[1 - F_z(1)] = .3174$

$100(1 - .3174)\% = 68.26\%$

8-10 a. $n = 9, \quad \bar{x} = 187.9, \quad \sigma = 32.4, \quad z_{.10} = 1.28$

$187.9 \pm 1.28(32.4/3) = 174.076$ up to 201.724

b. $210.0 - 187.9 = 22.1 = z_{\alpha/2}(32.4/3), \quad z_{\alpha/2} = 2.05$

$\alpha = 2[1 - F_z(2.05)] = .0404$

$100(1 - .0404)\% = 95.96\%$

8-12   a.
Results for: Sugar.xls
Descriptive Statistics: Weights

Variable	N	Mean	Median	TrMean	StDev	SE Mean
Weights	100	520.95	518.75	520.52	9.45	0.95

Variable	Minimum	Maximum	Q1	Q3		
Weights	504.70	544.80	513.80	527.28		

90% confidence interval:
Results for: Sugar.xls
One-Sample T: Weights

Variable	N	Mean	StDev	SE Mean	90.0% CI
Weights	100	520.948	9.451	0.945	(519.379, 522.517)

b. narrower since a smaller value of z will be used in generating the 80% confidence interval.

8-14 $n = 174, \quad \bar{x} = 6.06, \quad s = 1.43$

$6.16 - 6.06 = .1 = z_{\alpha/2}(1.43/\sqrt{174}), \quad z_{\alpha/2} = .922$

$\alpha = 2[1 - F_z(.92)] = .3576$

$100(1 - .3576)\% = 64.24\%$

8-16 $n = 7, \quad \bar{x} = 74.7143, \quad s = 6.3957, \quad t_{6,.025} = 2.447$

margin for error: $\pm 2.447(6.3957/\sqrt{7}) = \pm 5.9152$

8-18 $n = 25, \quad \bar{x} = 42,740, \quad s = 4,780, \quad t_{24,.05} = 1.711$

$42,740 \pm 1.711(4780/5) = 41,104.28$ up to $44,375.72$

8-20   a. unbiased point estimate of proportion:

Tally for Discrete Variables: Adequate Variety

Adequate Variety	Count	CumCnt	Percent	CumPct
1	135	135	37.92	37.92
2	221	356	62.08	100.00
N=	356			

$$p = \frac{x}{n} = \frac{135}{356} = .3792$$

b. 90% confidence interval:

$n = 356, \quad p = 135/356 = .3792, \quad z_{.05} = 1.645$

$$p \pm z_{\alpha/2} \sqrt{\frac{p(1-p)}{n}} \; = \; .3792 \pm (1.645)\sqrt{.3792(.6208)/356} \; =$$

.3369 up to .4215

8-22 $m \arg in \; for \; error = z \sqrt{\dfrac{p(1-p)}{n}}$

$.90 - .8790 = .021, \quad \sqrt{\dfrac{p(1-p)}{n}} = \sqrt{\dfrac{.8790(.121)}{600}} = .0133$

$.021 = z_{\alpha/2} \, (.0133), \quad z_{\alpha/2} = 1.58$

$\alpha = 2[1 - F_z(1.58)] = .1142$

$100(1-.1142)\% = 88.58\%$

8-24 $n = 95, \quad p = 67/95 = .7053, \quad z_{.005} = 2.58$

$$p \pm z_{\alpha/2} \sqrt{\frac{p(1-p)}{n}} \; = \; .7053 \pm (2.58)\sqrt{.7053(.2947)/95} \; =$$

99% confidence interval: .5846 up to .8260

Using PHStat, the result is:

Sample Proportion	0.705263158
Z Value	-2.57583451
Standard Error of the Proportion	0.046776854
Interval Half Width	0.120489435
Confidence Interval	
Interval Lower Limit	0.584773723
Interval Upper Limit	0.825752593

8-26 $m \arg in \ for \ error = z\sqrt{\dfrac{p(1-p)}{n}}$

$.545 - .445 = .100, \ p = .495, \ \sqrt{\dfrac{p(1-p)}{n}} = \sqrt{\dfrac{.495(.505)}{198}} = .0355$

$.05 = z_{\alpha/2} \ (.0355), \ z_{\alpha/2} = 1.41$

$\alpha = 2[1 - F_z(1.41)] = .0793$

$100(1 - .1586)\% = 84.14\%$

8-28 $n = 246, \quad p = 40/246 = .1626, \quad z_{.01} = 2.326$

$p \pm z_{\alpha/2}\sqrt{\dfrac{p(1-p)}{n}} = \ .1626 \pm (2.326)\sqrt{.1626(.8374)/246} \ =$

98% confidence interval: .1079 up to .2173

Using PHStat, the result is:

Sample Proportion	0.1626
Z Value	-2.3263
Standard Error of the Proportion	0.0235
Interval Half Width	0.0547
Confidence Interval	
Interval Lower Limit	**0.1079**
Interval Upper Limit	**0.2173**

8-30 $n = 50, \quad s^2 = (.000478)^2, \quad \chi^2_{49,.025} = 70.222, \quad \chi^2_{49,.975} = 31.555$

$\dfrac{(n-1)s^2}{\chi^2_{n-1,\alpha/2}} < \sigma^2 < \dfrac{(n-1)s^2}{\chi^2_{n-1,1-\alpha/2}} \ =$

$\dfrac{49(.000478)^2}{70.222} < \sigma^2 < \dfrac{49(.000478)^2}{31.555} \ =$

$1.59E\text{-}7 < \sigma^2 \ < 3.55E\text{-}7$

8-32 $n = 20$, $s^2 = 6.62$, $\chi^2_{19,.025} = 32.85$, $\chi^2_{19,.975} = 8.91$

$$\frac{(n-1)s^2}{\chi^2_{n-1,\alpha/2}} < \sigma^2 < \frac{(n-1)s^2}{\chi^2_{n-1,1-\alpha/2}} =$$

$$\frac{19(6.62)}{32.85} < \sigma^2 < \frac{19(6.62)}{8.91} =$$

3.8289 up to 14.1167

Bounds = 5.1439

Similar values are found with PHStat,

Degrees of Freedom	19
Sum of Squares	125.78
Single Tail Area	0.025
Lower Chi-Square Value	8.9065
Upper Chi-Square Value	32.852

Results	
Interval Lower Limit for Variance	3.8285
Interval Upper Limit for Variance	14.122

Assumption: Population from which sample was drawn has an approximate normal distribution.

8-34   a. $n = 15$, $s^2 = (2.36)^2$, $\chi^2_{14,.05} = 26.12$, $\chi^2_{14,.95} = 5.63$

$$\frac{14(5.5696)}{26.12} < \sigma^2 < \frac{14(5.5696)}{5.63} =$$

2.9852 up to 13.8498

From PHStat, similar results.

Interval Lower Limit for Variance	2.9854
Interval Upper Limit for Variance	13.853

Assumption: Population from which sample was drawn has an approximate normal distribution.

b. wider since the chi-square statistic for a 99% confidence interval is larger than for a 95% confidence interval

8-36   Let X = Without Passive Solar; Y = With Passive Solar; $d_i = x_i - y_i$

$n = 10$, $\sum d_i = 373$, $\bar{d} = 37.3$, $\sum d_i^2 = 16,719$, $t_{9,.05} = 1.833$

$s_d = \sqrt{[16,719 - (10)(37.3)^2]/9} = 17.6575$

$37.3 \pm 1.833(17.6575)/\sqrt{10}$

$27.0649 < \mu_x - \mu_y < 47.5351$

8-38   95% confidence interval: $(\bar{X}-\bar{Y})\pm t_{(v,\alpha/2)}\sqrt{\dfrac{s_x^2}{n_x}+\dfrac{s_y^2}{n_y}}=$

where $\quad v=\dfrac{\left[\left(\dfrac{s_x^2}{n_x}\right)+\left(\dfrac{s_y^2}{n_y}\right)\right]^2}{\left(\dfrac{s_x^2}{n_x}\right)^2/(n_x-1)+\left(\dfrac{s_y^2}{n_y}\right)^2/(n_y-1)}=$

$v=\dfrac{\left[\left(\dfrac{2.53^2}{6}\right)+\left(\dfrac{8.61^2}{9}\right)\right]^2}{\left(\dfrac{2.53^2}{6}\right)^2/(6-1)+\left(\dfrac{8.61^2}{9}\right)^2/(9-1)}=9.940$

$(76.12-74.61)\pm t_{10,.025}\sqrt{\dfrac{s_x^2}{n_x}+\dfrac{s_y^2}{n_y}}=$

$1.51\pm 2.228\sqrt{\dfrac{(2.53)^2}{6}+\dfrac{(8.61)^2}{9}}=$

-5.286 up to 8.306

8-40 $n_x=138,\quad \bar{x}=36,558,\quad s_x=11,624,\quad z_{.05}=1.645$

$n_y=266,\quad \bar{y}=37,499,\quad s_y=16,521$

$(36,558-37,499)\pm(1.645)\sqrt{\dfrac{(11,624)^2}{138}+\dfrac{(16,521)^2}{266}}$

-3,270.41 up to 1,388.41

8-42 $n_x=9,\quad \bar{x}=9.78,\quad s_x^2=17.64,\quad t_{17,.05}=1.74$

$n_y=10,\quad \bar{y}=15.1,\quad s_y^2=27.01$

$(9.78-15.10)\pm(1.74)\sqrt{\dfrac{8(17.64)+9(27.01)}{17}\dfrac{19}{90}}$

-9.1207 up to -1.5193

8-44 $n_x=21,\quad \bar{x}=72.1,\quad s_x=11.3,\quad t_{37,.10}=1.303$

$n_y=18,\quad \bar{y}=73.8,\quad s_y=10.6$

$(72.1-73.8)\pm(1.303)\sqrt{\dfrac{20(11.3)^2+17(10.6)^2}{37}\dfrac{39}{378}}$

-6.2971 up to 2.8971

8-46

Results for: Library.xls

Tabulated Statistics: Class, Adequate Variety

Rows: Class   Columns: Adequate
                1   2   All

	1	2	All
1	73	71	144
	50.69	49.31	100.00
	54.07	32.27	40.56
	20.56	20.00	40.56
2	26	76	102
	25.49	74.51	100.00
	19.26	34.55	28.73
	7.32	21.41	28.73
3	19	47	66
	28.79	71.21	100.00
	14.07	21.36	18.59
	5.35	13.24	18.59
4	17	26	43
	39.53	60.47	100.00
	12.59	11.82	12.11
	4.79	7.32	12.11
All	135	220	355
	38.03	61.97	100.00
	100.00	100.00	100.00
	38.03	61.97	100.00

Cell Contents --
                Count
                % of Row
                % of Col
                % of Tbl

$$p_{seniors} = 17/43 = .3953, \quad p_{freshmen} = 73/144 = .5069$$

$$(.3953 - .5069) \pm (1.645)\sqrt{\frac{(.3953)(.6047)}{43} + \frac{(.5069)(.4931)}{144}} =$$

$-.1116 \pm .1405 = -.2521$ up to $.0289$

8-48 $n_x = 100, \quad p_x = .61, \quad n_y = 100, \quad p_y = .54$

$$.1 - (.61 - .54) = .03 = z_{\alpha/2}\sqrt{\frac{(.61)(.39)}{100} + \frac{(.54)(.46)}{100}}, \quad z_{\alpha/2} = .43$$

$\alpha = 2[1 - F_z(.43)] = .6672, \quad 100(1 - .6672)\% = 33.28\%$ confidence level

8-50   a. $z_{.05} = 1.645, \quad B = .04$

$$n = \frac{.25(z_{\alpha/2})^2}{B^2} = \frac{(.25)(1.645)^2}{(.04)^2} = 422.8, \text{ take } n = 423$$

b. $\frac{(.25)(1.96)^2}{(.04)^2} = 600.25$, take $n = 601$

c. $\frac{(.25)(2.33)^2}{(.05)^2} = 542.89$, take $n = 543$

8-52 $z_{.05} = 1.645, \quad B = .03$

$$n = \frac{.25(z_{\alpha/2})^2}{B^2} = \frac{(.25)(1.645)^2}{(.03)^2} = 751.7, \text{ take n} = 752$$

8-54 $n = 16, \quad \bar{x} = 150, \quad s = 12, \quad t_{15,.025} = 2.131$

$$\bar{x} \pm t\left(\frac{s}{\sqrt{n}} \right) = 150 \pm 2.131(12/4) = 143.607 \text{ up to } 156.393$$

Using PHStat,

Standard Error of the Mean	3
Degrees of Freedom	15
t Value	2.131450856
Interval Half Width	6.394352567
Confidence Interval	
Interval Lower Limit	**143.61**
Interval Upper Limit	**156.39**

It is recommended that he stock 157 gallons.

8-56   Results from Minitab:

Descriptive Statistics: Passengers8_56

Variable	N	Mean	Median	TrMean	StDev	SE Mean
Passenge	50	136.22	141.00	136.75	24.44	3.46
Variable	Minimum	Maximum	Q1	Q3		
Passenge	86.00	180.00	118.50	152.00		

One-Sample T: Passengers8_56

Variable	N	Mean	StDev	SE Mean	95.0% CI	
Passengers8_	50	136.22	24.44	3.46	(129.27,	143.17)

Using results from PHStat,

Data	
Sample Standard Deviation	24.43925414
Sample Mean	136.22
Sample Size	50
Confidence Level	95%
Standard Error of the Mean	3.456232466
Degrees of Freedom	49
t Value	2.009574018
Interval Half Width	6.945554964
Confidence Interval	
Interval Lower Limit	**129.27**
Interval Upper Limit	**143.17**

8-58   a. $n_x = 225$, $p_x = .6222$, $n_y = 210$, $p_y = .5714$, $z_{.05} = 1.645$

$p_x - p_y = .6222 - .5714 = .0508$

b.   Minitab results:

Test and CI for Two Proportions
Sample   X   N   Sample p
1   140   225   0.622222
2   120   210   0.571429
Estimate for p(1) - p(2): 0.0507937
95% CI for p(1) - p(2): (-0.0413643, 0.142952)

8-60   Assume both populations are distributed normally with equal variances

$n_x = 15$, $\bar{x} = 470$, $s_x = 5$, $t_{25,.05} = 1.708$

$n_y = 12$, $\bar{y} = 460$, $s_y = 7$

$$(470 - 460) \pm (1.708) \sqrt{\frac{(n_x - 1)s_x^2 + (n_y - 1)s_y^2}{n_x + n_y - 2}} \sqrt{\frac{1}{n_x} + \frac{1}{n_y}}$$

$$(470 - 460) \pm (1.708) \sqrt{\frac{(15 - 1)5^2 + (12 - 1)7^2}{15 + 12 - 2}} \sqrt{\frac{1}{15} + \frac{1}{12}}$$

$10 \pm (1.708)(5.9632)(.3873)$

$10 \pm 3.9447 = 6.055$ up to 13.945

Since both endpoints of the confidence interval are positive, this provides evidence that the new machine provides a larger mean filling weight than the old

8-62 a.   The minimum variance unbiased point estimator of the population mean is the

sample mean: $\bar{X} = \dfrac{\sum X_i}{n} = \dfrac{27}{8} = 3.375$.   The unbiased point estimate of the

variance: $s^2{}_x = \dfrac{\sum x_i^2 - n\bar{x}^2}{n - 1} = \dfrac{94.62 - 8(3.375)^2}{7} = .4993$

b. $p_x = \dfrac{x}{n} = \dfrac{3}{8} = .375$

Chapter 9: Hypothesis Testing

9-2 $H_0: T_B \leq T_G$ No difference in the total number of votes between Bush and Gore

       $H_1: T_B > T_G$ Bush with more votes

9-4 $H_0: \pi_A \geq \pi_B$: There is no difference in the percentage of underfilled cereal packages

       $H_1: \pi_A < \pi_B$: Lower percentage after the change

9-6 $H_0: \mu \geq 50$; $H_1: \mu < 50$; reject H_0 if $Z_{.10} < -1.28$

$$Z = \frac{48.2 - 50}{3/\sqrt{9}} = -1.8,$$ therefore, Reject H_0 at the 10% level.

9-8 $H_0: \mu \geq 3$; $H_1: \mu < 3$;

$$Z = \frac{2.4 - 3}{1.8/\sqrt{100}} = -3.33,$$ p-value $= 1 - F_Z(3.33) = 1 - .9996 = .0004$,

therefore, reject H_0 at levels in excess of .04%

9-10 $H_0: \mu = 0$; $H_1: \mu \neq 0$;

$$Z = \frac{.078 - 0}{.201/\sqrt{76}} = 3.38,$$ p-value $= 2[1 - F_Z(3.38)] = 2[1 - .9996] = .0008$,

therefore, reject H_0 at levels in excess of .08%

9-12 $H_0: \mu = 0$; $H_1: \mu < 0$;

$$Z = \frac{-2.91 - 0}{11.33/\sqrt{170}} = -3.35,$$ p-value $= 1 - F_Z(3.35) = 1 - .9996 = .0004$,

therefore, reject H_0 at any common level of alpha.

9-14   a. No, the 95% confidence level provides for 2.5% of the area in either tail. This does not correspond to a one-tailed hypothesis test with an alpha of 5% which has 5% of the area in one of the tails.

       b. Yes.

9-16 $H_0: \mu = 20$; $H_1: \mu \neq 20$; reject H_0 if $|t_{8, .05/2}| > 2.306$

$$t = \frac{20.3556 - 20}{.6126/\sqrt{9}} = 1.741,$$ therefore, do not reject H_0 at the 5% level

9-18   The population values must be assumed to be normally distributed.

$H_0: \mu \geq 50; H_1: \mu < 50;$ reject H_0 if $t_{19, .05} < -1.729$

$t = \dfrac{41.3 - 50}{12.2/\sqrt{20}}$ = -3.189, therefore, reject H_0 at the 5% level

9-20 $H_0: \pi \leq .25; H_1: \pi > .25;$

$z = \dfrac{.2908 - .25}{\sqrt{(.25)(.75)/361}}$ = 1.79, p-value = $1 - F_Z(1.79) = 1 - .9633 = .0367$

Therefore, reject H_0 at alpha greater than 3.67%

9-22 $H_0: \pi = .5; H_1: \pi \neq .5;$

$z = \dfrac{.45 - .5}{\sqrt{(.5)(.5)/160}}$ = -1.26, p-value = $2[1 - F_Z(1.26)] = 2[1 - .8962] = .2076$

The probability of finding a random sample with a sample proportion this far or further from .5 if the null hypothesis is really true is .2076

9-24 $H_0: \pi = .5; H_1: \pi > .5;$

$z = \dfrac{.56 - .5}{\sqrt{(.5)(.5)/50}}$ = .85, p-value = $1 - F_Z(.85) = 1 - .8023 = .1977$

Therefore, reject H_0 at alpha levels in excess of 19.77%

9-25 $H_0: \pi = .75; H_1: \pi < .75;$

$z = \dfrac{.686 - .75}{\sqrt{(.25)(.75)/172}}$ = -1.94, p-value = $1 - F_Z(1.94) = 1 - .9738 = .0262$

Therefore, reject H_0 at alpha levels in excess of 2.62%

9-26 $H_0: \pi \geq .75; H_1: \pi < .75;$

$z = \dfrac{.6931 - .75}{\sqrt{(.75)(.25)/202}}$ = -1.87, p-value = $1 - F_Z(1.87) = 1 - .9693 = .0307$

Therefore, reject H_0 at alpha levels in excess of 3.07%

9-28   a. $s^2 = 5.1556$

   b. $H_0: \sigma^2 \leq 2.25; H_1: \sigma^2 > 2.25;$ reject H_0 if $\chi^2_{(9,.05)} > 16.92$

$\chi^2 = \dfrac{9(5.1556)}{2.25} = 20.6224,$

Therefore, reject H_0 at the 5% level

9-30   The hypothesis test assumes that the population values are normally distributed

$H_0: \sigma = 2.0; H_1: \sigma > 2.0;$ reject H_0 if $\chi^2_{(19,.05)} > 30.14$

$\chi^2 = \dfrac{19(2.36)^2}{(2)^2} = 26.4556,$ Therefore, do not reject H_0 at the 5% level

9-32 $H_o: \mu_x - \mu_y = 0; H_1: \mu_x - \mu_y > 0;$

$t = \dfrac{1475 - 0}{1862.985/\sqrt{8}} = 2.239,$ p-value $= .0301,$ Therefore, reject H_0 at levels in excess of

3%

9-34 $H_o: \mu_x - \mu_y = 0; H_1: \mu_x - \mu_y \neq 0;$

$t = \dfrac{.518 - 0}{.3055/\sqrt{145}} = 2.0417,$ p-value $= .043$

Therefore, reject H_0 at alpha levels in excess of 4.3%

9-36 $H_o: \mu_x - \mu_y = 0; H_1: \mu_x - \mu_y > 0;$

$z = \dfrac{1.91 - .21}{\sqrt{(1.32)^2/125 + (.53)^2/86}} = 12.96$

Therefore, reject H_0 at all common levels of alpha

9-38 $H_o: \mu_x - \mu_y = 0; H_1: \mu_x - \mu_y \neq 0;$

$s_p^{\,2} = \dfrac{(n_x - 1)s_x^{\,2} + (n_y - 1)s_y^{\,2}}{n_x + n_y - 2} = \dfrac{35(22.93)^2 + 35(27.56)^2}{36 + 36 - 2} = 642.66925$

$t = \dfrac{\bar{X} - \bar{Y} - D_0}{\sqrt{\dfrac{s_p^{\,2}}{n_x} + \dfrac{s_p^{\,2}}{n_y}}} = \dfrac{36.21 - 47.56}{\sqrt{\dfrac{642.66925}{36} + \dfrac{642.66925}{36}}} = -1.8995$

$t_{70}(1.8995) = .0308;$ p-value $= 2(.0308) = .0616$

Therefore, reject H_0 at levels in excess of 6.16%

9-40 $H_o: \mu_x - \mu_y = 0; H_1: \mu_x - \mu_y > 0;$

$s^2_p = \dfrac{9(2107)^2 + 9(1681)^2}{10 + 10 - 2} = 3{,}632{,}605$

$t = \dfrac{9254 - 8167}{\sqrt{\dfrac{3632605}{10} + \dfrac{3632605}{10}}} = 1.275,$

Therefore, do not reject H_0 at the 10% alpha level since $1.275 < 1.33 = t_{(18,.1)}$

9-42 $H_0 : \pi_x - \pi_y = 0; H_1 : \pi_x - \pi_y \neq 0;$ reject H_0 if $|z_{.025}| > 1.96$

$$p_o = \frac{368(.25) + 116(.319)}{368 + 116} = .266$$

$$z = \frac{.25 - .319}{\sqrt{\dfrac{(.266)(.734)}{368} + \dfrac{(.266)(.734)}{116}}} = -1.466$$

Therefore, do not reject H_0 at the 5% level

9-44 $H_0 : \pi_x - \pi_y = 0; H_1 : \pi_x - \pi_y \neq 0;$

$$p_o = \frac{191 + 145}{381 + 166} = .614$$

$$z = \frac{.501 - .873}{\sqrt{\dfrac{(.614)(.386)}{381} + \dfrac{(.614)(.386)}{166}}} = -8.216$$

Therefore, reject H_0 at all common levels of alpha

9-46 $H_0 : \pi_x - \pi_y = 0; H_1 : \pi_x - \pi_y < 0;$ reject H_0 if $z_{.01} < -2.33$

$$p_o = \frac{480 + 790}{1200 + 1000} = .577$$

$$z = \frac{.4 - .79}{\sqrt{\dfrac{(.577)(.423)}{1200} + \dfrac{(.577)(.423)}{1000}}} = -18.44$$

Therefore, reject H_0 at the 1% level

9-48 $H_0 : \sigma^2{}_x = \sigma^2{}_y; H_1 : \sigma^2{}_x > \sigma^2{}_y;$ reject H_0 if $F_{(3,6,.05)} > 4.76$

$F = 114.09/16.08 = 7.095$, Therefore, reject H_0 at the 5% level

9-50 $H_0 : \sigma^2{}_x = \sigma^2{}_y; H_1 : \sigma^2{}_x \neq \sigma^2{}_y;$ $F = (2107)^2/(1681)^2 = 1.57$

Therefore, do not reject H_0 at the 10% level since $1.57 < 3.18 \approx F_{(9,9,.05)}$

9-52 H_0 is rejected when $\dfrac{\bar{X} - 50}{3/\sqrt{9}} < -1.28$ or when $\bar{X} < 48.72$

power of the test $= 1 - \beta = 1 - P(Z > \dfrac{48.72 - 49}{3/\sqrt{9}}) = 1 - P(Z > -.28) = .3897$

9-54 H_0 is rejected when $-2.275 < \dfrac{\overline{X} - 4}{1.32/\sqrt{1562}} < 2.275$ or when $3.914 < \overline{X} < 4.086$

$\beta = P(\dfrac{3.914 - 3.95}{1.32/\sqrt{1562}} < Z < \dfrac{4.086 - 3.95}{1.32/\sqrt{1562}}) = P(-1.08 > Z > 4.07) = .8599$

9-56 H_0 is rejected when $\dfrac{p - .25}{\sqrt{(.25)(.75)/998}} < -1.645$ or when $p < .2275$

power of the test $= 1 - \beta = 1 - P(Z > \dfrac{.2275 - .2}{\sqrt{(.2)(.8)/998}}) =$

$1 - P(Z > 2.17) = .9850$

9-58   a. $\alpha = P(Z < \dfrac{30.8 - 32}{3/\sqrt{36}}) = P(Z < -2.4) = 0.0082$

b. $\alpha = P(Z < \dfrac{30.8 - 32}{3/\sqrt{9}}) = P(Z < -1.2) = 0.1151$

c. $\beta = P(Z > \dfrac{30.8 - 31}{3/\sqrt{36}}) = P(Z > -.4) = 0.6554$

9-60   a. The null hypothesis is the statement that is assumed to be true unless there is sufficient evidence to suggest that the null hypothesis can be rejected. The alternative hypothesis is that the statement that will be accepted if there is sufficient evidence to reject the null hypothesis

b. A simple hypothesis assumes a specific value for the population parameter that is being tested. A composite hypothesis assumes a range of values for the population parameter.

c. One sided alternatives can be either a one-tailed upper (> greater than) or a one-tailed lower (< less than) statement about the population parameter. Two sided alternatives are made up of both greater than or less than statements and are written as (≠ not equal to).

d. A Type I error is falsely rejecting the null hypothesis. To make a Type I error, the truth must be that the null hypothesis is really true and yet you conclude to reject the null and accept the alternative. A Type II error is falsely not rejecting the null hypothesis when in fact the null hypothesis is false. To make a Type II error, the null hypothesis must be false (the alternative is true) and yet you conclude to not reject the null hypothesis.

e. Significance level is the chosen level of significance that established the probability of a making a Type I error. This is represented by alpha. The power of the test is the ability of the hypothesis test to identify correctly a false null hypothesis and reject it.

9-62   The p-value indicates the likelihood of getting the sample result at least as far away from the hypothesized value as the one that was found, assuming that the distribution is really centered on the null hypothesis. The smaller the p-value, the stronger the evidence against the null hypothesis.

9-64   a. False. The significance level is the probability of making a Type I error – falsely rejecting the null hypothesis when in fact the null is true.

      b. True

      b. True

      c. False. The power of the test is the ability of the test to correctly reject a false null hypothesis.

      d. False. The rejection region is further away from the hypothesized value at the 1% level than it is at the 5% level. Therefore, it is still possible to reject at the 5% level but not at the 1% level.

      f. True

      g. False. The p-value tells the strength of the evidence against the null hypothesis.

9-66   a. Assume that the population is normally distributed

One-Sample T: Grams:9-66

```
Test of mu = 5 vs mu not = 5
Variable           N      Mean      StDev    SE Mean
Grams:9-66        12     4.9725    0.0936    0.0270

Variable              95.0% CI              T       P
Grams:9-66     (  4.9130,   5.0320)      -1.02   0.331
```

$$\bar{X} = 4.9725; s_x = .0936$$

$$H_0: \mu = 5; H_1: \mu \neq 5; \text{ reject } H_0 \text{ if } |t_{(11, .05)}| > 2.201$$

$$t = \frac{4.9725 - 5}{.0936/\sqrt{12}} = -1.018, \text{ Therefore, do not reject } H_0 \text{ at the 5\% level}$$

    b. $H_0: \sigma = .025; H_1: \sigma > .025; \text{ reject } H_0 \text{ if } \chi^2_{(11,.05)} > 19.68$

$$\chi^2 = \frac{11(.0936)^2}{(.025)^2} = 154.19, \text{ Therefore, reject } H_0 \text{ at the 5\% level}$$

9-68   a. $\alpha = P(Z < \dfrac{776 - 800}{1120/\sqrt{100)}}) = P(Z < -2) = .0228$

    b. $\beta = P(Z > \dfrac{776 - 740}{1120/\sqrt{100}}) = P(Z > 3) = .0014$

    c. i) smaller ii) smaller

    d. i) smaller ii) larger

9-70 $H_0: \pi = .5; H_1: \pi \neq .5;$

$$z = \frac{.4808 - .5}{\sqrt{(.5)(.5)/104}} = -.39, \text{ p-value} = 2[1\text{-}F_Z(.39)] = 2[1-.6517] = .6966$$

Therefore, reject H_0 at levels in excess of 69.66%

9-72 $H_0: \pi \leq .25; H_1: \pi > .25;$ reject H_0 if $z_{.05} > 1.645$

$$z = \frac{.3333 - .25}{\sqrt{(.25)(.75)/150}} = 2.356,$$

Therefore, reject H_0 at the 5% level

9-74 Assume that the population of matched differences are normally distributed

$H_o: \mu_x - \mu_y = 0; H_1: \mu_x - \mu_y \neq 0;$ reject H_0 if $|t_{(9,.05)}| > 1.833$

$\overline{X}$ of the matched differences = 1.13, s of the matched differences = 1.612

$$t = \frac{1.13 - 0}{1.612/\sqrt{10}} = 2.22$$

Therefore, reject H_0 at the 10% level

9-76 $H_o: \mu_x - \mu_y = 0; H_1: \mu_x - \mu_y \neq 0;$

$$z = \frac{2.21 - 1.47}{\sqrt{(2.21)^2/34 + (1.69)^2/86}} = 1.76, \text{ p-value} = 2[1\text{-}F_Z(1.76)] = 2[1 - .9608] = .0784$$

Therefore, reject H_0 at all levels in excess of 7.84%

9-78 $H_o: \mu_x - \mu_y = 0; H_1: \mu_x - \mu_y \neq 0;$ reject H_0 if $|z_{.05}| > 1.645$

$$z = \frac{35.02 - 36.34}{\sqrt{(18.2)^2/44 + (18.94)^2/68}} = -.369,$$

Therefore, do not reject H_0 at the 10% level

9-80 Assuming the populations are normally distributed with equal variances and independent random samples:

Scientific American: $\overline{X} = 10.968; s_x = 2.647$

Sports Illustrated: $\overline{Y} = 6.738; s_y = 1.636$

$H_o: \mu_x - \mu_y = 0; H_1: \mu_x - \mu_y > 0;$ reject H_0 if $t_{(10,.05)} > 1.812$

$$t = \frac{10.968 - 6.738}{\sqrt{\frac{5(2.647)^2 + 5(1.636)^2}{10} \cdot \frac{12}{36}}} = 3.33$$

Therefore, reject H_0 at the 5% level

9-82 $H_o : \mu_x - \mu_y = 0; H_1 : \mu_x - \mu_y > 0;$

$$z = \frac{2.83 - 3.0}{\sqrt{\frac{(.89)^2}{202} + \frac{(.67)^2}{291}}} = -2.30, \text{p-value} = 1 - F_Z(2.3) = 1 - .9893 = .0107$$

Therefore, reject H_0 at levels of alpha in excess of 1.07%

9-84   a. $H_0 : \pi \geq .5; H_1 : \pi < .5;$ reject H_0 if $z_{.05} < -1.645$

$$z = \frac{.455 - .5}{\sqrt{(.5)(.5)/178}} = -1.2,$$

Therefore, do not reject H_0 at the 5% level

b. $H_0 : \pi_x - \pi_y = 0; H_1 : \pi_x - \pi_y \neq 0;$ reject Ho if $|z_{.025}| > 1.96$

$$P_o = \frac{75 + 81}{148 + 178} = .478$$

$$z = \frac{.5068 - .455}{\sqrt{(.478)(.522)(\frac{1}{148} + \frac{1}{178})}} = .932$$

Therefore, do not reject H_0 at the 5% level

9-86 $H_0 : \pi_x - \pi_y = 0; H_1 : \pi_x - \pi_y < 0;$ reject Ho if $|z_{.01}| < -2.33$

$$P_o = \frac{11 + 27}{67 + 113} = .211$$

$$z = \frac{.164 - .239}{\sqrt{(.211)(.789)(\frac{1}{67} + \frac{1}{113})}} = -1.19$$

Therefore, do not reject H_0 at the 1% level

9-88 $H_0 : \pi_x - \pi_y = 0; H_1 : \pi_x - \pi_y > 0;$

$$P_o = \frac{53 + 47}{94 + 68} = .617$$

$$z = \frac{.564 - .691}{\sqrt{(.617)(.383)(\frac{1}{94} + \frac{1}{68})}} = -1.653, \text{p-value} = 1 - F_Z(1.65)] = .0495$$

Therefore, reject H_0 at levels of alpha in excess of 4.95%

9-90   No, equality of variances test is based on independent random samples being drawn.

9-92   The hypothesis test is: $H_0: \mu \geq 100$; $H_1: \mu < 100$; reject H_0 if $Z_{.05} > 1.645$

Note: two zero values can be removed since a loaf of bread cannot weigh zero grams:
Using Minitab:

One-Sample T: Dbread
```
Test of mu = 100 vs mu < 100
Variable          N        Mean      StDev    SE Mean
Dbread           37      101.19      32.79       5.39

Variable      95.0% Upper Bound          T      P
Dbread                      110.29       0.22   0.587
```

Using PHStat:

t Test for Hypothesis of the Mean

Data	
Null Hypothesis $\mu=$	100
Level of Significance	0.05
Sample Size	37
Sample Mean	101.1895132
Sample Standard Deviation	32.79143341
Intermediate Calculations	
Standard Error of the Mean	5.390878445
Degrees of Freedom	36
t Test Statistic	0.22065295
Lower-Tail Test	
Lower Critical Value	-1.688297289
p-Value	0.586695339
Do not reject the null hypothesis	

At the .05 level of significance, do not reject H_0

9-94   a. $H_o : \mu_1 - \mu_2 = 0; H_1 : \mu_1 - \mu_2 > 0;$

Results for: Ole.MTW

Two-Sample T-Test and CI: Olesales, Carlsale

Two-sample T for Olesales vs Carlsale

```
             N     Mean    StDev   SE Mean
Olesales   156     3791     5364       429
Carlsale   156     2412     4249       340
```

Difference = mu Olesales - mu Carlsale
Estimate for difference: 1379
95% lower bound for difference: 475
T-Test of difference = 0 (vs >): T-Value = 2.52   P-Value = 0.006   DF = 310
Both use Pooled StDev =   4839

Reject Ho at the .01 level of significance

b. $H_o : \mu_1 - \mu_2 = 0; H_1 : \mu_1 - \mu_2 \neq 0;$

Two-Sample T-Test and CI: Oleprice, Carlpric

Two-sample T for Oleprice vs Carlpric

```
N        Mean    StDev   SE Mean
Oleprice 156     0.819    0.139     0.011
Carlpric 156     0.819    0.120    0.0096
```

Difference = mu Oleprice - mu Carlpric
Estimate for difference: -0.0007
95% CI for difference: (-0.0297, 0.0283)
T-Test of difference = 0 (vs not =): T-Value = -0.05   P-Value = 0.962   DF = 310
Both use Pooled StDev = 0.130

Do not reject Ho at any common level of significance. Note that the 95% confidence interval contains 0, therefore, no evidence of a difference.

9-96   Cost Model where W = Total Cost: W = 1,000 + 5X

$\mu_W = 1,000 + 5(400) = 3,000$

$\sigma^2{}_W = (5)^2(625) = 15,625, \quad \sigma_W = 125, \quad \sigma_{\bar{W}} = \dfrac{125}{\sqrt{25}} = 25$

$H_0 : W \leq 3000; \quad H1 : W > 3000;$

Using the test statistic criteria: (3050 – 3000)/25 = 2.00 which yields a p-value of .0228, therefore, reject H_0 at the .05 level.

Using the sample statistic criteria: $\bar{X}_{crit} = 3,000 + (25)(1.645) = 3041.1, \; \bar{X}_{calc} = 3,050,$ since $\bar{X}_{calc} = 3,050 > \bar{X}_{crit} = 3041.1,$ therefore, reject H_0 at the .05 level.

9-98 $H_0 : \mu \le 40, H_1 : \mu > 40; \overline{X} = 49.73 > 42.86$ reject H_0

One-Sample T: Salmon Weight

```
Test of mu = 40 vs mu > 40

Variable          N        Mean      StDev    SE Mean
Salmon Weigh     39       49.73      10.60       1.70

Variable      95.0% Lower Bound          T        P
Salmon Weigh                 46.86     5.73    0.000
```

$\overline{X}_{crit} = Ho + t_{crit}(S_{\overline{x}})$: $40 + 1.686(1.70) = 42.8662$

Population mean for $\beta = .50$ (power=.50): tcrit = 0.0: $42.8662 + 0.0(1.70) = 42.8662$

Population mean for $\beta = .25$ (power=.75): tcrit = .681: $42.8662 + .681(1.70) = 44.0239$

Population mean for $\beta = .10$ (power=.90): tcrit = 1.28: $42.8662 + 1.28(1.70) = 45.0422$

Population mean for $\beta = .05$ (power=.95): tcrit = 1.645: $42.8662 + 1.645(1.70) = 45.6627$

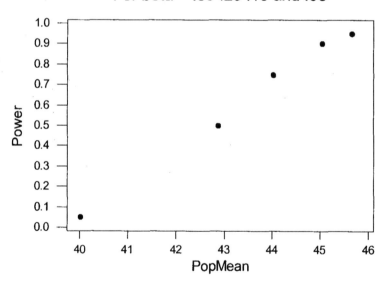

Power curve - 9_98
For beta = .50 .25 .10 and .05

Chapter 10: Simple Regression

10-2   a. $n = 13, \sum x = 7.2, \bar{X} = 7.2/13 = .5538, \sum x^2 = 80.06$

$\sum y = 153.6, \bar{Y} = 153.6/13 = 11.8154, \sum y^2 = 3718.76, \sum xy = -69.67$

$$r = \frac{-69.67 - (13)(.5538)(11.8154)}{\sqrt{(80.06 - (13)(.5538)^2)(3718.76 - (13)(11.8154)^2)}} = -.4066$$

b. $H_o : \rho = 0, H_1 : \rho \neq 0$

$$t = \frac{-.4066}{\sqrt{[1 - (-.4066)^2]/11}} = -1.4761$$

$t_{11,.10} = 1.363$, $t_{11,.05} = 1.796$

Therefore, do not reject Ho at the 10% level

10-4 $H_o : \rho = 0, H_1 : \rho \neq 0$

$n = 17, \sum x = 67.83, \bar{X} = 67.83/17 = 3.99, \sum x^2 = 365.3705$

$\sum y = 2716.07, \bar{Y} = 2716.07/17 = 159.7688, \sum y^2 = 485,829.5153, \sum xy = 10,964.5397$

$$r = \frac{10,964.5397 - (17)(3.99)(159.7688)}{\sqrt{(365.3705 - 17(3.99)^2)(485,829.5153 - (17)(159.7688)^2)}} = .0575$$

$$t = \frac{.0575}{\sqrt{[1 - (.0575)^2]/15}} = .2230$$

Therefore, do not reject Ho at the 20% level since $.2230 < 1.341 = t_{15,.10}$

10-6 $H_o : \rho = 0, H_1 : \rho > 0$

$$t = \frac{.11}{\sqrt{[1 - (.11)^2]/351}} = 2.07$$

Therefore, reject Ho at the 2.5% level since $2.07 > 1.96 = z_{.025} \approx t_{351,.025}$

10-8   A population regression equation consists of the true regression coefficients β_i's and the true model error ε_i. By contrast, the estimated regression model consists of the estimated regression coefficients b_i's and the residual term e_i. The population regression equation is a model that purports to measure the actual value of Y while the sample regression equation is an estimate of the predicted value of the dependent variable Y.

10-10 The constant represents an adjustment for the estimated model and not the number sold when the price is zero.

10.12   a. plot the data and estimate the linear regression of sales on price

Regression Plot

Sales = 644.516 - 42.5806 Price

S = 12.7423   R-Sq = 87.8 %   R-Sq(adj) = 85.8 %

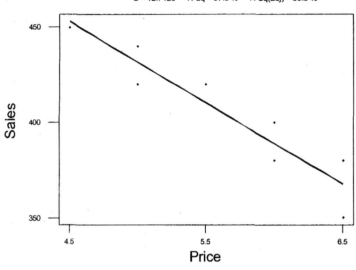

$$\hat{y} = 644.5 - 42.58x$$

b. For a one hundred dollar increase in price, we would expect that sales would fall by $42.5806

10.14   a. $\hat{y} = 1.89 + 0.0896x$

Regression Plot

Percent Loss = 1.88534 + 0.0895659 Percent Gain

S = 0.642483   R-Sq = 53.8 %   R-Sq(adj) = 51.8 %

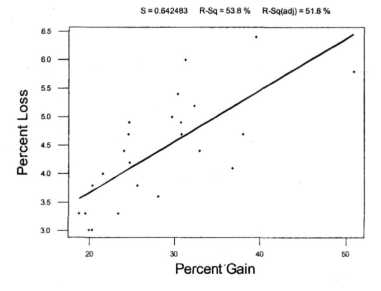

b. 0.0896%. For a one percent pre-November 13 gain, we would estimate that there would be a loss of .0896% on November 13.

10-16 a. $n = 20, n = 20, \bar{X} = 25.4/20 = 1.27, \bar{Y} = 22.6/20 = 1.13$

$$b = \frac{150.5 - (20)(1.13)(1.27)}{145.7 - (20)(1.27)^2} = 1.0737$$

$$a = 1.13 - 1.0737(1.27) = -.2336$$

b. For a one unit increase in the rate of return of the S&P 500 index, we estimate that the rate of return of the corporation's stock will increase by 1.07%

c. When the percentage rate of return of the S&P 500 index is zero, we estimate that the corporation's rate of return will be -.2336%

10-18 a. $b = 180/350 = .5143, a = 16 - .5143(25.5) = 2.8854$

b. For a one unit increase in the average cost of a meal, we would estimate that the number of bottles sold would increase by .5148%

c. Yes. 2.8854 bottles are estimated to be sold, regardless of the price paid for a meal.

10.20 a. $R^2 = \dfrac{\sum(\hat{y}_i - \bar{y})^2}{\sum(y_i - \bar{y})^2} = \dfrac{\sum[(b_i(x_i - \bar{x})]^2}{\sum(y_i - \bar{y})^2} = b_i^2 \dfrac{\sum(x_i - \bar{x})^2}{\sum(y_i - \bar{y})^2}$

b. $R^2 = b_i^2 \dfrac{\sum(x_i - \bar{x})^2}{\sum(y_i - \bar{y})^2} = b \dfrac{\sum(x_i - \bar{x})(y_i - \bar{y})}{\sum(y_i - \bar{y})^2} = \dfrac{[\sum(x_i - \bar{x})(y_i - \bar{y})]^2}{\sum(x_i - x)^2 \sum(y_i - y)^2} = r^2$

c. $b_1 b_1^* = \dfrac{\sum(x_i - \bar{x})(y_i - \bar{y})}{\sum(x_i - \bar{x})^2} \dfrac{\sum(x_i - \bar{x})(y_i - \bar{y})}{\sum(y_i - \bar{y})^2} = r^2$

10-22 $n = 13, \bar{x} = .5538, \sum x^2 = 80.06, \bar{y} = 11.8154, \sum y^2 = 3718.76, b = -2.0341$

Based on the result from Exercise 20.a: $R^2 = (2.0341)^2 \dfrac{80.06 - 13(.5538)^2}{3718.76 - 13(11.8154)^2} = .1653$

From Exercise 2: $r = -.4066, r^2 = .1653 = R^2$

Or, from the Minitab output:

Regression Analysis: Dow1Yr versus Dow5day

```
The regression equation is
Dow1Yr = 12.9 - 2.03 Dow5day
Predictor        Coef      SE Coef           T          P
Constant       12.942        3.420        3.78      0.003
Dow5day        -2.034        1.378       -1.48      0.168

S = 12.02      R-Sq = 16.5%      R-Sq(adj) = 8.9%

Analysis of Variance
Source              DF          SS          MS          F          P
Regression           1       314.8       314.8       2.18      0.168
Residual Error      11      1589.2       144.5
Total               12      1903.9
```

10-24   a. The Minitab output below shows the predicted value (Fit) and the residuals:
Regression Analysis: Change in Absence Rate versus Change in UN Rate
The regression equation is
CHANGE IN MEAN EMPLOYEE ABSENCE = 0.0449 - 0.224 CHANGE IN UNEMPLOYMENT RATE

Predictor	Coef	SE Coef	T	P
Constant	0.04485	0.06347	0.71	0.498
CHANGE I	-0.22426	0.05506	-4.07	0.003

S = 0.2073   R-Sq = 64.8%   R-Sq(adj) = 60.9%

Analysis of Variance

Source	DF	SS	MS	F	P
Regression	1	0.71315	0.71315	16.59	0.003
Residual Error	9	0.38685	0.04298		
Total	10	1.10000			

Obs	CHANGE I	CHANGE I	Fit	SE Fit	Residual	St Resid
1	-0.20	0.2000	0.0897	0.0663	0.1103	0.56
2	-0.10	0.2000	0.0673	0.0647	0.1327	0.67
3	1.40	0.2000	-0.2691	0.0910	0.4691	2.52R
4	1.00	-0.4000	-0.1794	0.0765	-0.2206	-1.14
5	-0.30	-0.1000	0.1121	0.0683	-0.2121	-1.08
6	-0.70	0.2000	0.2018	0.0798	-0.0018	-0.01
7	0.70	-0.1000	-0.1121	0.0683	0.0121	0.06
8	2.90	-0.8000	-0.6055	0.1613	-0.1945	-1.49 X
9	-0.80	0.2000	0.2243	0.0833	-0.0243	-0.13
10	-0.70	0.2000	0.2018	0.0798	-0.0018	-0.01
11	-1.00	0.2000	0.2691	0.0910	-0.0691	-0.37

R denotes an observation with a large standardized residual
X denotes an observation whose X value gives it large influence.

b. $SST = \sum y^2 - n\bar{y}^2 = 1.1 - 25(0.0)^2 = 1.1$

$SSR = \sum (\hat{y}_i - \bar{y})^2 = .713$

$SSE = \sum e_i^2 = .387$

$SST = 1.1 = .713 + .387 = SSR + SSE$

c. $R^2 = SSR / SST = .713 / 1.1 = .648$, 64.8% of the variation in the dependent variable mean employee absence rate due to own illness can be explained by the variation in the unemployment rate.

10-26 a. The Minitab output below shows the predicted value (Fit) and the residuals:
Regression Analysis: WklySales versus TestScores
```
The regression equation is
WklySales = - 11.5 + 0.402 TestScores
Predictor         Coef     SE Coef        T        P
Constant       -11.505       9.575    -1.20    0.275
TestScor        0.4018       0.1339     3.00    0.024

S = 4.279       R-Sq = 60.0%     R-Sq(adj) = 53.4%

Analysis of Variance
Source             DF          SS         MS        F        P
Regression          1      165.00     165.00     9.01    0.024
Residual Error      6      109.87      18.31
Total               7      274.88

Obs   TestScor   WklySale        Fit    SE Fit    Residual    St Resid
  1       55.0      10.00      10.60      2.58       -0.60       -0.17
  2       60.0      12.00      12.61      2.08       -0.61       -0.16
  3       85.0      28.00      22.65      2.45        5.35        1.52
  4       75.0      24.00      18.63      1.62        5.37        1.36
  5       80.0      18.00      20.64      1.97       -2.64       -0.70
  6       85.0      16.00      22.65      2.45       -6.65       -1.89
  7       65.0      15.00      14.61      1.69        0.39        0.10
  8       60.0      12.00      12.61      2.08       -0.61       -0.16
```

b. $SST = \sum y^2 - n\bar{y}^2 = 2553 - 8(16.8750)^2 = 274.875$

$SSR = \sum (\hat{y}_i - \bar{y})^2 = 164.9749$

$SSE = \sum e_i^2 = 109.8716$

$SST = 274.875 = 164.9749 + 109.8716 = SSR + SSE$

c. $R^2 = SSR/SST = 164.9749/274.875 = .6002$, 60.02% of the variation in the dependent variable weekly sales can be explained by the aptitude test scores.

d. $\sum xy = 9945$

$$r = \frac{9945 - 8(90.625)(16.875)}{\sqrt{(40925 - 8(70.625)^2 (2553 - 8(16.875)^2}} = .7748$$

10-28 a. $\sum e_i^2 = \sum (y_i - \bar{y})^2 - b^2 \sum (x_i - \bar{x})^2 = [1320200 - 8(405)^2] -$
$(42.5806)^2 [257 - 8(5.625)^2] = 974.2084$

$s_e^2 = SSE/(n-2) = 974.2084/6 = 162.3681$

b. $s_b^2 = \dfrac{s_e^2}{\sum x^2 - n\bar{x}^2} = \dfrac{162.3681}{257 - 8(5.625)^2} = 41.9014$

b. $t_{6,.05} = 1.943$. Therefore, the 95% confidence interval is: $-42.5806 \pm 1.943\sqrt{41.9014}$
-55.1578 up to -30.0033

10-30 a. $\sum e_i^2 = [509.86 - 25(4.424)^2] - (.0896)^2[21464.7 - 25(28.344)^2] = 9.4856$

$s_e^2 = SSE/(n-2) = 9 - 4856/23 = .4124$

b. $s_b^2 = \dfrac{.4124}{21464.7 - 25(28.344)^2} = .000299$

c. $t_{23,.05} = 1.714,\ t_{23,.025} = 2.069,\ t_{23,.005} = 2.807$

Therefore, the 90% confidence interval is: $.0896 \pm 1.714\sqrt{.000299}$, .05996 up to .1192

Therefore, the 95% confidence interval is: $.0896 \pm 2.069\sqrt{.000299}$, .05382 up to .1254

Therefore, the 99% confidence interval is: $.0896 \pm 2.807\sqrt{.000299}$, .0411 up to .1381

10-32 $n = 8, \bar{X} = 156.4/8 = 19.55, \sum x^2 = 3072$

$\bar{Y} = 162.3/8 = 20.2875, \sum y^2 = 3822.35, \sum xy = 3088$

$b = \dfrac{3088 - 8(19.55)(20.2875)}{3072 - 8(10.55)^2} = -5.903$

$a = 20.2875 + 5.903(19.55) = 135.691$

$\sum e_i^2 = [3822.35 - 8(20.2875)^2] - (5.903)^2[3072 - 8(19.55)^2] = 28.6118$

$s_e^2 = 28.6118/6 = 4.7686$

$s_b^2 = \dfrac{4.7686}{3072 - 8(19.55)^2} = .3316$

$t_{6,.025} = 2.447,$

Therefore, the 95% confidence interval is: $-5.903 \pm 2.447\sqrt{.3316}$, -7.3121 up to –4.4939

10-34 a. $n = 5, \bar{X} = 6.3/5 = 1.26, \sum x^2 = 8.09$

$\bar{Y} = 118/5 = 23.6, \sum y^2 = 3310, \sum xy = 139.8$

$b = \dfrac{139.8 - 5(1.26)(23.6)}{8.09 - 5(1.26)^2} = -58.4211$

$a = 23.6 + 58.4211(1.26) = 97.2105$

b. $s_e^2 = 6.4211/3 = 2.1404$

$s_b^2 = \dfrac{2.1404}{8.09 - 5(1.26)^2} = 14.8013$, $t_{3,.05} = 2.353$

$-58.4211 \pm 2.353\sqrt{14.8013}$, Interval is from –67.2507 up to –49.5914

c. A dosage of 2.5 grams is not close to the data that was used to estimate the regression equation, therefore, the prediction will be extrapolated outside of the data values and hence, not as likely to be useful.

10-36 $SSE = 109.8716$

$s^2_e = 109.8716/6 = 18.3119$

$s^2_b = \dfrac{18.3119}{40925 - 8(70.625)^2} = .0179$

$H_o : \beta = 0, H_1 : \beta > 0$

$t = \dfrac{.4018}{\sqrt{.0179}} = 3.002$,

Therefore, reject Ho at the 2.5% level

10-38 a. $\dfrac{1-r^2}{n-2} = \dfrac{1-R^2}{n-2} = \dfrac{1}{n-2}[1 - b^2 \dfrac{\sum(x_i - x)^2}{\sum(y_i - y)^2}]$

$= \dfrac{1}{n-2} \dfrac{\sum(yi - \bar{y})^2 - b^2 \sum(x_i - \bar{x})^2}{\sum(y_i - \bar{y})^2} = \dfrac{1}{n-2} \dfrac{\sum e_i^2}{\sum(y_i - \bar{y})^2} = \dfrac{s^2_e}{\sum(y_i - \bar{y})^2}$

b. $\dfrac{r}{\sqrt{(1-r^2)/(n-2)}} = \dfrac{1}{\sqrt{s^2_e / SST}} \dfrac{\sum(x_i - \bar{x})y_i - \bar{y})}{\sqrt{\sum(x_i - \bar{x})^2 \sum(y_i - \bar{y})^2}}$

$= \dfrac{\sum(x_i - \bar{x})(y_i - \bar{y})}{s_e \sqrt{\sum(x_i - \bar{x})^2}} = \dfrac{\sum(x_i - \bar{x})(y_i - \bar{y})}{\sum(x_i - \bar{x})^2} \dfrac{\sqrt{\sum(x_i - \bar{x})^2}}{s_e} = \dfrac{b}{s_e / \sqrt{\sum(x_i - \bar{x})^2}}$

c. Hypothesis test for r: (see equations 10.1-10.3): $t = \dfrac{r\sqrt{(n-2)}}{\sqrt{(1-r^2)}}$ which is equivalent to

the first term of the expression in part b. above.

Hypothesis test for b_1: (see equations 10.16 and 10.17)

$t = \dfrac{b_1}{S_{b_1^2}}$ where $S_{b^2} = \dfrac{S_e^2}{(n-1)S_x^2}$. Substituting in and simplifying yields:

$t = \dfrac{b_1}{Se / \sqrt{(n-1)S_x^2}} = \dfrac{b_1}{Se / \sqrt{(n-1)\dfrac{\sum(x_i - \bar{X})^2}{(n-1)}}} = \dfrac{b_1}{Se / \sqrt{\sum(x_i - \bar{X})^2}}$ which is equivalent

to the second term of the expression in part b. above.

10-40 $Ho : \beta = 0, H_1 : \beta > 0$

$t = \dfrac{1.11}{2.31} = .4805$

Therefore, do not reject Ho at the 10% level since t = .4805 < 1.282 = t $_{72,.10}$

10-42 a. $\hat{Y}_{n+1} = 644.5161 - 42.5806(4.8) = 440.129$

   b. $t_{6,.025} = 2.447$

   The 95% confidence interval for prediction of the actual value:

   $$440.129 \pm 2.447 \sqrt{[1 + \frac{1}{8} + \frac{(4.8 - 5.625)^2}{257 - 8(5.625)^2}]162.3681}$$

   440.129 ± 35.560
   404.569 up to 475.689
   The 95% confidence interval for prediction of the expected value:

   $$440.129 \pm 2.447 \sqrt{[\frac{1}{8} + \frac{(4.8 - 5.625)^2}{257 - 8(5.625)^2}]162.3681}$$

   440.129 ± 17.0967
   423.032 up to 457.226

10-44 $\hat{Y}_{n+1} = .0449 - .2243(0) = .0449$

   $t_{9,.05} = 1.833$

   The 90% confidence interval for prediction of the actual value:

   $$.0449 \pm 1.833 \sqrt{[1 + \frac{1}{11} + \frac{(.2)^2}{14.62 - 11(.2)^2}].043}$$

   $.0449 \pm .3975$, -.3526 up to .4424
   90% confidence interval for the prediction of the expected value:

   $$.0449 \pm 1.833 \sqrt{[\frac{1}{11} + \frac{(.2)^2}{14.62 - 11(.2)^2}].043}$$

   $.0449 \pm .1164$, -.0715 up to .1613

10.46 $\hat{Y}_{n+1} = -11.5046 + .4018(70) = 16.6214$

   $t_{6,.10} = 1.440, t_{6,.05} = 1.943$

   The 80% confidence interval for prediction of the actual value:

   $$16.6214 \pm 1.440 \sqrt{[1 + \frac{1}{8} + \frac{(70 - 70.625)^2}{40925 - 8(70.625)^2}]18.3119}$$

   16.6214 ± 6.537, 10.08 up to 23.16
   90% confidence interval for the prediction of the actual value

   $$16.6214 \pm 1.943 \sqrt{[1 + \frac{1}{8} + \frac{(70 - 70.625)^2}{40925 - 8(70.625)^2}]18.3119}$$

   16.6214 ± 8.8204, 7.80 up to 25.44

10-48

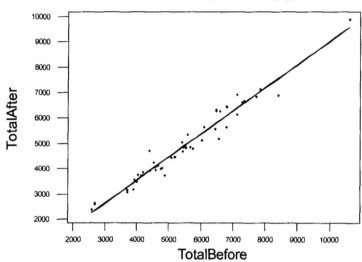

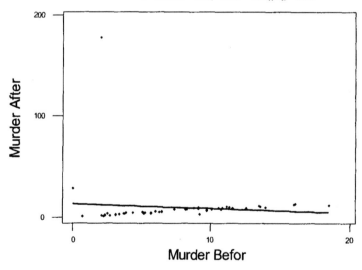

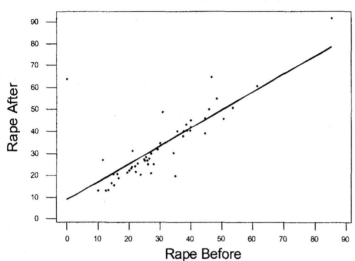

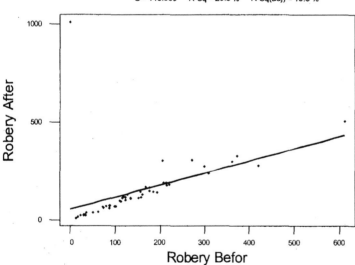

Crime rates before appear to be significant predictors of crime rates after. All of the regressions indicate positive associations. The explanatory power of the models will improve after investigating and (possibly) eliminating outliers.

10-50 a. $n = 5, \bar{x} = 0/5, \sum x^2 = 10, \bar{y} = 10/5, \sum y^2 = 36, \sum xy = 0$

$$r = \frac{0 - 5(0)(2)}{\sqrt{(10 - 5(0)^2)(36 - 5(2)^2)}} = 0$$

b. The correlation coefficient is a measure of the strength of the <u>linear</u> association between two variables. Because X and Y are non-linear, the correlation coefficient will show a strength of zero for the linear association.

10-52 $H_o : \rho = 0, H_1 : \rho \neq 0$

$$t = \frac{.1398}{\sqrt{[1 - (.1398)^2]/524}} = 3.232$$

Therefore, reject Ho at the 1% level since t = 3.232 > 2.576 ≈ t $_{524,.005}$

10-54 $H_o : \rho = 0, H_1 : \rho \neq 0$

$$t = \frac{-.18}{\sqrt{[1 - (.18)^2]/190}} = -2.522$$

Therefore, reject Ho at the 2% level since t = -2.522 < -2.326 ≈ t $_{190,.01}$

10-56

Regression Analysis: Supervisors Grade versus Aptitude Score
```
The regression equation is
Supervisors Grade = 43.9 + 0.425 Aptitude Score
Predictor         Coef     SE Coef           T          P
Constant         43.92       13.97        3.14      0.010
Aptitude        0.4250      0.1792        2.37      0.039

S = 6.490        R-Sq = 36.0%     R-Sq(adj) = 29.6%
Analysis of Variance
Source              DF          SS          MS          F          P
Regression           1      237.06      237.06       5.63      0.039
```

a. $\hat{y} = 43.9 + 0.425x$

b. For a one unit increase in the employee's aptitude score, we would estimate a .425 unit increase in the supervisor's score

c. No, factors other than aptitude score have an effect on the supervisor's grade

d. $R^2 = 36.0\%$. 36% of the variation in the aptitude score can explain the variation of the supervisor's grade

e. $H_o : \beta = 0, H_1 : \beta > 0$, $t = \frac{.425}{\sqrt{.0321}} = 2.372$

Therefore, reject Ho at 2.5% level since t = 2.372 > 2.228 = t $_{10,.025}$

f. 95% confidence interval for the prediction of an actual value
$\hat{y} = 43.9162 + .425(70) = 73.6662$

$$73.662 \pm 2.228 \sqrt{[1 + \frac{1}{12} + \frac{(73.6662 - 77.25)^2}{72923 - 12(77.25)^2}]41.1188}$$

73.6662 ± 14.9372, Interval runs from 58.729 up to 88.6034

10-58 a.

Regression Analysis: y_purchases_58 versus x_percent_58

```
The regression equation is
y_purchases_58 = - 8.5 + 9.03 x_percent_58
```

Predictor	Coef	SE Coef	T	P
Constant	-8.53	12.36	-0.69	0.516
x_percen	9.033	4.339	2.08	0.083

```
S = 5.537    R-Sq = 41.9%    R-Sq(adj) = 32.3%
Analysis of Variance
```

Source	DF	SS	MS	F	P
Regression	1	132.90	132.90	4.33	0.083
Residual Error	6	183.98	30.66		
Total	7	316.88			

b. For a one percent increase in the percentage buying in a year, we estimate that the coffee purchases of instant coffee per buyer will increase by 9.03 units.

c. $R^2 = 41.9\%$. 41.9% of the variation in purchases per buyer can be explained by variation in the percentage buying in a year

d. $9.03 \pm 1.943(4.339) = 9.03 \pm 8.431$. The interval runs from .599 up to 17.461. We are 90% confident we will capture the true overall rate of response that a change in the percentage buying in a year has on the purchases per buyer within the interval from .599 up to 17.461 purchases per buyer

e. $Y_{n+1} = b_o + b_1 x_{n+1} = -8.5 + 9.03(2) = 9.56$

The 90% confidence interval for the expected value of Y is

$$9.56 \pm 1.943 \sqrt{\frac{1}{8} + \frac{(2-2.8125)^2}{1.6287}} = 9.56 \pm 7.835 = 1.725 \text{ up to } 17.395$$

10-60 a. $R^2 = \frac{SSR}{SSR + SSE} = \frac{128}{128 + 286} = .3092$

b. $s^2_e = 286/28 = 10.2143$ and $s^2_b = 10.2143/70.56 = .1448$

$H_o : \beta = 0, H_1 : \beta \neq 0, \ t = \frac{8.4}{\sqrt{.1448}} = 22.078$

Therefore, reject Ho at any common level of alpha

c. $R^2 = b^2 \frac{\sum(x_i - \bar{x})^2}{\sum(y_i - \bar{y})^2}, therefore, \sum(x_i - \bar{x})^2 = \frac{(SST)(R^2)}{b^2}$

$\sum(x_i - \bar{x})^2 = \frac{414(.3092)}{(8.4)^2} = 70.56$

10-62 a. $r = \sqrt{R^2} = \sqrt{.72} = .8485$

b. $H_o : \rho = 0, H_1 : \rho \neq 0, \ t = \frac{r}{\sqrt{[1-r^2]/(n-2)}} = \frac{.8485}{\sqrt{[1-.72]/18}} = 6.8031$

Therefore, reject Ho at any common level of alpha

c. $\frac{s_e}{\sqrt{\sum(x_i - \bar{x})^2}} = \frac{b}{t} = .47/6.8031 = .0691$

10-64 a.

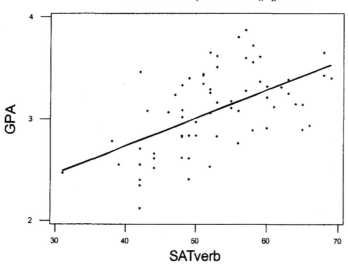

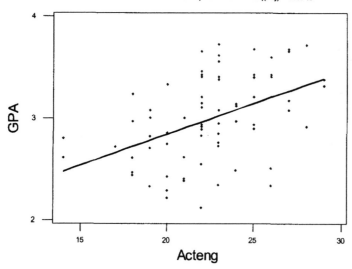

Regression Plot

GPA = 1.71968 + 0.0222434 SATmath

S = 0.351314   R-Sq = 22.4 %   R-Sq(adj) = 21.2 %

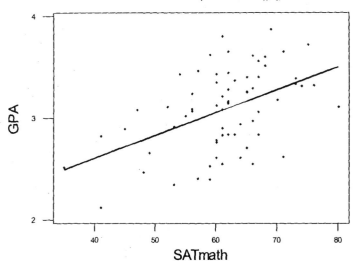

Regression Plot

GPA = 1.88634 + 0.0414748 ACTmath

S = 0.391302   R-Sq = 15.4 %   R-Sq(adj) = 14.2 %

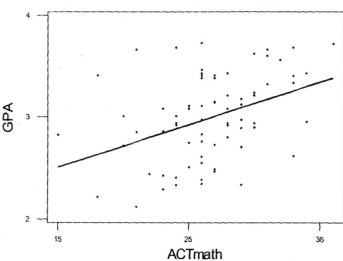

b. Out of the four measures, it appears that the SAT Verbal is the better single predictor followed by the SAT Math, ACT Verbal and ACT Math respectively.

Results for: Student GPA.XLS
Regression Analysis: EconGPA versus SATverb

The regression equation is
EconGPA = 1.48 + 0.0293 SATverb
67 cases used 45 cases contain missing values

Predictor	Coef	SE Coef	T	P
Constant	1.4836	0.3558	4.17	0.000
SATverb	0.029345	0.006682	4.39	0.000

S = 0.4387   R-Sq = 22.9%   R-Sq(adj) = 21.7%
Analysis of Variance

Source	DF	SS	MS	F	P
Regression	1	3.7109	3.7109	19.29	0.000
Residual Error	65	12.5072	0.1924		
Total	66	16.2181			

Regression Analysis: EconGPA versus Acteng

The regression equation is
EconGPA = 1.36 + 0.0705 Acteng
73 cases used 39 cases contain missing values

Predictor	Coef	SE Coef	T	P
Constant	1.3566	0.4521	3.00	0.004
Acteng	0.07054	0.01997	3.53	0.001

S = 0.5372   R-Sq = 15.0%   R-Sq(adj) = 13.8%

Analysis of Variance

Source	DF	SS	MS	F	P
Regression	1	3.6019	3.6019	12.48	0.001
Residual Error	71	20.4878	0.2886		
Total	72	24.0897			

Regression Analysis: GPA versus SATverb, SATmath

The regression equation is
GPA = 1.02 + 0.0220 SATverb + 0.0148 SATmath
67 cases used 45 cases contain missing values

Predictor	Coef	SE Coef	T	P	VIF
Constant	1.0183	0.3244	3.14	0.003	
SATverb	0.022001	0.005066	4.34	0.000	1.1
SATmath	0.014789	0.004863	3.04	0.003	1.1

S = 0.3112   R-Sq = 40.1%   R-Sq(adj) = 38.2%

Analysis of Variance

Source	DF	SS	MS	F	P
Regression	2	4.1403	2.0702	21.38	0.000
Residual Error	64	6.1964	0.0968		
Total	66	10.3368			

Regression Analysis: GPA versus Acteng, ACTmath

The regression equation is
GPA = 1.19 + 0.0479 Acteng + 0.0275 ACTmath
73 cases used 39 cases contain missing values

Predictor	Coef	SE Coef	T	P	VIF
Constant	1.1853	0.3624	3.27	0.002	
Acteng	0.04790	0.01468	3.26	0.002	1.2
ACTmath	0.02747	0.01166	2.36	0.021	1.2

S = 0.3671   R-Sq = 26.5%   R-Sq(adj) = 24.4%

Analysis of Variance

Source	DF	SS	MS	F	P
Regression	2	3.4086	1.7043	12.64	0.000
Residual Error	70	9.4357	0.1348		
Total	72	12.8444			

Regression Analysis: GPA versus Acteng, ACTmath, SATverb, SATmath

The regression equation is
GPA = 0.773 + 0.0156 Acteng + 0.0494 ACTmath + 0.0163 SATverb - 0.0055 SATmath
34 cases used 78 cases contain missing values

Predictor	Coef	SE Coef	T	P	VIF
Constant	0.7727	0.5341	1.45	0.159	
Acteng	0.01556	0.02705	0.58	0.570	1.8
ACTmath	0.04940	0.02587	1.91	0.066	3.2
SATverb	0.016290	0.007841	2.08	0.047	1.7
SATmath	-0.00554	0.01191	-0.47	0.645	3.3

S = 0.3204   R-Sq = 45.6%   R-Sq(adj) = 38.1%

Analysis of Variance

Source	DF	SS	MS	F	P
Regression	4	2.4947	0.6237	6.08	0.001
Residual Error	29	2.9764	0.1026		
Total	33	5.4711			

Regression Analysis: GPA versus Acteng, SATverb

The regression equation is
GPA = 1.41 + 0.0269 Acteng + 0.0189 SATverb
34 cases used 78 cases contain missing values

Predictor	Coef	SE Coef	T	P	VIF
Constant	1.4150	0.4968	2.85	0.008	
Acteng	0.02689	0.02817	0.95	0.347	1.7
SATverb	0.018876	0.008365	2.26	0.031	1.7

S = 0.3446   R-Sq = 32.7%   R-Sq(adj) = 28.4%

Analysis of Variance

Source	DF	SS	MS	F	P
Regression	2	1.7906	0.8953	7.54	0.002
Residual Error	31	3.6806	0.1187		
Total	33	5.4711			

Regression Analysis: GPA versus SATmath, ACTmath

The regression equation is
GPA = 1.51 - 0.0019 SATmath + 0.0586 ACTmath
34 cases used 78 cases contain missing values

Predictor	Coef	SE Coef	T	P	VIF
Constant	1.5070	0.4709	3.20	0.003	
SATmath	-0.00190	0.01308	-0.15	0.885	3.2
ACTmath	0.05864	0.02866	2.05	0.049	3.2

S = 0.3574   R-Sq = 27.6%   R-Sq(adj) = 22.9%

Analysis of Variance

Source	DF	SS	MS	F	P
Regression	2	1.5107	0.7553	5.91	0.007
Residual Error	31	3.9605	0.1278		
Total	33	5.4711			

c.

Descriptive Statistics: GPA, SATverb, SATmath, Acteng, ACTmath

Variable	N	N*	Mean	Median	TrMean	StDev
GPA	112	0	3.0436	3.0650	3.0475	0.4114
SATverb	67	45	52.642	52.000	52.689	8.080
SATmath	67	45	61.28	62.00	61.61	8.42
Acteng	73	39	22.425	22.000	22.462	3.171
ACTmath	73	39	26.630	26.000	26.708	3.991

Variable	SE Mean	Minimum	Maximum	Q1	Q3
GPA	0.0389	2.1200	3.8700	2.7525	3.3875
SATverb	0.987	31.000	69.000	48.000	58.000
SATmath	1.03	35.00	80.00	57.00	66.00
Acteng	0.371	14.000	29.000	20.000	25.000
ACTmath	0.467	15.000	36.000	24.000	29.000

10-66 a.

Regression Analysis: deaths versus prurpop

The regression equation is
deaths = 0.0989 + 0.184 prurpop

Predictor	Coef	SE Coef	T	P
Constant	0.09895	0.01759	5.62	0.000
prurpop	0.18397	0.03631	5.07	0.000

S = 0.06519   R-Sq = 35.3%   R-Sq(adj) = 33.9%

Analysis of Variance

Source	DF	SS	MS	F	P
Regression	1	0.10908	0.10908	25.67	0.000
Residual Error	47	0.19973	0.00425		
Total	48	0.30881			

Regression Analysis: deaths versus Ruspeed

The regression equation is
deaths = - 0.671 + 0.0145 Ruspeed

Predictor	Coef	SE Coef	T	P
Constant	-0.6706	0.3853	-1.74	0.088
Ruspeed	0.014525	0.006619	2.19	0.033

S = 0.07720   R-Sq = 9.3%   R-Sq(adj) = 7.4%

Analysis of Variance

Source	DF	SS	MS	F	P
Regression	1	0.028703	0.028703	4.82	0.033
Residual Error	47	0.280106	0.005960		
Total	48	0.308809			

Regression Analysis: deaths versus Prsurf

The regression equation is
deaths = 0.359 - 0.231 Prsurf

Predictor	Coef	SE Coef	T	P
Constant	0.35929	0.04138	8.68	0.000
Prsurf	-0.23148	0.05043	-4.59	0.000

S = 0.06736   R-Sq = 30.9%   R-Sq(adj) = 29.5%

Analysis of Variance

Source	DF	SS	MS	F	P
Regression	1	0.095574	0.095574	21.07	0.000
Residual Error	47	0.213235	0.004537		
Total	48	0.308809			

b.

Correlations: deaths, prurpop, Ruspeed, Prsurf

```
           deaths   prurpop  Ruspeed
prurpop     0.594
            0.000

Ruspeed     0.305    0.224
            0.033    0.121

Prsurf     -0.556   -0.207   -0.232
            0.000    0.153    0.109
```

Crash deaths are positively related to both percent urban population and rural speed. Deaths are negatively related to percent of rural roads that are surfaced. Percent urban population has the strongest linear association followed closely by percentage of rural roads that are surfaced and then by rural speed.

10-68   a. Retail sales file

Regression Plot

retsal84 = 2127.13 + 0.277669 perinc84

S = 635.000   R-Sq = 40.1 %   R-Sq(adj) = 38.8 %

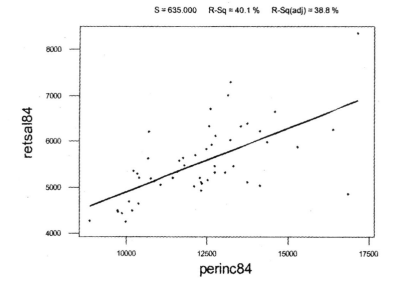

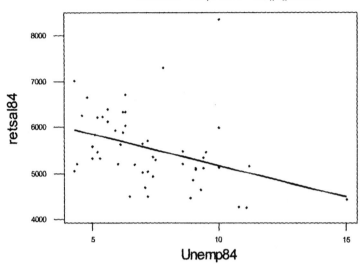

Regression Plot

retsal84 = 6529.53 - 135.437 Unemp84

S = 762.058   R-Sq = 13.7 %   R-Sq(adj) = 11.9 %

Regression Analysis: retsal84 versus perinc84

```
The regression equation is
retsal84 = 2127 + 0.278 perinc84
Predictor       Coef      SE Coef         T         P
Constant       2127.1       602.3      3.53     0.001
perinc84      0.27767     0.04852      5.72     0.000

S = 635.0        R-Sq = 40.1%     R-Sq(adj) = 38.8%

Analysis of Variance
Source          DF         SS          MS        F         P
Regression       1   13203228    13203228    32.74     0.000
Residual Error  49   19758042      403225
Total           50   32961271
```

The regression analysis shows a significant F-calc on the test of the explanatory power of the model as well as a significant t-test on the test for the individual regression slope coefficient. Therefore, there is a significant positive relationship between retail sales and per capita personal income.

95% confidence interval for the slope coefficient:

$$\hat{\beta}_1 \pm t_{.025,49}(S_{\hat{\beta}_1}) = .278 \pm 2.01(.04852): \quad .278 \pm .0975 = .1805 \text{ up to } .3755$$

Regression Analysis: retsal84 versus Unemp84

```
The regression equation is
retsal84 = 6530 - 135 Unemp84
Predictor         Coef      SE Coef          T          P
Constant        6529.5        372.3      17.54      0.000
Unemp84         -135.44        48.62      -2.79      0.008

S = 762.1       R-Sq = 13.7%      R-Sq(adj) = 11.9%

Analysis of Variance
Source           DF           SS           MS          F          P
Regression        1      4505400      4505400       7.76      0.008
Residual Error   49     28455871       580732
Total            50     32961271
```

The regression analysis shows a significant F-calc on the test of the explanatory power of the model as well as a significant t-test on the test for the individual regression slope coefficient. Therefore, there is a significant negative relationship between retail sales and unemployment rate.

95% confidence interval for the slope coefficient:

$$\hat{\beta}_1 \pm t_{.025,49}(S_{\hat{\beta}_1}) = -135.44 \pm 2.01(48.62): \quad -135.44 \pm 97.73 = -233.17 \text{ up to } -37.71$$

b. The effect of a $1,000 decrease in per capita income is to have an estimated decrease of $278 in per capita retail sales

c.

Descriptive Statistics: retsal84, perinc84, Unemp84

Variable	N	Mean	Median	TrMean	StDev	SE Mean
retsal84	51	5536	5336	5483	812	114
perinc84	51	12277	12314	12166	1851	259
Unemp84	51	7.335	7.000	7.196	2.216	0.310

Variable	Minimum	Maximum	Q1	Q3
retsal84	4250	8348	5059	6037
perinc84	8857	17148	10689	13218
Unemp84	4.300	15.000	5.600	9.100

```
Predicted Values for New Observations

New Obs    Fit    SE Fit        90.0% CI            90.0% PI
1       2404.8    554.4  ( 1475.3,  3334.3)  (  991.6,  3818.1)
```

Letting Y be the level of retail sales and X being the level of per capita income, the predicted value at the mean:

$$\hat{Y}_{\bar{X}=12277} = 2127 + (.27767)(12277) = 5536$$

$$\text{and } S_{\hat{Y}_{\bar{X}}} = \sqrt{\left(\frac{1}{n} + \frac{(Xp - \bar{X})}{(n-1)S^2_x}\right)S^2_{Y|X}} = \sqrt{\left(\frac{1}{51} + 0\right)(635)^2} = 88.92$$

$$= 5536 \pm 2.01(88.92) = 5536 \pm 178.729: \quad 5357.27 \text{ up to } 5714.729$$

At $1,000 above the mean:

$$\hat{Y}_{\bar{X}=12277} = 2127 + (.27767)(13277) = 5814$$

$$\text{and } S_{\hat{Y}_{\bar{X}}} = \sqrt{\left(\frac{1}{n} + \frac{(Xp - \bar{X})}{(n-1)S^2_x}\right)S^2_{Y|X}} = \sqrt{\left(\frac{1}{51} + \frac{(1000)^2}{(50)(1851)}\right)(635)^2} = 101.29$$

$$= 5814 \pm 2.01(101.29) = 5814 \pm 203.593: \quad 5610.407 \text{ up to } 6017.593$$

Chapter 11: Multiple Regression

11-2   The estimated regression slope coefficients are interpreted as follows:
$b_1 = .057$: All else equal, an increase of one unit in the change over the quarter in equity purchases by financial institutions results in an estimated .057 increase in the change over the quarter in the Financial Times stock price index

$b_2 = -.065$: All else equal, an increase of one unit in the change over the quarter in equity sales by financial institutions results in an estimated .065 decrease in the change over the quarter in the Financial Times stock price index

11-4   a. $b_1 = .653$: All else equal, a one unit increase in the average number of meals eaten per week will result in an estimated .653 pounds gained during the freshman year.

$b_2 = -1.345$: All else equal, a one unit increase in the average number of hours of exercise per week will result in an estimated 1.345 pound weight loss.
$b_3 = .613$: All else equal, a one unit increase in the average number of beers consumed per week will result in an estimated .613 pound weight gain.

11-6   a. Electricity sales as a function of number of customers and price
Regression Analysis: salesmw2 versus priclec2, numcust2
```
The regression equation is
salesmw2 = - 647363 + 19895 priclec2 + 2.35 numcust2
Predictor       Coef     SE Coef          T         P
Constant     -647363      291734      -2.22     0.030
priclec2       19895       22515       0.88     0.380
numcust2      2.3530      0.2233      10.54     0.000

S = 66399      R-Sq = 79.2%     R-Sq(adj) = 78.5%

Analysis of Variance
Source          DF          SS          MS          F         P
Regression       2 1.02480E+12 5.12400E+11     116.22     0.000
Residual Error  61 2.68939E+11  4408828732
Total           63 1.29374E+12

Source      DF      Seq SS
priclec2     1 5.35306E+11
numcust2     1 4.89494E+11
```

All else equal, for every one unit increase in the price of electricity, we estimate that sales will increase by 19895 mwh. Note that this estimated coefficient is not significantly different from zero.

All else equal, for every additional residential customer who uses electricity in the heating of their home, we estimate that sales will increase by 2.353 mwh.

b. Electricity sales as a function of number of customers

Regression Analysis: salesmw2 versus numcust2

```
The regression equation is
salesmw2 = - 410202 + 2.20 numcust2
Predictor       Coef     SE Coef        T        P
Constant      -410202      114132    -3.59    0.001
numcust2       2.2027      0.1445     15.25    0.000


S = 66282       R-Sq = 78.9%     R-Sq(adj) = 78.6%


Analysis of Variance
Source          DF          SS          MS        F        P
Regression       1  1.02136E+12  1.02136E+12   232.48    0.000
Residual Error  62  2.72381E+11   4393240914
Total           63  1.29374E+12
```

All else equal, an additional residential customer will add 2.2027 mwh to electricity sales.
The two models have roughly equivalent explanatory power; therefore, adding price as a variable
does not add a significant amount of explanatory power to the model. There appears to be a
problem of multicollinearity between price and customers.

c.

Regression Analysis: salesmw2 versus priclec2, degrday2

```
The regression equation is
salesmw2 = 2312260 - 165275 priclec2 + 56.1 degrday2
Predictor       Coef     SE Coef        T        P
Constant      2312260      148794     15.54    0.000
priclec2      -165275       24809     -6.66    0.000
degrday2        56.06       60.37      0.93    0.357


S = 110725      R-Sq = 42.2%     R-Sq(adj) = 40.3%


Analysis of Variance
Source          DF          SS          MS        F        P
Regression       2  5.45875E+11  2.72938E+11    22.26    0.000
Residual Error  61  7.47863E+11  12260053296
Total           63  1.29374E+12


Source       DF       Seq SS
priclec2      1  5.35306E+11
degrday2      1  10569514277
```

All else equal, an increase in the price of electricity will reduce electricity sales by 165,275 mwh.
All else equal, an increase in the degree days (departure from normal weather) by one unit will
increase electricity sales by 56.06 mwh.
Note that the coefficient on the price variable is now negative, as expected, and it is significantly
different from zero (p-value = .000)

d.

Regression Analysis: salesmw2 versus Yd872, degrday2

```
The regression equation is
salesmw2 = 293949 + 326 Yd872 + 58.4 degrday2
Predictor        Coef     SE Coef        T          P
Constant       293949       67939     4.33      0.000
Yd872          325.85       21.30    15.29      0.000
degrday2        58.36       35.79     1.63      0.108

S = 66187      R-Sq = 79.3%      R-Sq(adj) = 78.7%

Analysis of Variance
Source         DF          SS          MS          F          P
Regression      2  1.02652E+12  5.13259E+11     117.16      0.000
Residual Error 61  2.67221E+11  4380674677
Total          63  1.29374E+12

Source        DF        Seq SS
Yd872          1  1.01487E+12
degrday2       1   11651638615
```

All else equal, an increase in personal disposable income by one unit will increase electricity sales by 325.85 mwh.

All else equal, an increase in degree days by one unit will increase electricity sales by 58.36 mwh.

11-8   a. Horsepower as a function of weight, cubic inches of displacement

Regression Analysis: horspwr versus weight, displace

```
The regression equation is
horspwr = 23.5 + 0.0154 weight + 0.157 displace
151 cases used 4 cases contain missing values
Predictor        Coef     SE Coef        T          P        VIF
Constant       23.496       7.341     3.20      0.002
weight       0.015432    0.004538     3.40      0.001        6.0
displace      0.15667     0.03746     4.18      0.000        6.0

S = 13.64      R-Sq = 69.2%      R-Sq(adj) = 68.8%

Analysis of Variance
Source         DF          SS          MS          F          P
Regression      2       61929       30964     166.33      0.000
Residual Error 148       27551         186
Total         150       89480
```

All else equal, a 100 pound increase in the weight of the car is associated with a 1.54 increase in horsepower of the auto.

All else equal, a 10 cubic inch increase in the displacement of the engine is associated with a 1.57 increase in the horsepower of the auto.

b. Horsepower as a function of weight, displacement, number of cylinders

Regression Analysis: horspwr versus weight, displace, cylinder

```
The regression equation is
horspwr = 16.7 + 0.0163 weight + 0.105 displace + 2.57 cylinder
151 cases used 4 cases contain missing values
Predictor        Coef      SE Coef         T        P       VIF
Constant       16.703        9.449      1.77    0.079
weight       0.016261     0.004592      3.54    0.001       6.2
displace      0.10527      0.05859      1.80    0.074      14.8
cylinder        2.574        2.258      1.14    0.256       7.8

S = 13.63       R-Sq = 69.5%      R-Sq(adj) = 68.9%

Analysis of Variance
Source           DF           SS          MS         F        P
Regression        3        62170       20723    111.55    0.000
Residual Error  147        27310         186
Total           150        89480
```

All else equal, a 100 pound increase in the weight of the car is associated with a 1.63 increase in horsepower of the auto.

All else equal, a 10 cubic inch increase in the displacement of the engine is associated with a 1.05 increase in the horsepower of the auto.

All else equal, one additional cylinder in the engine is associated with a 2.57 increase in the horsepower of the auto.

Note that adding the independent variable number of cylinders has not added to the explanatory power of the model. R square has increased marginally. Engine displacement is no longer significant at the .05 level (p-value of .074) and the estimated regression slope coefficient on the number of cylinders is not significantly different from zero. This is due to the strong correlation that exists between cubic inches of engine displacement and the number of cylinders.

c. Horsepower as a function of weight, displacement and fuel mileage

Regression Analysis: horspwr versus weight, displace, milpgal

```
The regression equation is
horspwr = 93.6 + 0.00203 weight + 0.165 displace - 1.24 milpgal
150 cases used 5 cases contain missing values
Predictor        Coef      SE Coef         T        P       VIF
Constant        93.57        15.33      6.11    0.000
weight       0.002031     0.004879      0.42    0.678       8.3
displace      0.16475      0.03475      4.74    0.000       6.1
milpgal       -1.2392       0.2474     -5.01    0.000       3.1

S = 12.55       R-Sq = 74.2%      R-Sq(adj) = 73.6%

Analysis of Variance
Source           DF           SS          MS         F        P
Regression        3        66042       22014    139.77    0.000
Residual Error  146        22994         157
Total           149        89036
```

All else equal, a 100 pound increase in the weight of the car is associated with a .203 increase in horsepower of the auto.

All else equal, a 10 cubic inch increase in the displacement of the engine is associated with a 1.6475 increase in the horsepower of the auto.

All else equal, an increase in the fuel mileage of the vehicle by 1 mile per gallon is associated with a reduction in horsepower of 1.2392.

Note that the negative coefficient on fuel mileage indicates the trade-off that is expected between horsepower and fuel mileage. The displacement variable is significantly positive, as expected, however, the weight variable is no longer significant. Again, one would expect high correlation among the independent variables.

      d. Horsepower as a function of weight, displacement, mpg and price

Regression Analysis: horspwr versus weight, displace, milpgal, price

```
The regression equation is
horspwr = 98.1 - 0.00032 weight + 0.175 displace - 1.32 milpgal +0.000138 price
150 cases used 5 cases contain missing values
Predictor         Coef      SE Coef          T        P       VIF
Constant         98.14        16.05       6.11    0.000
weight       -0.000324     0.005462      -0.06    0.953      10.3
displace       0.17533      0.03647       4.81    0.000       6.8
milpgal        -1.3194       0.2613      -5.05    0.000       3.5
price        0.0001379    0.0001438       0.96    0.339       1.3


S = 12.55       R-Sq = 74.3%      R-Sq(adj) = 73.6%

Analysis of Variance
Source              DF           SS          MS        F        P
Regression           4        66187       16547   105.00    0.000
Residual Error     145        22849         158
Total              149        89036
```

      e. Explanatory power has marginally increased from the first model to the last. The estimated coefficient on price is not significantly different from zero. Displacement and fuel mileage have the expected signs. The coefficient on weight has the wrong sign; however, it is not significantly different from zero (p-value of .953).

11-10 a. $R^2 = 1 - \dfrac{88.2}{162.1} = .4559$, therefore, 45.59% of the variability in milk consumption can

      be explained by the variations in weekly income and family size.

     b. $\bar{R}^2 = 1 - \dfrac{88.2/(30-3)}{162.1/29} = .4156$

     c. $R = \sqrt{.4559} = .6752$. This is the sample correlation between observed and predicted values of milk consumption.

11-12 a.

Regression Analysis: Y profit versus X2 offices

```
The regression equation is
Y profit = 1.55 -0.000120 X2  offices
Predictor          Coef      SE Coef          T        P
Constant         1.5460       0.1048      14.75    0.000
X2  offi    -0.00012033   0.00001434      -8.39    0.000


S = 0.07049     R-Sq = 75.4%      R-Sq(adj) = 74.3%

Analysis of Variance
Source              DF           SS          MS        F        P
Regression           1      0.34973     0.34973    70.38    0.000
Residual Error      23      0.11429     0.00497
Total               24      0.46402
```

b.

Regression Analysis: X1 revenue versus X2 offices

```
The regression equation is
X1 revenue = - 0.078 +0.000543 X2  offices

Predictor          Coef     SE Coef           T        P
Constant        -0.0781      0.2975       -0.26    0.795
X2  offi     0.00054280  0.00004070       13.34    0.000

S = 0.2000      R-Sq = 88.5%     R-Sq(adj) = 88.1%
Analysis of Variance
Source            DF          SS          MS        F        P
Regression         1      7.1166      7.1166   177.84    0.000
Residual Error    23      0.9204      0.0400
Total             24      8.0370
```

c.

Regression Analysis: Y profit versus X1 revenue

```
The regression equation is
Y profit = 1.33 - 0.169 X1 revenue
Predictor          Coef     SE Coef           T        P
Constant         1.3262      0.1386        9.57    0.000
X1 reven       -0.16913      0.03559       -4.75    0.000

S = 0.1009      R-Sq = 49.5%     R-Sq(adj) = 47.4%
Analysis of Variance
Source            DF          SS          MS        F        P
Regression         1     0.22990     0.22990    22.59    0.000
Residual Error    23     0.23412     0.01018
Total             24     0.46402
```

d.

Regression Analysis: X2 offices versus X1 revenue

```
The regression equation is
X2  offices = 957 + 1631 X1 revenue
Predictor          Coef     SE Coef           T        P
Constant          956.9       476.5        2.01    0.057
X1 reven         1631.3       122.3       13.34    0.000

S = 346.8       R-Sq = 88.5%     R-Sq(adj) = 88.1%
Analysis of Variance
Source            DF          SS          MS        F        P
Regression         1    21388013    21388013   177.84    0.000
Residual Error    23     2766147      120267
Total             24    24154159
```

e. Using the residuals obtained from a, b: $r = .6731$

f. Using the residuals obtained from c, d: $r = -.8562$

11-14 a. $H_0 : \beta_1 = 0; H_1 : \beta_1 > 0$

$$t = \frac{.052}{.023} = 2.26$$

$t_{27,.025/.01} = 2.052, 2.473$

Therefore, reject H_0 at the 2.5% level but not at the 1% level

b. $t_{27,.05/.025/.005} = 1.703, 2.052, 2.771$

90% CI: $1.14 \pm 1.703(.35)$; .5439 up to 1.7361

95% CI: $1.14 \pm 2.052(.35)$; .4218 up to 1.8582

99% CI: $1.14 \pm 2.771(.35)$; .1701 up to 2.1099

11-16   a. $H_0 : \beta_3 = 0, H_1 : \beta_3 \neq 0$

$$t = \frac{-.000191}{.000446} = -.428$$

$t_{16,.10} = -1.337$

Therefore, do not reject H_0 at the 20% level

b. $H_0 : \beta_1 = \beta_2 = \beta_3 = 0, H_1 :$ At least one $\beta_i \neq 0, (i = 1, 2, 3)$

$$F = \frac{16}{3} \frac{.71}{1-.71} = 13.057$$

$F_{3,16,.01} = 5.29$

Therefore, reject H_0 at the 1% level

11-18   a.   All else being equal, an extra \$1 in mean per capita personal income leads to an expected extra \$.04 of net revenue per capita from the lottery

b. $b_2 = .8772, s_{b_2} = .3107, n = 29, t_{24,.025} = 2.064$

95% CI: $.8772 \pm 2.064(.3107)$, .2359 up to 1.5185

c. $H_0 : \beta_3 = 0, H_1 : \beta_3 < 0$

$$t = \frac{-365.01}{263.88} = -1.383$$

$t_{24,.10/.05} = -1.318, -1.711$

Therefore, reject H_0 at the 10% level but not at the 5% level

11-20   a. $n = 19, b_1 = .2, s_{b_1} = .0092, t_{16,.025} = 2.12$

95% CI: $.2 \pm 2.12(.0092)$, .1805 up to .2195

b. $H_0 : \beta_2 = 0, H_1 : \beta_2 < 0$

$$t = \frac{-.1}{.084} = -1.19, \quad t_{16,.10} = -1.337$$

Therefore, do not reject H_0 at the 10% level

11-22   a. $n = 39, b_5 = .0495, s_{b_1} = .01172, t_{30,.005} = 2.750$

99% CI: $.0495 \pm 2.750(.01172)$, .0173 up to .0817

b. $H_0 : \beta_4 = 0, H_1 : \beta_4 \neq 0$

$$t = \frac{.48122}{.77954} = .617, \quad t_{30,.10} = 1.31$$

Therefore, do not reject H_0 at the 20% level

c. $H_0 : \beta_7 = 0, H_1 : \beta_7 \neq 0$

$$t = \frac{.00645}{.00306} = 2.108, \quad t_{30,.025/.01} = 2.042, 2.457$$

Therefore, reject H_0 at the 5% level but not at the 2% level

11-24 a. SST = 3.881, SSR = 3.549, SSE = .332

$H_0 : \beta_1 = \beta_2 = \beta_3 = 0, H_1 :$ At least one $\beta_i \neq 0, (i = 1, 2, 3)$

$F = \dfrac{3.549/3}{.332/23} = 81.955$

$F_{3,23,.01} = 4.76$

Therefore, reject H_0 at the 1% level

b. Analysis of Variance table:

Sources of variation	Sum of Squares	Degress of Freedom	Mean Squares	F-Ratio
Regressor	3.549	3	1.183	81.955
Error	.332	23	.014435	
Total	3.881	26		

11-26 a. SST = 162.1, SSR = 73.9, SSE = 88.2

$H_0 : \beta_1 = \beta_2 = 0, H_1 :$ At least one $\beta_i \neq 0, (i = 1, 2)$

$F = \dfrac{73.9/2}{88.2/27} = 11.311$, $F_{2,27,.01} = 5.49$

Therefore, reject H_0 at the 1% level

b.

Sources of variation	Sum of Squares	Degress of Freedom	Mean Squares	F-Ratio
Regressor	73.9	2	36.95	11.311
Error	88.2	27	3.266667	
Total	162.1	29		

11-28 $H_0 : \beta_1 = \beta_2 = \beta_3 = \beta_4 = 0, H_1 :$ At least one $\beta_i \neq 0, (i = 1, 2, 3, 4)$

$F = \dfrac{24}{4} \dfrac{.51}{1 - .51} = 6.2449$

$F_{4,24,.01} = 4.22$

Therefore, reject H_0 at the 1% level

11-30 $H_0 : \beta_1 = \beta_2 = 0, H_1 :$ At least one $\beta_i \neq 0, (i = 1, 2)$

$F = \dfrac{16}{2} \dfrac{.96 + (2/16)}{1 - .96} = 217$, $F_{2,16,.01} = 6.23$

Therefore, reject H_0 at the 1% level

11-32 $\dfrac{(SSE* - SSE)k_1}{SSE/(n-k-1)} = \dfrac{n-k-1}{k_1} \dfrac{(SSE* - SSE)/SST}{SSE/SST}$

$= \dfrac{n-k-1}{k_1} \dfrac{1 - R^2* - (1 - R^2)}{1 - R^2} = \dfrac{n-k-1}{k_1} \dfrac{R^2 - R^2*}{1 - R^2}$

11-34 $\hat{Y} = 7.35 + .653(20) - 1.345(10) + .613(6) = 10.638$ pounds

11-36 $\hat{Y} = .578 + .661(1) + .065(7) - .018(50) = .794$ million worker=hours

11-38   There are many possible answers. Relationships that can be approximated by a non-linear quadratic model include many supply functions, production functions and cost functions including average cost versus the number of units produced.

11-40   Linear model:

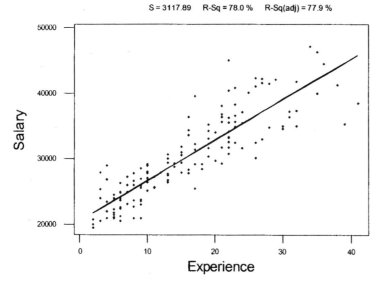

Regression Plot

Salary = 20544.5 + 616.113 Experience

S = 3117.89   R-Sq = 78.0 %   R-Sq(adj) = 77.9 %

Quadratic model:

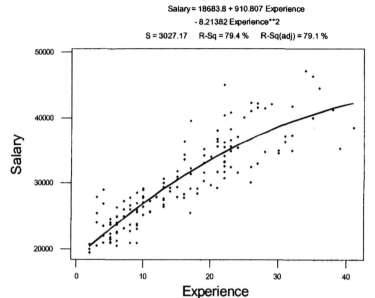

Cubic model:

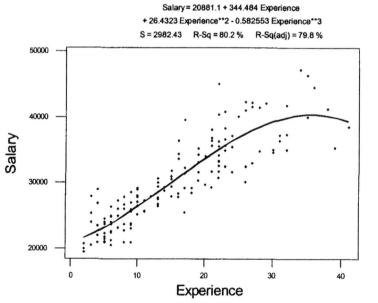

All three of the models appear to fit the data well. The cubic model appears to fit the data the best as the standard error of the estimate is lowest. In addition, explanatory power is marginally higher for the cubic model than the other models.

11-42 a. A 1% increase in median income leads to an expected .68% increase in store size.

b. $H_0 : \beta_1 = 0, H_1 : \beta_1 > 0$

$$t = \frac{.68}{.077} = 8.831$$

Therefore, reject H_0 at the 1% level

11-44

Results for: GermanImports.xls

Regression Analysis: LogYt versus LogX1t, LogX2t

```
The regression equation is
LogYt = - 4.07 + 1.36 LogX1t + 0.101 LogX2t
Predictor          Coef      SE Coef          T        P      VIF
Constant        -4.0709       0.3100     -13.13    0.000
LogX1t          1.35935       0.03005      45.23    0.000      4.9
LogX2t          0.10094       0.05715       1.77    0.088      4.9

S = 0.04758     R-Sq = 99.7%     R-Sq(adj) = 99.7%

Analysis of Variance
Source            DF          SS          MS          F        P
Regression         2      21.345      10.673    4715.32    0.000
Residual Error    28       0.063       0.002
Total             30      21.409

Source          DF      Seq SS
LogX1t           1      21.338
LogX2t           1       0.007
```

11-46

11-48 a. All else being equal, expected selling price is higher by $3,219 if house has a fireplace.

b. All else being equal, expected selling price is higher by $2,005 if house has brick siding.

c. 95% CI: $3219 \pm 1.96(947) = \$1,362.88$ up to $5,075.12

b. $H_0 : \beta_5 = 0, H_1 : \beta_5 > 0$

$$t = \frac{2005}{768} = 2.611$$

$t_{809,.005} = 2.576$

Therefore, reject H_0 at the .5% level

11-50 35.6% of the variation in overall performance in law school can be explained by the variation in undergraduate gpa, scores on the LSATs and whether the student's letter of recommendation are unusually strong. The overall model is significant since we can reject the null hypothesis that the model has no explanatory power in favor of the alternative hypothesis that the model has significant explanatory power. The individual regression coefficients that are significantly different than zero include the scores on the LSAT and whether the student's letters of recommendation were unusually strong. The coefficient on undergraduate gpa was not found to be significant at the 5% level.

11-52

Results for: Student Performance.xls
Regression Analysis: Y versus X1, X2, X3, X4, X5

```
The regression equation is
Y = 2.00 + 0.0099 X1 + 0.0763 X2 - 0.137 X3 + 0.064 X4 + 0.138 X5

Predictor       Coef     SE Coef        T        P        VIF
Constant        1.997      1.273      1.57    0.132
X1            0.00990    0.01654      0.60    0.556      1.3
X2            0.07629    0.05654      1.35    0.192      1.2
X3           -0.13652    0.06922     -1.97    0.062      1.1
X4            0.0636      0.2606      0.24    0.810      1.4
X5            0.13794    0.07521      1.83    0.081      1.1

S = 0.5416     R-Sq = 26.5%     R-Sq(adj) = 9.0%

Analysis of Variance
Source            DF        SS        MS        F        P
Regression         5    2.2165    0.4433     1.51    0.229
Residual Error    21    6.1598    0.2933
Total             26    8.3763
```

The model is not significant (p-value of the F-test = .229). The model only explains 26.5% of the variation in gpa with the hours spent studying, hours spent preparing for tests, hours spent in bars, whether or not students take notes or mark highlights when reading tests and the average number of credit hours taken per semester. The only independent variables that are marginally significant (10% level but not the 5% level) include number of hours spent in bars and whether or not students take notes or mark highlights when reading tests. The other independent variables are not significant at common levels of alpha.

11-54   34.4% of the variation in a test on understanding college economics can be explained by the student's gpa, the teacher that taught the course, the gender of the student, the pre-test score, the number of credit hours completed and the age of the student. The regression model has significant explanatory power:

$$H_0 : \beta_1 = \beta_2 = \beta_3 = \beta_4 = \beta_5 = \beta_6 = \beta_7 = 0, H_1 : \text{At least one } \beta_i \neq 0, (i = 1, 2, 3, 4, 5, 6, 7)$$

$$F = \frac{n-k-1}{k} \frac{R^2}{1-R^2} = \frac{342}{7} \frac{.344}{1-.344} = 25.62$$

11-56   Analyze the correlation matrix first:

Correlations: Sales Pizza1, Price Pizza1, Promotion Pi, Sales B2, Price B2, Sale

	Sales Pi	Price Pi	Promotio	Sales B2	Price B2	Sales B3	Price B3	Sales B4
Price Pi	-0.263							
	0.001							
Promotio	0.570	-0.203						
	0.000	0.011						
Sales B2	0.136	0.170	0.031					
	0.090	0.034	0.700					
Price B2	0.118	0.507	0.117	-0.370				
	0.143	0.000	0.146	0.000				
Sales B3	0.014	0.174	0.045	0.103	0.199			
	0.862	0.029	0.581	0.199	0.013			
Price B3	0.179	0.579	0.034	0.162	0.446	-0.316		
	0.026	0.000	0.675	0.043	0.000	0.000		
Sales B4	0.248	0.102	0.123	0.310	0.136	0.232	0.081	
	0.002	0.205	0.127	0.000	0.091	0.004	0.313	
Price B4	0.177	0.509	0.124	0.229	0.500	0.117	0.523	-0.158
	0.027	0.000	0.124	0.004	0.000	0.147	0.000	0.049

Strongest correlation with sales of Pizza1 is the type of promotion. Price of Pizza1 has the correct 'negative' association with sales. Prices of the competing brands are expected to be positive since they are substitutes with Pizza1; however, the sales of the competing brands are expected to be negatively related to the sales of Pizza1.

Regression Analysis: Sales Pizza1 versus Price Pizza1, Promotion Pi, ...

The regression equation is
Sales Pizza1 = - 6406 - 24097 Price Pizza1 + 1675 Promotion Pizza1
              + 0.0737 Sales B2 + 4204 Price B2 + 0.177 Sales B3 + 18003 Price B3
              + 0.345 Sales B4 + 11813 Price B4

Predictor	Coef	SE Coef	T	P	VIF
Constant	-6406	2753	-2.33	0.021	
Price Pi	-24097	3360	-7.17	0.000	2.5
Promotio	1674.6	283.9	5.90	0.000	1.2
Sales B2	0.07370	0.08281	0.89	0.375	3.1
Price B2	4204	4860	0.87	0.388	4.3
Sales B3	0.17726	0.09578	1.85	0.066	1.9
Price B3	18003	4253	4.23	0.000	3.0
Sales B4	0.3453	0.1392	2.48	0.014	1.9
Price B4	11813	6151	1.92	0.057	3.0

S = 3700   R-Sq = 54.9%   R-Sq(adj) = 52.4%

Analysis of Variance

Source	DF	SS	MS	F	P
Regression	8	2447394873	305924359	22.35	0.000
Residual Error	147	2012350019	13689456		
Total	155	4459744891			

The multiple regression with all of the independent variables indicates that 54.9% of the variation in the sales of Pizza1 can be explained by all of the independent variables. However, not all of the independent variables are significantly different from zero. It appears that neither the price of Brand 2, nor the sales of Brand 2 has a statistically significant effect on Pizza1. Eliminating those variables that are insignificant yields:

Regression Analysis: Sales Pizza1 versus Price Pizza1, Promotion Pi, ...

```
The regression equation is
Sales Pizza1 =  - 6546 - 23294 Price Pizza1 + 1701 Promotion Pizza1
             + 0.197 Sales B3 + 18922 Price B3 + 0.418 Sales B4 + 15152 Price B4
```

Predictor	Coef	SE Coef	T	P	VIF
Constant	-6546	2676	-2.45	0.016	
Price Pi	-23294	3210	-7.26	0.000	2.3
Promotio	1701.0	279.9	6.08	0.000	1.2
Sales B3	0.19737	0.09234	2.14	0.034	1.8
Price B3	18922	4092	4.62	0.000	2.8
Sales B4	0.4183	0.1137	3.68	0.000	1.3
Price B4	15152	4978	3.04	0.003	2.0

```
S = 3686       R-Sq = 54.6%     R-Sq(adj) = 52.8%
Analysis of Variance
```

Source	DF	SS	MS	F	P
Regression	6	2435527670	405921278	29.88	0.000
Residual Error	149	2024217221	13585350		
Total	155	4459744891			

All of the variables are now significant at the .05 level and all have the correct sign excepting the sales of brand 3 and 4.

11-58   Reports can be written by following the extended Case Study on the data file Cotton – see Section 11.9

11-60

Regression Analysis: y_deathrate versus x1_totmiles, x2_avgspeed

```
The regression equation is
y_deathrate =  - 2.97 - 0.00447 x1_totmiles + 0.219 x2_avgspeed
```

Predictor	Coef	SE Coef	T	P	VIF
Constant	-2.969	3.437	-0.86	0.416	
x1_totmi	-0.004470	0.001549	-2.89	0.023	11.7
x2_avgsp	0.21879	0.08391	2.61	0.035	11.7

```
S = 0.1756       R-Sq = 55.1%     R-Sq(adj) = 42.3%
Analysis of Variance
```

Source	DF	SS	MS	F	P
Regression	2	0.26507	0.13254	4.30	0.061
Residual Error	7	0.21593	0.03085		
Total	9	0.48100			

55.1% of the variation in death rates can be explained by the variation in total miles traveled and in average travel speed. The overall model is significant at the 10% but not the 5% level since the p-value of the F-test is .061.

All else equal, the average speed variable has the expected sign since as average speed increases, the death rate also increases. The total miles traveled variable is negative which indicates that the more miles traveled, the lower the death rate. Both of the independent variables are significant at the 5% level (p-values of .023 and .035 respectively). There appears to be some correlation between the independent variables.

Due to the high correlation between the independent variables, an alternative model using a quadratic model is as follows:

Regression Analysis: y_deathrate versus x1_totmiles, x1_totsquared
The regression equation is
y_deathrate = - 6.54 + 0.0268 x1_totmiles -0.000015 x1_totsquared

Predictor	Coef	SE Coef	T	P	VIF
Constant	-6.539	1.296	-5.04	0.001	
x1_totmi	0.026800	0.002835	9.45	0.000	285.5
x1_totsq	-0.00001480	0.00000153	-9.68	0.000	285.5

S = 0.06499   R-Sq = 93.9%   R-Sq(adj) = 92.1%

Analysis of Variance

Source	DF	SS	MS	F	P
Regression	2	0.45143	0.22572	53.44	0.000
Residual Error	7	0.02957	0.00422		
Total	9	0.48100			

Source	DF	Seq SS
x1_totmi	1	0.05534
x1_totsq	1	0.39609

11.62
Regression Analysis: y_money versus x1_pcincome, x2_ir
The regression equation is
y_money = - 1158 + 0.253 x1_pcincome - 19.6 x2_ir

Predictor	Coef	SE Coef	T	P	VIF
Constant	-1158.4	587.9	-1.97	0.080	
x1_pcinc	0.25273	0.03453	7.32	0.000	1.3
x2_ir	-19.56	21.73	-0.90	0.391	1.3

S = 84.93   R-Sq = 89.8%   R-Sq(adj) = 87.5%

Analysis of Variance

Source	DF	SS	MS	F	P
Regression	2	570857	285429	39.57	0.000
Residual Error	9	64914	7213		
Total	11	635771			

Source	DF	Seq SS
x1_pcinc	1	565012
x2_ir	1	5845

11-64 The method of least squares regression yields estimators that are BLUE – Best Linear
Unbiased Estimators. This result holds when the assumptions regarding the behavior of the
error term are true. BLUE estimators are the most efficient (best) estimators out of the class
of all unbiased estimators. The advent of computing power incorporating the method of
least squares has dramatically increased its use.

11-66 a. False. If the regression model does not explain a large enough portion of the
variability of the dependent variable, then the error sum of squares can be larger than the
regression sum of squares
   b. False – the sum of several simple linear regressions will not equal a multiple regression
   since the assumption of 'all else equal' will be violated in the simple linear regressions.
   The multiple regression 'holds' all else equal in calculating the partial effect that a
   change in one of the independent variables has on the dependent variable.
   c. True

d. False – While the regular coefficient of determination (R^2) cannot be negative, the adjusted coefficient of determination $\bar{R}^2$ can become negative. If the independent variables added into a regression equation have very little explanatory power, the loss of degrees of freedom may more than offset the added explanatory power.

e. True

11-68   This is a classic example of what happens when there is a high degree of multicollinearity between the independent variables. The overall model can be shown to have significant explanatory power and yet none of the slope coefficients on the independent variables are significantly different from zero.

11-70   a. All else equal, a unit change in population, industry size, measure of economic quality, measure of health and social life results in a respective 4.983, 2.198, 3.816, 3.215, and .085 increase in the new business starts in the industry.

b. $R^2 = .766$

c. $t_{62,.05} = 1.67$, therefore, the 90% CI: $3.816 \pm 1.67(2.063) = .3708$ up to 7.2612

d. $H_0 : \beta_5 = 0, H_1 : \beta_5 \neq 0$

$$t = \frac{-.886}{3.055} = -.29$$

$t_{62,.10} = -1.295$

Therefore, do not reject H_0 at the 20% level

e. $H_0 : \beta_6 = 0, H_1 : \beta_6 \neq 0$

$$t = \frac{3.125}{1.568} = 2.05, \quad t_{62,.025} = 1.999$$

Therefore, reject H_0 at the 5% level

f. $H_0 : \beta_1 = \beta_2 = \beta_3 = \beta_4 = \beta_5 = \beta_6 = \beta_7 = 0, H_1 :$ At least one $\beta_i \neq 0, (i = 1, 2, 3, 4, 5, 6, 7)$

$$F = \frac{n-k-1}{k} \frac{R^2}{1-R^2} = \frac{62}{2} \frac{.766}{1-.766} = 28.99$$

$F_{7,62,.01} = 2.79$, Therefore, reject H_0 at the 1% level

11-72   a. All else equal, a 1% increase in course time spent in group discussion results in an expected increase of .3817 in the average rating of the course. All else equal, a unit increase in money spent on the course results in an expected increase of .5172 in the average rating by participants of the course. All else equal, a unit increase in expenditure on non-course activities results in an expected increase of .0753 in the average rating of the course.

b. 57.9% of the variation in the average rating can be explained by the linear relationship with % of class time spent on discussion, money spent on class activities and money spent on non-class activities.

c. $H_0 : \beta_1 = \beta_2 = \beta_3 = 0, H_1 :$ At least one $\beta_i \neq 0, (i = 1, 2, 3)$

$$F = \frac{n-k-1}{k} \frac{R^2}{1-R^2} = \frac{21}{3} \frac{.579}{1-.579} = 9.627$$

$F_{2,21,.01} = 4.87$

Therefore, reject H_0 at the 1% level

d. $t_{21,.05} = 1.721$, 90% CI: $.3817 \pm 1.721(.2018)$ .0344 up to .729

e. t = 2.64, $t_{21,.01/.005} = 2.518, 2.831$

Therefore, reject H_0 at the 1% level but not at the .5% level

   f. t = 1.09, $t_{21,.10} = 1.323$

Therefore, do not reject H_0 at the 20% level

11.74   Use the result from exercise 32

$H_0 : \beta_4 = \beta_5 = \beta_6 = \beta_7 = 0, H_1 :$ At least one $\beta_i \neq 0, (i = 4, 5, 6, 7,)$

$$F = \frac{n-k-1}{k} \frac{R^2}{1-R^2} = \frac{55}{4} \frac{.467 - .242}{1-.467} = 5.804$$

$F_{4,55,.01} = 3.68$

Therefore, reject H_0 at the 1% level

11-76   a. $t_{22,.01} = 2.819$, therefore, the 99% CI: $.0974 \pm 2.819(0.0215) = .0368$ up to .1580

   b. $H_0 : \beta_2 = 0, H_1 : \beta_2 > 0$

$$t = \frac{.374}{.209} = 1.789$$

$t_{22,.05/.025} = 1.717, 2.074$, therefore, reject H_0 at the 5% level but not the 2.5% level

   c. $R^2 = \frac{22(.91) + 2}{24} = .9175$

   d. $H_0 : \beta_1 = \beta_2 = 0, H_1 :$ At least one $\beta_i \neq 0, (i = 1, 2)$

$$F = \frac{n-k-1}{k} \frac{R^2}{1-R^2} = \frac{22}{2} \frac{.9175}{1-.9175} = 122.33$$

$F_{2,22,.01} = 5.72$

Reject H_0 at any common levels of alpha

   e. $R = \sqrt{.9175} = .9579$

11-78   a. $H_0 : \beta_1 = 0, H_1 : \beta_1 \neq 0$

$$t = \frac{-.052}{.019} = -2.737$$

$t_{60,.005} = 2.66$, therefore, reject H_0 at the 1% level

b. $H_0 : \beta_2 = 0, H_1 : \beta_2 \neq 0$

$t = \dfrac{-.005}{.042} = -.119$

$t_{60,.10} = 1.296$, therefore, do not reject H_0 at the 20% level

c. 17% of the variation in the growth rate in GDP can be explained by the variations in real income per capita and the average tax rate, as a proportion of GNP.

d. $R = \sqrt{.17} = .4123$

11-80 a. Start with the correlation matrix:

Correlations: EconGPA, SATverb, SATmath, HSPct

```
           EconGPA   SATverb   SATmath
SATverb    0.478
           0.000

SATmath    0.427     0.353
           0.000     0.003

HSPct      0.362     0.201     0.497
           0.000     0.121     0.000
```

Regression Analysis: EconGPA versus SATverb, SATmath, HSPct

```
The regression equation is
EconGPA = 0.612 + 0.0239 SATverb + 0.0117 SATmath + 0.00530 HSPct
61 cases used 51 cases contain missing values
Predictor        Coef      SE Coef           T        P        VIF
Constant       0.6117       0.4713        1.30    0.200
SATverb      0.023929     0.007386        3.24    0.002        1.2
SATmath      0.011722     0.007887        1.49    0.143        1.5
HSPct        0.005303     0.004213        1.26    0.213        1.3

S = 0.4238      R-Sq = 32.9%      R-Sq(adj) = 29.4%

Analysis of Variance
Source            DF           SS          MS        F        P
Regression         3       5.0171      1.6724     9.31    0.000
Residual Error    57      10.2385      0.1796
Total             60      15.2556

Source        DF     Seq SS
SATverb        1     3.7516
SATmath        1     0.9809
HSPct          1     0.2846
```

The regression model indicates positive coefficients, as expected, for all three independent variables. The greater the high school rank, and the higher the SAT verbal and SAT math scores, the larger the Econ GPA. The high school rank variable has the smallest t-statistic and is removed from the model:

Regression Analysis: EconGPA versus SATverb, SATmath

```
The regression equation is
EconGPA = 0.755 + 0.0230 SATverb + 0.0174 SATmath
67 cases used 45 cases contain missing values
Predictor         Coef      SE Coef        T         P        VIF
Constant        0.7547       0.4375      1.72     0.089
SATverb        0.022951     0.006832     3.36     0.001       1.1
SATmath        0.017387     0.006558     2.65     0.010       1.1

S = 0.4196      R-Sq = 30.5%      R-Sq(adj) = 28.3%

Analysis of Variance
Source             DF          SS         MS         F         P
Regression          2      4.9488     2.4744     14.05     0.000
Residual Error     64     11.2693     0.1761
Total              66     16.2181

Source        DF      Seq SS
SATverb        1      3.7109
SATmath        1      1.2379
```

Both SAT variables are now statistically significant at the .05 level and appear to pick up separate influences on the dependent variable. The simple correlation coefficient between SAT math and SAT verbal is relatively low at .353. Thus, multicollinearity will not be dominant in this regression model.

The final regression model, with conditional t-statistics in parentheses under the coefficients, is:

$$\hat{Y} = .755 + .023(SATverbal) + .0174(SATmath)$$

$$(3.36) \qquad\qquad (2.65)$$

$$S = .4196 \quad R^2 = .305 \quad n = 67$$

   b. Start with the correlation matrix:

Correlations: EconGPA, Acteng, ACTmath, ACTss, ACTcomp, HSPct

```
          EconGPA   Acteng   ACTmath    ACTss   ACTcomp
Acteng      0.387
            0.001

ACTmath     0.338    0.368
            0.003    0.001

ACTss       0.442    0.448     0.439
            0.000    0.000     0.000

ACTcomp     0.474    0.650     0.765    0.812
            0.000    0.000     0.000    0.000

HSPct       0.362    0.173     0.290    0.224     0.230
            0.000    0.150     0.014    0.060     0.053
```

Regression Analysis: EconGPA versus Acteng, ACTmath, ...

```
The regression equation is
EconGPA = - 0.207 + 0.0266 Acteng - 0.0023 ACTmath + 0.0212 ACTss
          + 0.0384 ACTcomp + 0.0128 HSPct
71 cases used 41 cases contain missing values
```

Predictor	Coef	SE Coef	T	P	VIF
Constant	-0.2069	0.6564	-0.32	0.754	
Acteng	0.02663	0.02838	0.94	0.352	2.2
ACTmath	-0.00229	0.03031	-0.08	0.940	4.2
ACTss	0.02118	0.02806	0.75	0.453	4.6
ACTcomp	0.03843	0.07287	0.53	0.600	12.7
HSPct	0.012817	0.005271	2.43	0.018	1.2

```
S = 0.5034      R-Sq = 31.4%      R-Sq(adj) = 26.1%
```

Analysis of Variance

Source	DF	SS	MS	F	P
Regression	5	7.5253	1.5051	5.94	0.000
Residual Error	65	16.4691	0.2534		
Total	70	23.9945			

Source	DF	Seq SS
Acteng	1	3.5362
ACTmath	1	1.0529
ACTss	1	1.4379
ACTcomp	1	0.0001
HSPct	1	1.4983

The regression shows that only high school rank is significant at the .05 level. We may suspect multicollinearity between the variables, particularly since there is a 'total' ACT score (ACT composite) as well as the components that make up the ACT composite. Since conditional significance is dependent on which other independent variables are included in the regression equation, drop one variable at a time. ACTmath has the lowest t-statistic and is removed:

Regression Analysis: EconGPA versus Acteng, ACTss, ACTcomp, HSPct

```
The regression equation is
EconGPA = - 0.195 + 0.0276 Acteng + 0.0224 ACTss + 0.0339 ACTcomp
          + 0.0127 HSPct
71 cases used 41 cases contain missing values
```

Predictor	Coef	SE Coef	T	P	VIF
Constant	-0.1946	0.6313	-0.31	0.759	
Acteng	0.02756	0.02534	1.09	0.281	1.8
ACTss	0.02242	0.02255	0.99	0.324	3.0
ACTcomp	0.03391	0.04133	0.82	0.415	4.2
HSPct	0.012702	0.005009	2.54	0.014	1.1

```
S = 0.4996      R-Sq = 31.4%      R-Sq(adj) = 27.2%
```

Analysis of Variance

Source	DF	SS	MS	F	P
Regression	4	7.5239	1.8810	7.54	0.000
Residual Error	66	16.4706	0.2496		
Total	70	23.9945			

Source	DF	Seq SS
Acteng	1	3.5362
ACTss	1	2.1618
ACTcomp	1	0.2211
HSPct	1	1.6048

Again, high school rank is the only conditionally significant variable. ACTcomp has the lowest t-statistic and is removed:

Regression Analysis: EconGPA versus Acteng, ACTss, HSPct

```
The regression equation is
EconGPA = 0.049 + 0.0390 Acteng + 0.0364 ACTss + 0.0129 HSPct
71 cases used 41 cases contain missing values
Predictor          Coef     SE Coef          T       P      VIF
Constant         0.0487      0.5560       0.09   0.930
Acteng          0.03897     0.02114       1.84   0.070      1.3
ACTss           0.03643     0.01470       2.48   0.016      1.3
HSPct          0.012896    0.004991       2.58   0.012      1.1

S = 0.4983      R-Sq = 30.7%     R-Sq(adj) = 27.6%

Analysis of Variance
Source              DF          SS         MS       F       P
Regression           3      7.3558     2.4519    9.87   0.000
Residual Error      67     16.6386     0.2483
Total               70     23.9945

Source         DF    Seq SS
Acteng          1    3.5362
ACTss           1    2.1618
HSPct           1    1.6579
```

Now ACTss and high school rank are conditionally significant. ACTenglish has a t-statistic less than 2 and is removed:

Regression Analysis: EconGPA versus ACTss, HSPct

```
The regression equation is
EconGPA = 0.566 + 0.0479 ACTss + 0.0137 HSPct
71 cases used 41 cases contain missing values
Predictor          Coef     SE Coef          T       P      VIF
Constant         0.5665      0.4882       1.16   0.250
ACTss           0.04790     0.01355       3.53   0.001      1.1
HSPct          0.013665    0.005061       2.70   0.009      1.1

S = 0.5070      R-Sq = 27.1%     R-Sq(adj) = 25.0%

Analysis of Variance
Source              DF          SS         MS       F       P
Regression           2      6.5123     3.2562   12.67   0.000
Residual Error      68     17.4821     0.2571
Total               70     23.9945

Source         DF    Seq SS
ACTss           1    4.6377
HSPct           1    1.8746
```

Both of the independent variables are statistically significant at the .05 level and hence, the final regression model, with conditional t-statistics in parentheses under the coefficients, is:

$$\hat{Y} = .567 + .0479(ACTss) + .0137(HSPct)$$
$$\qquad\quad (3.53) \qquad\qquad (2.70)$$
$$S = .5070 \quad R^2 = .271 \quad n = 71$$

c. The regression model with the SAT variables is the better predictor because the standard error of the estimate is smaller than for the ACT model (.4196 vs. .5070). The R^2 measure cannot be directly compared due to the sample size differences.

11-82

Correlations: hseval, Comper, Homper, Indper, sizehse, incom72

```
          hseval    Comper    Homper    Indper   sizehse
Comper   -0.335
          0.001

Homper    0.145    -0.499
          0.171     0.000

Indper   -0.086    -0.140    -0.564
          0.419     0.188     0.000

sizehse   0.542    -0.278     0.274    -0.245
          0.000     0.008     0.009     0.020

incom72   0.426    -0.198    -0.083     0.244     0.393
          0.000     0.062     0.438     0.020     0.000
```

The correlation matrix indicates that the size of the house, income and percent homeowners have a positive relationship with house value. There is a negative relationship between the percent industrial and percent commercial and house value.

Regression Analysis: hseval versus Comper, Homper, ...

The regression equation is

hseval = - 19.0 - 26.4 Comper - 12.1 Homper - 15.5 Indper + 7.22 sizehse + 0.00408 incom72

Predictor	Coef	SE Coef	T	P	VIF
Constant	-19.02	13.20	-1.44	0.153	
Comper	-26.393	9.890	-2.67	0.009	2.2
Homper	-12.123	7.508	-1.61	0.110	3.0
Indper	-15.531	8.630	-1.80	0.075	2.6
sizehse	7.219	2.138	3.38	0.001	1.5
incom72	0.004081	0.001555	2.62	0.010	1.4

S = 3.949   R-Sq = 40.1%   R-Sq(adj) = 36.5%

Analysis of Variance

Source	DF	SS	MS	F	P
Regression	5	876.80	175.36	11.25	0.000
Residual Error	84	1309.83	15.59		
Total	89	2186.63			

All variables are conditionally significant with the exception of Indper and Homper. Since Homper has the smaller t-statistic, it is removed:

Regression Analysis: hseval versus Comper, Indper, sizehse, incom72

The regression equation is

hseval = - 30.9 - 15.2 Comper - 5.73 Indper + 7.44 sizehse + 0.00418 incom72

Predictor	Coef	SE Coef	T	P	VIF
Constant	-30.88	11.07	-2.79	0.007	
Comper	-15.211	7.126	-2.13	0.036	1.1
Indper	-5.735	6.194	-0.93	0.357	1.3
sizehse	7.439	2.154	3.45	0.001	1.5
incom72	0.004175	0.001569	2.66	0.009	1.4

S = 3.986   R-Sq = 38.2%   R-Sq(adj) = 35.3%

Analysis of Variance

Source	DF	SS	MS	F	P
Regression	4	836.15	209.04	13.16	0.000
Residual Error	85	1350.48	15.89		
Total	89	2186.63			

Indper is not significant and is removed:

Regression Analysis: hseval versus Comper, sizehse, incom72

```
The regression equation is
hseval = - 34.2 - 13.9 Comper + 8.27 sizehse + 0.00364 incom72
Predictor        Coef     SE Coef          T         P       VIF
Constant       -34.24       10.44      -3.28     0.002
Comper        -13.881       6.974      -1.99     0.050       1.1
sizehse         8.270       1.957       4.23     0.000       1.2
incom72      0.003636    0.001456       2.50     0.014       1.2


S = 3.983       R-Sq = 37.6%      R-Sq(adj) = 35.4%

Analysis of Variance
Source            DF          SS         MS         F         P
Regression         3      822.53     274.18     17.29     0.000
Residual Error    86     1364.10      15.86
Total             89     2186.63
```

This becomes the final regression model. The selection of a community with the objective of having larger house values would include communities where the percent of commercial property is low, the median rooms per residence is high and the per capita income is high.

11.84   a. Correlation matrix:

Correlations: deaths, Purbanpop, Ruspeed, Prsurf

```
          deaths  Purbanpo   Ruspeed
Purbanpo  -0.594
           0.000

Ruspeed    0.305    -0.224
           0.033     0.121

Prsurf    -0.556     0.207    -0.232
           0.000     0.153     0.109
```

Descriptive Statistics: deaths, Purbanpop, Prsurf, Ruspeed

```
Variable       N      Mean    Median     TrMean     StDev    SE Mean
deaths        49    0.1746    0.1780     0.1675    0.0802     0.0115
Purbanpo      49    0.5890    0.6311     0.5992    0.2591     0.0370
Prsurf        49    0.7980    0.8630     0.8117    0.1928     0.0275
Ruspeed       49    58.186    58.400     58.222     1.683      0.240

Variable   Minimum   Maximum        Q1         Q3
deaths      0.0569    0.5505    0.1240     0.2050
Purbanpo    0.0000    0.9689    0.4085     0.8113
Prsurf      0.2721    1.0000    0.6563     0.9485
Ruspeed     53.500    62.200    57.050     59.150
```

The proportion of urban population and rural roads that are surfaced are negatively related to crash deaths. Average rural speed is positively related, but the relationship is not as strong as the proportion of urban population and surfaced roads. The simple correlation coefficients among the independent variables are relatively low and hence multicollinearity should not be dominant in this model. Note the relatively narrow range for average rural speed. This would indicate that there is not much variability in this independent variable.

b.

Regression Analysis: deaths versus Purbanpop, Prsurf, Ruspeed
```
The regression equation is
deaths = 0.141 - 0.149 Purbanpop - 0.181 Prsurf + 0.00457 Ruspeed

Predictor        Coef      SE Coef         T        P       VIF
Constant       0.1408       0.2998      0.47    0.641
Purbanpo      -0.14946      0.03192     -4.68    0.000       1.1
Prsurf        -0.18058      0.04299     -4.20    0.000       1.1
Ruspeed       0.004569     0.004942      0.92    0.360       1.1

S = 0.05510     R-Sq = 55.8%     R-Sq(adj) = 52.8%

Analysis of Variance
Source           DF          SS          MS         F        P
Regression        3    0.172207    0.057402     18.91    0.000
Residual Error   45    0.136602    0.003036
Total            48    0.308809
```

The model has conditionally significant variables for percent urban population and percent surfaced roads. Since average rural speed is not conditionally significant, it is dropped from the model:

Regression Analysis: deaths versus Purbanpop, Prsurf
```
The regression equation is
deaths = 0.416 - 0.155 Purbanpop - 0.188 Prsurf
Predictor        Coef      SE Coef         T        P       VIF
Constant       0.41609      0.03569     11.66    0.000
Purbanpo      -0.15493      0.03132     -4.95    0.000       1.0
Prsurf        -0.18831      0.04210     -4.47    0.000       1.0

S = 0.05501     R-Sq = 54.9%     R-Sq(adj) = 53.0%

Analysis of Variance
Source           DF          SS          MS         F        P
Regression        2    0.169612    0.084806     28.03    0.000
Residual Error   46    0.139197    0.003026
Total            48    0.308809
```

This becomes the final model since both variables are conditionally significant.

c. Conclude that the proportions of urban populations and the percent of rural roads that are surfaced are important independent variables in explaining crash deaths. All else equal, increases in the proportion of urban population, the lower the crash deaths. All else equal, increases in the proportion of rural roads that are surfaced will result in lower crash deaths. The average rural speed is not conditionally significant.

11-86 a. Correlation matrix
Correlations: retsal84, Unemp84, perinc84
```
         retsal84   Unemp84
Unemp84   -0.370
           0.008
perinc84   0.633     -0.232
           0.000      0.101
```

There is a positive association between per capita income and retail sales. There is a negative association between unemployment and retail sales. Multicollinearity does not appear to be a problem since the correlation between the independent variables is relatively low.

Descriptive Statistics: retsal84, perinc84, Unemp84

Variable	N	Mean	Median	TrMean	StDev	SE Mean
retsal84	51	5536	5336	5483	812	114
perinc84	51	12277	12314	12166	1851	259
Unemp84	51	7.335	7.000	7.196	2.216	0.310

Variable	Minimum	Maximum	Q1	Q3
retsal84	4250	8348	5059	6037
perinc84	8857	17148	10689	13218

Regression Analysis: retsal84 versus Unemp84, perinc84

The regression equation is
retsal84 = 3054 - 86.3 Unemp84 + 0.254 perinc84

Predictor	Coef	SE Coef	T	P	VIF
Constant	3054.3	724.4	4.22	0.000	
Unemp84	-86.25	40.20	-2.15	0.037	1.1
perinc84	0.25368	0.04815	5.27	0.000	1.1

S = 612.9   R-Sq = 45.3%   R-Sq(adj) = 43.0%

Analysis of Variance

Source	DF	SS	MS	F	P
Regression	2	14931938	7465969	19.88	0.000
Residual Error	48	18029333	375611		
Total	50	32961271			

This is the final model since all of the independent variables are conditionally significant at the .05 level. The 95% confidence intervals for the regression slope coefficients:

$$\hat{\beta}_1 \pm t(S_{\hat{\beta}_1}): \quad -86.25 +/- 2.011(40.2) = -86.25 +/- 80.84$$

$$\hat{\beta}_2 \pm t(S_{\hat{\beta}_2}): \quad .254 + / - 2.011(.04815) = .254 + / - .0968$$

b. All things equal, the condition effect of a $1,000 decrease in per capita income on retail sales would be to reduce retail sales by $254.

c. Adding state population as a predictor yields the following regression results:

Regression Analysis: retsal84 versus Unemp84, perinc84, Totpop84

The regression equation is
retsal84 = 2828 - 71.3 Unemp84 + 0.272 perinc84 - 0.0247 Totpop84

Predictor	Coef	SE Coef	T	P	VIF
Constant	2828.4	737.9	3.83	0.000	
Unemp84	-71.33	41.40	-1.72	0.091	1.1
perinc84	0.27249	0.04977	5.47	0.000	1.1
Totpop84	-0.02473	0.01845	-1.34	0.187	1.1

S = 607.8   R-Sq = 47.3%   R-Sq(adj) = 44.0%

Analysis of Variance

Source	DF	SS	MS	F	P
Regression	3	15595748	5198583	14.07	0.000
Residual Error	47	17365523	369479		
Total	50	32961271			

The population variable is not conditionally significant and adds little explanatory power, therefore, it will not improve the multiple regression model.

11-88 a.

Correlations: Infmrt82, Phys82, Perinc84, Perhosp

```
           Infmrt82    Phys82 Perinc84
Phys82      0.434
            0.001
Perinc84    0.094     0.614
            0.511     0.000
Perhosp     0.411     0.285     0.267
            0.003     0.042     0.058
```

The correlation matrix shows a positive association with Phys82 and Perhosp. These variables are the number of physicians per 100,000 population and the total per capita expenditures for hospitals. One would expect a negative association, therefore, examine the scatterdiagram of infant mortality vs. phys82:

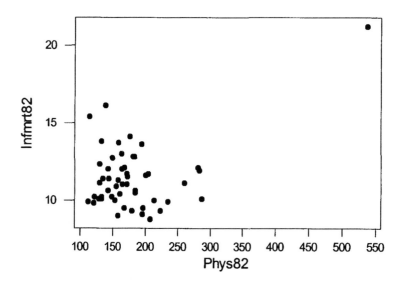

The graph shows an obvious outlier which, upon further investigation, is the District of Columbia. Due to the outlier status, this row is dropped from the analysis and the correlation matrix is recalculated:

Correlations: Infmrt82, Phys82, Perinc84, Perhosp

```
           Infmrt82    Phys82 Perinc84
Phys82     -0.147
            0.309
Perinc84   -0.192     0.574
            0.181     0.000
Perhosp     0.199    -0.065     0.140
            0.166     0.654     0.331
```

The physicians per 100,000 population now has the correct sign, however, none of the independent variables has a statistically significant linear association with the dependent variable. Per capita expenditures for hospitals is an unexpected positive sign; however, it is not conditionally significant. The multiple regression results are likely to yield low explanatory power with insignificant independent variables:

Regression Analysis: Infmrt82 versus Phys82, Perinc84, Perhosp

```
The regression equation is
Infmrt82 = 12.7 - 0.00017 Phys82 -0.000206 Perinc84 + 6.30 Perhosp
Predictor        Coef      SE Coef          T        P       VIF
Constant       12.701        1.676       7.58    0.000
Phys82       -0.000167     0.006647      -0.03    0.980       1.5
Perinc84     -0.0002064    0.0001637     -1.26    0.214       1.6
Perhosp         6.297        3.958       1.59    0.118       1.1

S = 1.602        R-Sq = 8.9%      R-Sq(adj) = 3.0%
Analysis of Variance
Source           DF           SS          MS        F        P
Regression        3       11.546       3.849     1.50    0.227
Residual Error   46      118.029       2.566
Total            49      129.575
```

As expected, the model explains less than 9% of the variability in infant mortality. None of the independent variables are conditionally significant and multicollinearity does not appear to be a significant problem. The standard error of the estimate is very large (1.602) relative to the size of the infant mortality rates and hence the model would not be a good predictor. Sequentially dropping the independent variable with the lowest t-statistic confirms the conclusion that none of the independnet variables is conditionally significant. The search is on for better independent variables.

b. The two variables to include are per capita spending on education (PerEduc) and per capita spending on public welfare (PerPbwel). Since the conditional significance of the independent variables is a function of other independent variables in the model, we will include the original set of variables:

Regression Analysis: Infmrt82 versus Phys82, Perinc84, ...

```
The regression equation is
Infmrt82 = 12.2 - 0.00122 Phys82 +0.000015 Perinc84 + 8.87 Perhosp
           - 1.96 PerEduc - 4.56 PerPbwel
Predictor        Coef      SE Coef          T        P       VIF
Constant       12.167        1.654       7.35    0.000
Phys82       -0.001219     0.008028      -0.15    0.880       2.4
Perinc84      0.0000152    0.0001942      0.08    0.938       2.4
Perhosp         8.872        4.010       2.21    0.032       1.2
PerEduc        -1.960        1.315      -1.49    0.143       1.8
PerPbwel       -4.555        3.360      -1.36    0.182       1.7

S = 1.550        R-Sq = 18.4%     R-Sq(adj) = 9.1%
Analysis of Variance
Source           DF           SS          MS        F        P
Regression        5       23.848       4.770     1.98    0.100
Residual Error   44      105.727       2.403
Total            49      129.575
```

The model shows low explanatory power and only one independent variable that is conditionally significant (Perhosp). Dropping sequentially the independent variable with the lowest t-statistic yields a model with no conditionally significant independent variables. This problem illustrates that in some applications, the variables that have been identified as theoretically important predictors do not meet the statistical test.

11-90

Regression Analysis: hseval versus sizehse, taxrate, incom72, Homper

```
The regression equation is
hseval = - 32.7 + 6.74 sizehse - 223 taxrate + 0.00464 incom72 + 11.2 Homper
Predictor        Coef     SE Coef        T        P      VIF
Constant      -32.694       8.972     -3.64    0.000
sizehse         6.740       1.880      3.58    0.001      1.4
taxrate      -222.96       45.39      -4.91    0.000      1.2
incom72      0.004642    0.001349      3.44    0.001      1.2
Homper         11.215       4.592      2.44    0.017      1.3

S = 3.610       R-Sq = 49.3%     R-Sq(adj) = 47.0%

Analysis of Variance
Source              DF          SS         MS         F        P
Regression           4     1079.08     269.77     20.70    0.000
Residual Error      85     1107.55      13.03
Total               89     2186.63
```

All of the independent variables are conditionally significant. Now add the percent of commercial property to the model to see if it is significant:

Regression Analysis: hseval versus sizehse, taxrate, ...

```
The regression equation is
hseval = - 31.6 + 6.76 sizehse - 218 taxrate + 0.00453 incom72 + 10.3 Homper
         - 2.18 Comper
Predictor        Coef     SE Coef        T        P      VIF
Constant      -31.615       9.839     -3.21    0.002
sizehse         6.757       1.892      3.57    0.001      1.4
taxrate      -217.63       49.58      -4.39    0.000      1.4
incom72      0.004534    0.001412      3.21    0.002      1.4
Homper         10.287       5.721      1.80    0.076      2.0
Comper         -2.182       7.940     -0.27    0.784      1.7

S = 3.630       R-Sq = 49.4%     R-Sq(adj) = 46.4%

Analysis of Variance
Source              DF          SS         MS         F        P
Regression           5     1080.07     216.01     16.40    0.000
Residual Error      84     1106.56      13.17
Total               89     2186.63
```

With a t-statistic of -.27 we have not found strong enough evidence to reject H_0 that the slope coefficient on percent commercial property is significantly different from zero. The conditional F test:

$$F_{Comper} = \frac{SSR_F - SSR_R}{S^2_{Y|X}} = \frac{1080.07 - 1079.08}{(3.63)^2} = .075 ,$$ Thus, at any common level of alpha,

do not reject H_0 that the percent commercial property has no effect on house values.

Add percent industrial property to the base model:

Regression Analysis: hseval versus sizehse, taxrate, ...

```
The regression equation is
hseval = - 28.6 + 6.10 sizehse - 232 taxrate + 0.00521 incom72 + 8.68 Homper
           - 7.50 Indper
Predictor        Coef     SE Coef         T         P        VIF
Constant      -28.643       9.602     -2.98     0.004
sizehse         6.096       1.956      3.12     0.003        1.5
taxrate      -232.34       46.00      -5.05     0.000        1.2
incom72      0.005208    0.001431      3.64     0.000        1.4
Homper         8.681       5.070       1.71     0.091        1.6
Indper        -7.505       6.427      -1.17     0.246        1.7

S = 3.602      R-Sq = 50.2%     R-Sq(adj) = 47.2%
Analysis of Variance
Source             DF         SS        MS         F         P
Regression          5    1096.77    219.35     16.91     0.000
Residual Error     84    1089.86     12.97
Total              89    2186.63
```

Likewise, the percent industrial property is not significantly different from zero. The conditional F test:

$$F_{Indper} = \frac{RSS_5 - RSS_4}{S^2_{Y|X}} = \frac{1096.77 - 1079.08}{(3.602)^2} = 1.36,$$ Again this is lower than the

critical value of F based on common levels of alpha, therefore, do not reject H_0 that the percent industrial property has no effect on house values.

Tax rate models:

Regression Analysis: taxrate versus taxbase, expercap, Homper

```
The regression equation is
taxrate = - 0.0174 -0.000000 taxbase +0.000162 expercap + 0.0424 Homper
Predictor         Coef      SE Coef         T         P        VIF
Constant     -0.017399     0.007852     -2.22     0.029
taxbase      -0.00000000  0.00000000    -0.80     0.426        1.2
expercap      0.00016204  0.00003160     5.13     0.000        1.1
Homper        0.042361     0.009378      4.52     0.000        1.2

S = 0.007692     R-Sq = 31.9%     R-Sq(adj) = 29.5%
Analysis of Variance
Source             DF          SS           MS         F         P
Regression          3    0.00237926   0.00079309    13.41     0.000
Residual Error     86    0.00508785   0.00005916
Total              89    0.00746711
```

Since taxbase is not significant, it is dropped from the model:

Regression Analysis: taxrate versus expercap, Homper

```
The regression equation is
taxrate = - 0.0192 +0.000158 expercap + 0.0448 Homper
Predictor         Coef      SE Coef         T         P        VIF
Constant     -0.019188     0.007511     -2.55     0.012
expercap      0.00015767  0.00003106     5.08     0.000        1.1
Homper        0.044777     0.008860      5.05     0.000        1.1

S = 0.007676     R-Sq = 31.4%     R-Sq(adj) = 29.8%
Analysis of Variance
Source             DF         SS           MS         F         P
Regression          2    0.0023414    0.0011707     19.87     0.000
Residual Error     87    0.0051257    0.0000589
Total              89    0.0074671
```

Both of the independent variables are significant. This becomes the base model that we now add percent commercial property and percent industrial property sequentially:

Regression Analysis: taxrate versus expercap, Homper, Comper

```
The regression equation is
taxrate = - 0.0413 +0.000157 expercap + 0.0643 Homper + 0.0596 Comper
Predictor        Coef      SE Coef          T        P      VIF
Constant     -0.041343     0.008455      -4.89    0.000
expercap    0.00015660   0.00002819       5.55    0.000      1.1
Homper        0.064320     0.009172       7.01    0.000      1.4
Comper        0.05960      0.01346        4.43    0.000      1.3

S = 0.006966    R-Sq = 44.1%    R-Sq(adj) = 42.2%

Analysis of Variance
Source           DF          SS           MS         F        P
Regression        3   0.0032936    0.0010979     22.62    0.000
Residual Error   86   0.0041735    0.0000485
Total            89   0.0074671
```

Percent commercial property is conditionally significant and an important independent variable as shown by the conditional F-test:

$$F_{Comper} = \frac{RSS_3 - RSS_2}{S^2_{Y|X}} = \frac{.003294 - .00234}{(.006966)^2} = 19.62$$

With 1 degree of freedom in the numberator and (90-3-1) = 86 degrees of freedom in the denominator, the critical value of F at the .05 level is 3.95. Hence we would conclude that the percentage of commercial property has a statistically significant positive impact on tax rate.

We now add industrial property to test the effect on tax rate:

Regression Analysis: taxrate versus expercap, Homper, Indper

```
The regression equation is
taxrate = - 0.0150 +0.000156 expercap + 0.0398 Homper - 0.0105 Indper
Predictor        Coef      SE Coef          T        P      VIF
Constant     -0.015038     0.009047      -1.66    0.100
expercap    0.00015586   0.00003120       5.00    0.000      1.1
Homper        0.03982      0.01071        3.72    0.000      1.6
Indper       -0.01052      0.01273       -0.83    0.411      1.5

S = 0.007690    R-Sq = 31.9%    R-Sq(adj) = 29.5%

Analysis of Variance
Source           DF          SS           MS         F        P
Regression        3   0.00238178   0.00079393    13.43    0.000
Residual Error   86   0.00508533   0.00005913
Total            89   0.00746711
```

The percent industrial property is insignificant with a t-statistic of only -.83. The F-test confirms that the variable does not have a significant impact on tax rate:

$$F_{Indper} = \frac{RSS_3 - RSS_2}{S^2_{Y|X}} = \frac{.002382 - .00234}{(.00769)^2} = .683$$

With 1 degree of freedom in the numberator and (90-3-1) = 86 degrees of freedom in the denominator, the critical value of F at the .05 level is 3.95. Hence we would conclude that the percentage of commercial property has no statistically significant impact on tax rate.

In conclusion, we found no evidence to back three of the activists claims and strong evidence to reject one of them. We concluded that commercial development will have no effect on house value, while it will actually increase tax rate. In addition, we concluded that industrial development will have no effect on house value or tax rate.

It was important to include all of the other independent variables in the regression models because the conditional significance of any one variable is influenced by which other independent variables are in the regression model. Therefore, it is important to test if direct relationships can be 'explained' by the relationships with other predictor variables.

11-92

92.7% of the total variation in gross revenue from a medical practice can be explained by the variations in number of hours worked, number of physicians, number of allied health personnel and the number of rooms used in the practice. The regression model indicates that gross revenue from a medical practice is positively associated with the number of hours worked, the number of physicians in the the practice, the number of allied health personnel and the number of rooms used in the practice. All of these variables are expected to have a positive effect on gross revenue. With df $= (50 - 4 - 1) = 45$, the critical value of t for a two-tailed test at an alpha of .05 is approximately 2.021. Therefore, one can conclude that all of the independent variables are conditionally significant with the sole exception of the number of rooms used in the practice. This variable, while a positive estimated coefficient, is not significantly different from zero.

The number of physicians in the practice has a large effect on gross revenue since, all else equal, for a 1% increase in the number of physicians in the practice, we estimate an increase in the gross revenue from the medical practice by .673%.

Note however that before additional physicians are hired, the analysis should be extended to include not only gross revenue but also profits.

Chapter 12: Additional Topics in Regression Analysis

12-2 $Y_i = \beta_0 + \beta_1 X_{1i} + \beta_2 X_{2i} + \beta_3 X_{3i} + \beta_4 X_{4i} + \beta_5 X_{5i} + \varepsilon_i$
where Y_i = wages
    X_1 = Years of experience
    X_2 = 1 for Germany, 0 otherwise
    X_3 = 1 for Great Britain, 0 otherwise
    X_4 = 1 for Japan, 0 otherwise
    X_5 = 1 for Turkey, 0 otherwise
The excluded category consists of wages in the United States

12-4   a. For any observation, the values of the dummy variables sum to one. Since the equation has an intercept term, there is perfect multicollinearity and the existence of the "dummy variable trap".

    b. β_3 measures the expected difference between demand in the first and fourth quarters, all else equal. β_4 measures the expected difference between demand in the second and fourth quarters, all else equal. β_5 measures the expected difference between demand in the third and fourth quarters, all else equal.

12-6

Regression Analysis: Y Retail Sales versus X Income, Ylag1
The regression equation is
Y Retail Sales = 1752 + 0.367 X Income + 0.053 Ylag1
21 cases used 1 cases contain missing values

Predictor	Coef	SE Coef	T	P
Constant	1751.6	500.0	3.50	0.003
X Incom	0.36734	0.08054	4.56	0.000
Ylag1	0.0533	0.2035	0.26	0.796

S = 153.4 R-Sq = 91.7% R-Sq(adj) = 90.7%

$t = \dfrac{.0533}{.2035} = .2619$; $t_{18,.10} = 1.33$, therefore, do not reject H_0 at the 20% level

12-8

Regression Analysis: Y_%stocks versus X_Return, Y_lag%stocks

The regression equation is
Y_%stocks = 1.65 + 0.228 X_Return + 0.950 Y_lag%stocks
24 cases used 1 cases contain missing values

Predictor	Coef	SE Coef	T	P
Constant	1.646	2.414	0.68	0.503
X_Return	0.22776	0.03015	7.55	0.000
Y_lag%st	0.94999	0.04306	22.06	0.000

S = 2.351   R-Sq = 95.9%   R-Sq(adj) = 95.5%
Analysis of Variance

Source	DF	SS	MS	F	P
Regression	2	2689.6	1344.8	243.38	0.000
Residual Error	21	116.0	5.5		
Total	23	2805.6			

12-10

Regression Analysis: Y_Birth versus X_1stmarriage, Y_lagBirth

The regression equation is
Y_Birth = 21262 + 0.485 X_1stmarriage + 0.192 Y_lagBirth

19 cases used 1 cases contain missing values

Predictor	Coef	SE Coef	T	P
Constant	21262	5720	3.72	0.002
X_1stmar	0.4854	0.1230	3.94	0.001
Y_lagBir	0.1923	0.1898	1.01	0.326

S = 2513   R-Sq = 93.7%   R-Sq(adj) = 93.0%

Analysis of Variance

Source	DF	SS	MS	F	P
Regression	2	1515082551	757541276	119.93	0.000
Residual Error	16	101062160	6316385		
Total	18	1616144711			

Source	DF	Seq SS
X_1stmar	1	1508597348
Y_lagBir	1	6485203

Unusual Observations

Obs	X_1stmar	Y_Birth	Fit	SE Fit	Residual	St Resid
15	105235	95418	89340	982	6078	2.63R

12-12

Regression Analysis: Y_logCons versus X_LogDI, Y_laglogCons

The regression equation is
Y_logCons = 0.405 + 0.373 X_LogDI + 0.558 Y_laglogCons

28 cases used 1 cases contain missing values

Predictor	Coef	SE Coef	T	P
Constant	0.4049	0.1051	3.85	0.001
X_LogDI	0.3734	0.1075	3.47	0.002
Y_laglog	0.5577	0.1243	4.49	0.000

S = 0.03023   R-Sq = 99.6%   R-Sq(adj) = 99.6%

Analysis of Variance

Source	DF	SS	MS	F	P
Regression	2	6.1960	3.0980	3389.90	0.000
Residual Error	25	0.0228	0.0009		
Total	27	6.2189			

Source	DF	Seq SS
X_LogDI	1	6.1776
Y_laglog	1	0.0184

Unusual Observations

Obs	X_LogDI	Y_logCon	Fit	SE Fit	Residual	St Resid
9	5.84	5.80814	5.72298	0.01074	0.08517	3.01R

Durbin-Watson statistic = 1.63

12-14

Results for: CITYDAT.XLS

Regression Analysis: hseval versus Comper, Homper, ...

The regression equation is
hseval = - 19.0 - 26.4 Comper - 12.1 Homper - 15.5 Indper + 7.22 sizehse
        + 0.00408 incom72

Predictor	Coef	SE Coef	T	P
Constant	-19.02	13.20	-1.44	0.153
Comper	-26.393	9.890	-2.67	0.009
Homper	-12.123	7.508	-1.61	0.110
Indper	-15.531	8.630	-1.80	0.075
sizehse	7.219	2.138	3.38	0.001
incom72	0.004081	0.001555	2.62	0.010

S = 3.949   R-Sq = 40.1%   R-Sq(adj) = 36.5%

Analysis of Variance

Source	DF	SS	MS	F	P
Regression	5	876.80	175.36	11.25	0.000
Residual Error	84	1309.83	15.59		
Total	89	2186.63			

Source	DF	Seq SS
Comper	1	245.47
Homper	1	1.38
Indper	1	112.83
sizehse	1	409.77
incom72	1	107.36

Durbin-Watson statistic = 1.03

Dropping the insignificant independent variables: Homper and Indper yields:
Regression Analysis: hseval versus Comper, sizehse, incom72
```
The regression equation is
hseval = - 34.2 - 13.9 Comper + 8.27 sizehse + 0.00364 incom72

Predictor          Coef      SE Coef          T        P
Constant         -34.24        10.44      -3.28    0.002
Comper          -13.881         6.974      -1.99    0.050
sizehse           8.270         1.957       4.23    0.000
incom72        0.003636      0.001456       2.50    0.014

S = 3.983       R-Sq = 37.6%      R-Sq(adj) = 35.4%

Analysis of Variance

Source             DF          SS          MS         F        P
Regression          3      822.53      274.18     17.29    0.000
Residual Error     86     1364.10       15.86
Total              89     2186.63

Source       DF      Seq SS
Comper        1      245.47
sizehse       1      478.09
incom72       1       98.98


Durbin-Watson statistic = 1.02
```

Excluding median rooms per residence (Sizehse):
Regression Analysis: hseval versus Comper, incom72
```
The regression equation is
hseval = 4.69 - 20.4 Comper + 0.00585 incom72
Predictor          Coef      SE Coef          T        P
Constant          4.693        5.379        0.87    0.385
Comper          -20.432        7.430       -2.75    0.007
incom72        0.005847      0.001484       3.94    0.000

S = 4.352       R-Sq = 24.7%      R-Sq(adj) = 22.9%
Analysis of Variance

Source             DF          SS          MS         F        P
Regression          2      539.20      269.60     14.24    0.000
Residual Error     87     1647.44       18.94
Total              89     2186.63

Durbin-Watson statistic = 0.98
```

Note that the coefficient on percent of commercial property for both of the models is negative; however, it is larger in the second model where the median rooms variable is excluded.

12-16   a.   In the special case where the sample correlations between x_1 and x_2 is zero, the estimate for β_1 will be the same whether or not x_2 is included in the regression equation. In the simple linear regression of y on x_1, the intercept term will embody the influence of x_2 on y, under these special circumstances.

b.

$$b_1 = \frac{\sum(x_{2i} - \bar{x}_2)^2 \sum(x_{1i} - \bar{x}_1)(y_{1i} - \bar{y}) - \sum(x_{1i} - \bar{x}_1)(x_{2i} - \bar{x}_2)\sum(x_{2i} - \bar{x}_2)(y_i - \bar{y})}{\sum(x_{1i} - \bar{x}_1)^2 \sum(x_{2i} - \bar{x}_2)^2 - [\sum(x_{1i} - \bar{x}_1)\sum(x_{2i} - \bar{x}_2)]^2}$$

If the sample correlation between x_1 and x_2 is zero, then $\sum (x_{1i} - \bar{x}_1)(x_{2i} - \bar{x}_2) = 0$ and the slope

coefficient equation can be simplified. The result is $b_1 = \dfrac{\sum (x_{1i} - \bar{x}_1)(y_{1i} - \bar{y})}{\sum (x_{1i} - \bar{x}_1)^2}$ which is the

estimated slope coefficient for the bivariate linear regression of y on x_1.

12-18   If y is, in fact, strongly influenced by x2, dropping it from the regression equation could lead to serious specification bias. Instead of dropping the variable, it is preferable to acknowledge that, while the group as a whole is clearly influential, the data does not contain information to alow the disentangling of the separate effects of each of the explanatory variables with some degree of precision.

12-20 a. Graphical check for heteroscedasticity shows no evidence of strong heteroscedasticity.

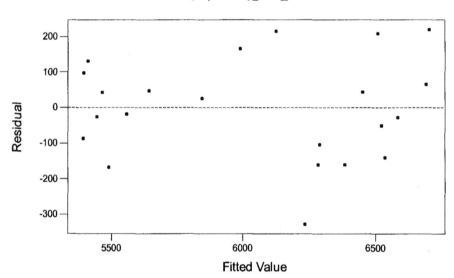

b.   The auxiliary regression is $\hat{e}^2 = -63310.41 + 13.75\hat{y}$

$n = 22, \quad R^2 = .06954, \quad nR^2 = 1.5299 < 2.71 = \chi^2_{1,.1}$, therefore, do not reject H_0 the error terms have constant variance at the 10% level.

12-22   a. Graphical check for heteroscedasticity shows no evidence of strong heteroscedasticity

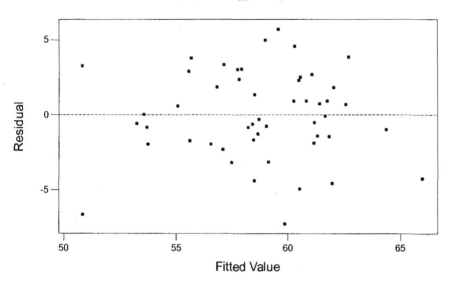

Residuals Versus the Fitted Values
(response is y_Female)

b. The auxiliary regression is $e^2 = 20.34 - .201\hat{y}$

$n = 50$, $R^2 = .00322$, $nR^2 = .161 < 2.71 = \chi^2_{1,1}$, therefore, do not reject the H_0 that the error terms have constant variance at the 10% level.

12-24   Given that $Var(\varepsilon_i) = Kx^2_i$ $(K > 0)$, $Var(\varepsilon_i / x_i) = \dfrac{1}{x^2_i} Var(\varepsilon_i) = \dfrac{1}{x^2_i} Kx^2_i = K$

If the squared relationship can be found between the variance of the error terms and x_i such as $Var(\varepsilon_i) = Kx^2_i$, the problem of heteroscedasticity can be removed by dividing both sides of the regression equation by x_i

12-26 $H_0 : \rho = 0, H_1 : \rho > 0$,   d=1.71, n=25, K = 2, $\alpha = .05$: $d_L = 1.21$ and $d_U = 1.55$

        Do not reject H_0 at the 5% level

12-28   The regression model associated with Exercise 12-12 includes the lagged value of the dependent variable as an independent variable. In the presence of a lagged dependent variable used as an independent variable, the Durbin-Watson statistic is no longer valid. Instead, use of Durbin's h statistic is appropriate:

$$H_0 : \rho = 0, H_1 : \rho > 0, \ r = 1 - \frac{d}{2} = 1 - \frac{1.63}{2} = .185, \quad s_c^2 = (.1243)^2 = .01545$$

$$h = r\sqrt{\frac{n}{1 - n(s_c^2)}} = .185\sqrt{\frac{28}{1 - 28(.01545)}} = 1.30$$

$z_{.1} = 1.28$, therefore, reject H_0 at the 10% level but not at the 5% level

12-30   With a low Durbin-Watson statistic of .85, test for the presence of positive autocorrelation of the residuals.

$H_0 : \rho = 0, H_1 : \rho > 0$, d=.85, n=24, K = 4

$\alpha = .05$: $d_L = 1.01$ and $d_U = 1.78$, $\alpha = .01$: $d_L = .80$ and $d_U = 1.53$

Reject H_0 at the 5% level, test is inconclusive at the 1% level.

12-32   d = .8529

$H_0 : \rho = 0, H_1 : \rho > 0$

d = .88, n=25, K = 1

$\alpha = .01$: $d_L = 1.05$ and $d_U = 1.21$

Reject H_0 at the 1% level, therefore, a misspecified regression model with an omitted variable can result in the presence of autocorrelation of the residuals

12-34   a. Dummy Variables: Dummy variables are used whenever a factor is not readily quantifiable. For example, if we wished to determine the effect of trade barriers on output growth rates, we could include a dummy variable which takes the value of one when trade barriers are imposed and zero otherwise. This could then be used to distinguish between different trade barrier levels.

b. Lagged dependent variables: Lagged dependent variables are useful when time series data are analyzed. For example, one might wish to include lagged growth rates in a model used to explain fluctuations in output

c. Logarithmic transformation: Logarithmic transformations allows inherently linear statistical techniques such as least squares linear regression to estimate non-linear functions. For example, cost functions where cost is some function of output produced is typically non-linear. The log transformation allows us to express non-linear relationships in linear form and hence use linear estimation techniques to estimate the model.

12-36   The statement is not valid. The summation of several bivariate (simple) linear regressions does not equal the results obtained from a multiple regression. Therefore, while separating the independent variables may give some indication of the statistical significance of the individual effects, they will not provide any information about the influence on the dependent variable when the independent variables are taken together. It is preferable to acknowledge that the group as a whole is clearly influential but the data are not sufficiently informative to allow the disentangling, with any precision, of each independent variable's separate effects.

12-38   a. $H_0 : \beta_1 = 0$, $H_1 : \beta_1 > 0$, $t = \dfrac{2.11}{1.79} = 1.179$

Do not reject H_0 at the 10% level since $t < 1.282 \approx t_{84,.1}$

b. $H_0 : \beta_2 = 0$, $H_1 : \beta_2 \neq 0$, $t = \dfrac{.96}{1.94} = .495$

Do not reject H_0 at the 10% level since $t < 1.282 \approx t_{84,.1}$

c. The difference in results are likely due to the existence of multicollinearity between earnings per share (x_1) and funds flow per share (x_2)

12-40 Nothing has been learned because x_5 & x_6 are perfectly collinear, therefore, the model estimates are invalid.

12-42 a. All else being equal, a 1% increase in value of new orders leads to expected decrease of .82% in number of failures.
   b. $H_0 : \rho = 0, H_1 : \rho > 0$, d = .49, n=30, K = 3, $\alpha = .01$: $d_L = 1.01$ and $d_U = 1.42$
       Reject H_0 at the 1% level
   c. Given that the residuals are autocorrelated, the hypothesis test results of part b are not valid. The model must be reestimated taking into account the autocorrelated errors
   d. $r = 1 - \dfrac{.49}{2} = .755$

12-44 a. 95% CI: $.253 \pm 2.052(.106)$: $.035 < \beta < .471$
   b. $.253 increase in current period, further $.138 increase next period, $.075 increase two periods ahead, and so on. Total expected increase of $.557.
   c. $H_0 : \rho = 0, H_1 : \rho > 0$
       Note that due to the presence of a lagged dependent variable used as an independent variable, Durbin's h statistic is relevant
   $$r = 1 - \frac{d}{2} = 1 - \frac{1.86}{2} = .07, \quad s^2_c = (.134)^2 = .01796, h = r\sqrt{\frac{n}{1 - ns_c^2}} = .07\sqrt{\frac{30}{1 - 30(.01796)}} = .56449$$
       $z_{.1} = 1.28$, therefore, do not reject H_0 at the 10% level

12-46
Regression Analysis: y_log versus x1_log, x2_log
```
The regression equation is
y_log = - 2.14 + 0.909 x1_log + 0.195 x2_log
Predictor        Coef      SE Coef          T        P
Constant      -2.1415       0.2000     -10.71    0.000
x1_log        0.90947       0.03518      25.85    0.000
x2_log        0.19451       0.07126       2.73    0.018

S = 0.07721       R-Sq = 99.6%      R-Sq(adj) = 99.5%
Analysis of Variance
Source           DF         SS          MS         F        P
Regression        2     16.7802      8.3901   1407.52    0.000
Residual Error    12      0.0715      0.0060
Total             14     16.8517

Durbin-Watson statistic = 1.67
```
   $H_0 : \rho = 0, H_1 : \rho > 0$, d = 1.67, n=15, K = 2, $\alpha = .05$: $d_L = .95$ and $d_U = 1.54$
   Do not reject H_0 at the 5% level

12-48

Regression Analysis: y_log versus x1_log, x2_log, y_laglog_1
The regression equation is
y_log = 0.435 - 0.101 x1_log + 0.237 x2_log + 0.666 y_laglog_1
34 cases used 1 cases contain missing values

Predictor	Coef	SE Coef	T	P
Constant	0.4352	0.4360	1.00	0.326
x1_log	-0.10116	0.03822	-2.65	0.013
x2_log	0.2365	0.1017	2.32	0.027
y_laglog	0.6658	0.1174	5.67	0.000

S = 0.04039   R-Sq = 75.1%   R-Sq(adj) = 72.6%
Analysis of Variance

Source	DF	SS	MS	F	P
Regression	3	0.147751	0.049250	30.18	0.000
Residual Error	30	0.048952	0.001632		
Total	33	0.196704			

Durbin-Watson statistic = 2.22

Test for autocorrelation:

$$r = 1 - \frac{d}{2} = 1 - \frac{2.22}{2} = -.11, \quad s^2_c = (.1174)^2 = .01378,$$

$$h = r\sqrt{\frac{n}{1 - ns_c^2}} = -.11\sqrt{\frac{35}{1 - 35(.01378)}} = -.904$$

p-value = 2[1-Fz(.904))] = .3682, do not reject H_0 at any common level of alpha

12-50

Regression Analysis: y_log versus x1_log, x2_log, x3_log
The regression equation is
y_log = 2.72 - 0.0252 x1_log + 0.315 x2_log + 0.379 x3_log

Predictor	Coef	SE Coef	T	P
Constant	2.71584	0.08821	30.79	0.000
x1_log	-0.02519	0.04049	-0.62	0.543
x2_log	0.31472	0.05689	5.53	0.000
x3_log	0.3788	0.2009	1.89	0.078

S = 0.03611   R-Sq = 91.7%   R-Sq(adj) = 90.2%

Analysis of Variance

Source	DF	SS	MS	F	P
Regression	3	0.231282	0.077094	59.14	0.000
Residual Error	16	0.020859	0.001304		
Total	19	0.252140			

Source	DF	Seq SS
x1_log	1	0.158727
x2_log	1	0.067919
x3_log	1	0.004636

Durbin-Watson statistic = 1.75

Test for autocorrelation:

$$H_0 : \rho = 0, H_1 : \rho > 0$$

d = 1.75, n=20, K = 3

$\alpha = .05$: $d_L = 1.00$ and $d_U = 1.68$

$\alpha = .01$: $d_L = .77$ and $d_U = 1.41$

Do not reject H_0 at the 1% level or 5% level

12-52 a. predict consumption of service goods (CSH) as a function of GDP (GDPH)

Regression Analysis: CSH versus GDPH
The regression equation is
CSH = - 207 + 0.417 GDPH
214 cases used 4 cases contain missing values

Predictor	Coef	SE Coef	T	P
Constant	-207.440	6.920	-29.98	0.000
GDPH	0.416931	0.001430	291.66	0.000

S = 44.42   R-Sq = 99.8%   R-Sq(adj) = 99.8%

Analysis of Variance

Source	DF	SS	MS	F	P
Regression	1	167815352	167815352	85064.28	0.000
Residual Error	212	418235	1973		
Total	213	168233587			

Durbin-Watson statistic = 0.11

Test for autocorrelation:

$$H_0 : \rho = 0, H_1 : \rho > 0$$

d = .11, n=214, K = 1

$\alpha = .01$: $d_L = 1.52$ and $d_U = 1.56$

Reject H_0 at the 1% level and accept the alternative that significant first order positive autocorrelation exists in the residuals.

The model shows extremely large explanatory power ($R^2 = 99.8\%$); however, there is significant autocorrelation in the residuals (d = .11).

b.

Regression Analysis: CSH versus GDPH, FBPR, CSH_lag

```
The regression equation is
CSH = - 4.30 + 0.0178 GDPH - 0.504 FBPR + 0.965 CSH_lag
210 cases used 8 cases contain missing values
```

Predictor	Coef	SE Coef	T	P
Constant	-4.302	2.661	-1.62	0.108
GDPH	0.017760	0.004441	4.00	0.000
FBPR	-0.5040	0.1676	-3.01	0.003
CSH_lag	0.96547	0.01077	89.64	0.000

```
S = 6.976      R-Sq = 100.0%    R-Sq(adj) = 100.0%
```

Analysis of Variance

Source	DF	SS	MS	F	P
Regression	3	162823334	54274445	1.115E+06	0.000
Residual Error	206	10024	49		
Total	209	162833358			

Source	DF	Seq SS
GDPH	1	162421749
FBPR	1	10585
CSH_lag	1	391000

```
Durbin-Watson statistic = 1.66
```

Test for autocorrelation:

$$r = 1 - \frac{d}{s} = 1 - \frac{1.66}{2} = .17, \quad s^2_c = (.01077)^2 = .000116$$

$$h = r \sqrt{\frac{n}{1 - ns_c^2}} = .17 \sqrt{\frac{210}{1 - 210(.000116)}} = 2.494$$

p-value = $2[1 - Fz(2.49)] = .0128$, therefore, do not reject H_0 at the 1% level, reject at the 5% level

Including the lagged value of the dependent variable as an independent variable has reduced the problem of autocorrelation of the residuals, however, multicollinearity has likely resulted between the independent variables.

12.54 a. Estimate with the statistically significant independent variables

Regression Analysis: hseval versus sizehse, taxrate, totexp, Comper

```
The regression equation is
hseval = - 23.4 + 9.21 sizehse - 178 taxrate +0.000001 totexp - 20.4 Comper
```

Predictor	Coef	SE Coef	T	P
Constant	-23.433	8.986	-2.61	0.011
sizehse	9.210	1.564	5.89	0.000
taxrate	-177.53	39.87	-4.45	0.000
totexp	0.00000142	0.00000030	4.80	0.000
Comper	-20.370	6.199	-3.29	0.001

```
S = 3.400      R-Sq = 55.1%     R-Sq(adj) = 52.9%
Analysis of Variance
```

Source	DF	SS	MS	F	P
Regression	4	1203.84	300.96	26.03	0.000
Residual Error	85	982.79	11.56		
Total	89	2186.63			

Source	DF	Seq SS
sizehse	1	643.12
taxrate	1	244.06
totexp	1	191.82
Comper	1	124.84

```
Unusual Observations
```

Obs	sizehse	hseval	Fit	SE Fit	Residual	St Resid
23	5.70	20.003	27.850	0.806	-7.847	-2.38R
49	5.60	29.810	28.522	1.708	1.288	0.44 X
50	5.60	30.061	28.178	1.687	1.883	0.64 X
75	5.70	35.976	24.490	0.535	11.486	3.42R
76	5.70	35.736	25.093	0.553	10.643	3.17R

```
R denotes an observation with a large standardized residual
X denotes an observation whose X value gives it large influence.

Durbin-Watson statistic = 1.20
```

Since all of the independent variables are statistically, significant, leave all of the independent variables in the regression model.

b.

The auxiliary regression is

Regression Analysis: ResiSq versus FITS1

```
The regression equation is
ResiSq = - 15.1 + 1.24 FITS1
```

Predictor	Coef	SE Coef	T	P
Constant	-15.09	11.96	-1.26	0.210
FITS1	1.2370	0.5604	2.21	0.030

```
S = 19.44      R-Sq = 5.2%     R-Sq(adj) = 4.2%
```

$$e^2 = -15.1 + 1.24\hat{y}$$

$$n = 90, \quad R^2 = .052$$

$nR^2 = 4.68 > 3.84 = \chi^2_{1,.05}$, therefore, reject the null hypothesis that the error terms have constant variance at the 5% level and the economist is correct that heteroscedasticity is likely to be a problem.

Chapter 13: Nonparametric Statistics

13-2 $H_0 : \pi = .5$ (there is no overall improvement in comprehension levels following completion of the program)

$H_1 : \pi > .5$ (the level of comprehension is increased by the program)

n = 9. For 8 scores higher "After" and a one-sided test,

$P(X \geq 8) = .0176 + .002 = .0196$

Therefore, reject H_0 at levels of alpha in excess of 1.96%

13-4 $H_0 : \pi = .5$ (positive and negative returns are equally likely)

$H_1 : \pi > .5$ (positive returns are more likely)

n = 57. $p_x = 39/57 = .6842$

$\mu = n\pi = 57(.5) = 28.5$ $\sigma = .5\sqrt{n} = .5\sqrt{57} = 3.7749$

$Z = \dfrac{S*-\mu}{\sigma} = \dfrac{38.5 - 28.5}{3.7749} = 2.65$

p-value = $1 - F_z(2.65) = 1 - .9960 = .0040$

Therefore, reject H_0 at levels of alpha in excess of .40%

13-6 $H_0 : \pi = .5$ (economists' profession is equally divided on whether the inflation rate will increase)

$H_1 : \pi \neq .5$ (otherwise)

n = 49, $p_x = 29/49 = .5918$

$\mu = n\pi = 49(.5) = 24.5$ $\sigma = .5\sqrt{n} = .5\sqrt{49} = 3.50$

$Z = \dfrac{S*-\mu}{\sigma} = \dfrac{28.5 - 24.5}{3.50} = 1.14$

p-value = $2[1 - F_z(1.14)] = 2[1 - .8729] = .2542$

Therefore, reject H_0 at levels of alpha in excess of 25.42%

13-8 H_0: no preference for domestic vs. imported beer

H_1: imported beer is preferred

Wilcoxon Signed Rank Test: Diff_13-8

Test of median = 0.000000 versus median < 0.000000

	N	N for Test	Wilcoxon Statistic	P	Estimated Median
Diff_13-8	10	9	7.0	0.038	-1.500

$n = 9$, $T = 7.0$, $T_{.05} = 9$

Therefore, reject H_0 at levels of alpha in excess of 3.8%

13-10 H_0: both courses rated equally interesting

H_1: statistics course is rated more interesting

$T = 281,$ $\mu_T = n(n+1)/4 = 40(41)/4 = 410$

$\sigma^2_T = n(n+1)(2n+1)/24 = 40(41)(81)/24 = 5535$

$z = \dfrac{281-410}{\sqrt{5535}} = -1.73$

p-value = $1\text{-}F_Z(1.73) = 1\text{-}.9582 = .0418$

Therefore, reject H_0 at levels in excess of 4.18%

13-12 H_0: time allocated equally

H_1: time not allocated equally

$T = 1502,$ $\mu_T = 80(81)/4 = 1620,$ $\sigma^2_T = 80(81)(161)/24 = 43,470$

$z = \dfrac{1502-1620}{\sqrt{43470}} = -.57$

p-value = $2[1\text{-}F_Z(.57)] = 2[1\text{-}.7157] = .5686$

Therefore, do not reject H_0 at any common level

13-14 H_0: there is no difference in returns

H_1: the 'buy list' has a higher percentage return (one-tailed test)

Sum of ranks for 'buy list' = 137

$R_1 = 137, n_1 = 10, n_2 = 10$

$U = n_1 n_2 + n_1(n_1+1)/2 - R_1 = 100 + 110/2 - 137 = 18$

$\mu_U = n_1 n_2 / 2 = 100/2 = 50, \sigma^2_U = n_1 n_2(n_1 + n_2 + 1)/12 = 100(21)/12 = 175$

$z = \dfrac{18-50}{\sqrt{175}} = -2.42$, p-value = $1\text{-}F_Z(2.42) = 1\text{-}.9922 = .0078$

Therefore, reject H_0 at levels in excess of .78%

13-16 H_0: no preference between marketing and finance majors

H_1: finance majors are preferred (one-tailed test)

Sum of ranks for the finance students = 171

$R_1 = 171, n_1 = 14, n_2 = 10$

$U = 14(10) + 14(15)/2 - 171 = 74$

$\mu_U = 140/2 = 70, \sigma^2_U = 14(10)(25)/12 = 291.667$

$z = \dfrac{74-70}{\sqrt{291.667}} = .234$

p-value = $1\text{-}F_Z(.23) = 1\text{-}.5910 = .4090$

Therefore, reject H_0 at levels in excess of 40.9%

13-18 H_0: population rates of return are equal

H_1: 'Highest rated' funds achieve higher rates of return

Sum of ranks for 'Highest rated' = 113.5

$R_1 = 113.5, n_1 = 10, n_2 = 10$

$U = 10(10) + 110/2 - 113.5 = 41.5$, $\mu_U = 100/5 = 50, \sigma^2_U = 100(21)/12 = 175$

$z = \dfrac{41.5 - 50}{\sqrt{175}} = -.64$, p-value = $1 - F_Z(.64) = 1 - .7389 = .2611$

Therefore, reject H_0 at levels in excess of 26.11%

13-20 H_0: time taken in days from year-end to release a preliminary profit report is no different for firms with clean audit reports vs. 'subject to' conditions

H_1: 'subject to' firms take longer

$R_1 (subject\ to) = 9686, n_1 = 86, n_2 = 120$

$U = 86(120) + 86(87)/2 - 9686 = 4375$

$\mu_U = 86(120)/2 = 5160, \sigma^2_U = 86(120)(207)/12 = 178,020$

$z = \dfrac{4375 - 5160}{\sqrt{178020}} = -1.8605$, p-value = $1 - F_Z(1.86) = 1 - .9686 = .0314$

Therefore, reject H_0 at levels in excess of 3.14%

13-22 a. Obtain rankings of the two variables

RankExam	RankProject
6	5.5
1	3.0
4	2.0
5	5.5
10	9.0
2	1.0
3	8.0
7	4.0
9	10.0
8	7.0

Therefore, pearson correlation between rankings of variables is the spearman rank correlation coefficient:

Correlations: RankExam, RankProject

Pearson correlation of RankExam and RankProject = 0.717

b. H_0: no association between scores on the exam vs on the project

H_1: an association exists (two-tailed test)

$n = 10, r_{s.025} = .648, r_{s.010} = .745$

Therefore, reject H_0 of no association between the two variables at the .05 level but not at the .02 level. (two-tailed test)

13-24 Nonparametric tests make no assumption about the behavior of the population distribution. The advantages of the tests are less restrictive assumptions, easily calculated tests that can be used on nominal or ordinal data. And less weight is placed on outliers by nonparametric tests.

13-26 $H_0 : \pi = .5$ (sales next year are the same as this year)

$H_1 : \pi \neq .5$ (otherwise)

n = 9. For 2 "in favor" and a two-sided test,

$P(2 \geq X \geq 7) = 2P(X \leq 2) = 2[.002 + .0176 + .0703] = .1798$

Therefore, reject H_0 at levels of alpha in excess of 17.98%

13-28 $H_0 : \pi = .5$ (more students expect a higher standard of living)

$H_1 : \pi < .5$ (more students expect a lower standard of living, compared with their parents)

$n = 78, \ p_x = 35 / 78 = .4487$

$\mu = n\pi = 78(.5) = 39 \quad \sigma = .5\sqrt{n} = .5\sqrt{78} = 4.4159$

$Z = \dfrac{S^* - \mu}{\sigma} = \dfrac{35.5 - 39}{4.4159} = -.79$

p-value= $1 - F_z(.79) = 1 - .7852 = .2148$

Therefore, reject H_0 at levels of alpha in excess of 21.48%

13-30 H_0 : corporate analysts are more optimistic about the prospects for their own companies than for the economy at large

H_1 : otherwise (one-tailed test)

$n = 8, \quad T = 11, \quad T_{.10} = 9$

Therefore, do not reject H_0 at the 10% level

Chapter 14: Goodness-of-Fit Tests and Contingency Tables

14-2 H_0: Mutual fund performance is equally likely to be in the 5 performance quintiles.

  H_1: otherwise

Mutual funds14-2	Top 20%	2nd 20%	3rd 20%	4th 20%	5th 20%	Total
Observed Number	13	20	18	11	13	75
Probability (Ho)	0.2	0.2	0.2	0.2	0.2	1
Expected Number	15	15	15	15	15	75
Chi-square calculation	0.266667	1.666667	0.6	1.066667	0.266667	3.8667

Chi-square calculation: $\chi^2 = \sum \frac{(O_i - E_i)^2}{Ei} = 3.8667$

$\chi^2_{(4,.1)} = 7.78$ Therefore, fail to reject H_0 at the 10% level

14-4 H_0: Quality of the output conforms to the usual pattern

  H_1: otherwise

Electronic component14-4	No faults	1 fault	>1 fault	Total
Observed Number	458	30	12	500
Probability (Ho)	0.93	0.05	0.02	1
Expected Number	465	25	10	500
Chi-square calculation	0.105376344	1	0.4	1.505376

Chi-square calculation: $\chi^2 = \sum \frac{(O_i - E_i)^2}{Ei} = 1.505$

$\chi^2_{(2,.05)} = 5.99$ Therefore, do not reject H_0 at the 5% level

14-6 H_0: Student opinion of business courses is the same as that for all courses

  H_1: otherwise

Opinion14-6	Very useful	Somewhat	Worthless	Total
Observed Number	68	18	14	100
Probability (Ho)	0.6	0.2	0.2	1
Expected Number	60	20	20	100
Chi-square calculation	1.066666667	0.2	1.8	3.066667

Chi-square calculation: $\chi^2 = \sum \frac{(O_i - E_i)^2}{Ei} = 3.067$

$\chi^2_{(2,.10)} = 4.61$ Therefore, do not reject H_0 at the 10% level

14-8 H_0: Consumer preferences for soft drinks is equally spread across 5 different soft drinks

   H_1: otherwise

Drink14-8	A	B	C	D	E	Total
Observed Number	20	25	28	15	27	115
Probability (Ho)	0.2	0.2	0.2	0.2	0.2	1
Expected Number	23	23	23	23	23	115
Chi-square calculation	0.391304	0.173913	1.086957	2.782609	0.695652	5.130435

Chi-square calculation: $\chi^2 = \sum \frac{(O_i - E_i)^2}{Ei} = 5.130$

$\chi^2_{(4,.10)} = 7.78$ Therefore, do not reject H_0 at the 10% level

14-10 H_0: Statistics professors preferences for software packages are equally divided across 4 packages

   H_1: otherwise

Software14-10	M	E	S	P	Total
Observed Number	100	80	35	35	250
Probability (Ho)	0.25	0.25	0.25	0.25	1
Expected Number	62.5	62.5	62.5	62.5	250
Chi-square calculation	22.5	4.9	12.1	12.1	51.6

Chi-square calculation: $\chi^2 = \sum \frac{(O_i - E_i)^2}{Ei} = 51.6$

$\chi^2_{(3,.005)} = 12.84$ Therefore, reject H_0 at the .5% level

14-12 H_0: population distribution of arrivals per minute is Poisson

   H_1: otherwise

Arrivals	0	1	2	3	4+	Total
Observed Number	10	26	35	24	5	100
Probability (Ho)	0.1496	0.2842	0.27	0.171	0.1252	1
Expected Number	14.96	28.42	27	17.1	12.52	100

Chi-square calculation: $\chi^2 = \sum \frac{(O_i - E_i)^2}{Ei} = 11.52$

$\chi^2_{(3,.01)} = 11.34$ $\chi^2_{(3,.005)} = 12.84$ Therefore, reject H_0 at the 1% level but not at the .5% level

14-14 H_0: resistance of electronic components is normally distributed

H_1: otherwise

$$B = 100 \left[\frac{(.63)^2}{6} + \frac{(3.85-3)^2}{24} \right] = 9.625$$

From Table 14.7 – Significance points of the Bowman-Shelton statistic; 5% point (n=100) is 4.29

Therefore, reject H_0 at the 5% level

14-16 H_0: monthly balances for credit card holders of a particular card are normally distributed

H_1: otherwise

$$B = 125 \left[\frac{(.55)^2}{6} + \frac{(2.77-3)^2}{24} \right] = 6.578$$

From Table 14.7 – Significance points of the Bowman-Shelton statistic; 5% point (n = 125) is 4.34

Therefore, reject H_0 at the 5% level

14-18   a. H_0: No association exists between gpa and major

   H_1: otherwise

   b.   PHStat results:

Chi-Square Test

Observed Frequencies			
	GPA		
School of Major	GPA <3.0	GPA 3.0+	Total
Arts & Sciences	50	35	85
Business	45	30	75
Music	15	25	40
Total	110	90	200

Expected Frequencies			
	GPA		
School of Major	GPA <3.0	GPA 3.0+	Total
Arts & Sciences	46.75	38.25	85
Business	41.25	33.75	75
Music	22	18	40
Total	110	90	200

Data	
Level of Significance	0.05
Number of Rows	3
Number of Columns	2
Degrees of Freedom	2

Results	
Critical Value	5.991476
Chi-Square Test Statistic	6.20915
p-Value	0.044844
Reject the null hypothesis	

Expected frequency assumption

   is met.

   Minitab results:

Chi-Square Test: GPA<3, GPA3+

Expected counts are printed below observed counts

```
     GPA<3  GPA3+  Total
 1      50     35     85
      46.75  38.25

 2      45     30     75
      41.25  33.75

 3      15     25     40
      22.00  18.00

Total  110     90    200
```

Chi-Sq = 0.226 + 0.276 + 0.341 + 0.417 + 2.227 + 2.722 = 6.209

DF = 2, P-Value = 0.045

$\chi^2_{(2,.05)} = 5.99$ Therefore, reject H_0 of no association at the 5% level

14-20   a. Complete the contingency table:

Age	Method of learning about product		
	Friend	Ad	col. total
<21	30	20	50
21-35	60	30	90
35+	18	42	60
row total	108	92	200

b. H_0: No association exists between the method of learning about the product and the age of the respondent

H_1: otherwise

Minitab results:

Chi-Square Test: Friend_20, Ad_20

Expected counts are printed below observed counts

	Friend_2	Ad_20	Total
1	30	20	50
	27.00	23.00	
2	60	30	90
	48.60	41.40	
3	18	42	60
	32.40	27.60	
Total	108	92	200

Chi-Sq = 0.333 + 0.391 +2.674 + 3.139 +6.400 + 7.513 = 20.451
DF = 2, P-Value = 0.000

$\chi^2_{(2,.005)} = 10.6$ Therefore, reject H_0 of no association at the .5% level

14-22 H_0: No association exists between write-downs of assets and merger activity

H_1: otherwise

Minitab results:

Chi-Square Test: Yes_22, No_22

Expected counts are printed below observed counts

	Yes_22	No_22	Total
1	32	48	80
	28.15	51.85	
2	25	57	82
	28.85	53.15	
Total	57	105	162

Chi-Sq = 0.527 + 0.286 +
    0.514 + 0.279 = 1.607
DF = 1, P-Value = 0.205

$\chi^2_{(1,.10)} = 2.71$ Therefore, do not reject H_0 at the 10% level

14-24 H_0: No association exists between personnel rating and college major

H_1: otherwise

Minitab results:

Chi-Square Test: Excellent, Strong, Average

Expected counts are printed below observed counts

	Excellen	Strong	Average	Total
1	21	18	10	49
	19.11	18.42	11.47	
2	19	15	5	39
	15.21	14.66	9.13	
3	10	5	5	20
	7.80	7.52	4.68	
4	5	15	13	33
	12.87	12.40	7.72	
Total	55	53	33	141

Chi-Sq = 0.186 + 0.010 + 0.188 +
     0.943 + 0.008 + 1.867 +
     0.620 + 0.843 + 0.022 +
     4.814 + 0.543 + 3.605 = 13.648
DF = 6, P-Value = 0.034
1 cells with expected counts less than 5.0

$\chi^2_{(6,.05)}$ = 12.59 Therefore, reject H_0 at the 5% level

14-26 H_0: No association exists between graduate studies and college major

H_1: otherwise

Minitab results:

Chi-Square Test: Business, Law, Theology

Expected counts are printed below observed counts

	Business	Law	Theology	Total
1	30	20	10	60
	18.00	27.00	15.00	
2	6	34	20	60
	18.00	27.00	15.00	
Total	36	54	30	120

Chi-Sq = 8.000 + 1.815 + 1.667 +
     8.000 + 1.815 + 1.667 = 22.963
DF = 2, P-Value = 0.000

$\chi^2_{(2,.005)}$ = 10.60 Therefore, reject H_0 at the .5% level

14-28 H_0: No association exists between primary election candidate preferences and voting district

H_1: otherwise

Minitab results:

Chi-Square Test: A_28, B_28, C_28, D_28

Expected counts are printed below observed counts

	A_28	B_28	C_28	D_28	Total
1	52	34	80	34	200
	46.46	31.69	92.00	29.85	
2	33	15	78	24	150
	34.85	23.77	69.00	22.38	
3	66	54	141	39	300
	69.69	47.54	138.00	44.77	
Total	151	103	299	97	650

Chi-Sq = 0.660 + 0.168 + 1.565 + 0.578 +
0.098 + 3.235 + 1.174 + 0.117 +
0.196 + 0.878 + 0.065 + 0.743 = 9.478

DF = 6, P-Value = 0.148

$\chi^2_{(6,.10)} = 10.64$ Therefore, do not reject H_0 at the 10% level

14-30 H_0: No association exists between years of experience and parts produced per hour

H_1: otherwise

Minitab results:

Chi-Square Test: Subgroup1_30, Subgroup2_30, Subgroup3_30

Expected counts are printed below observed counts

	Subgroup	Subgroup	Subgroup	Total
1	10	30	10	50
	10.00	20.00	20.00	
2	10	20	20	50
	10.00	20.00	20.00	
3	10	10	30	50
	10.00	20.00	20.00	
Total	30	60	60	150

Chi-Sq = 0.000 + 5.000 + 5.000 +
0.000 + 0.000 + 0.000 +
0.000 + 5.000 + 5.000 = 20.000

DF = 4, P-Value = 0.000

$\chi^2_{(4,.005)} = 14.86$ Therefore, reject H_0 at the .5% level

14-32   a. H_0: No association exists between package weight and package source

H_1: otherwise

Minitab results:

Chi-Square Test: <3lb_32, 4-10lb_32, 11-75lb_32

Expected counts are printed below observed counts

	<3 lb	4-10lb	11-75lb	Total
1	40	40	20	100
	37.85	36.62	25.54	
2	119	63	18	200
	75.69	73.23	51.08	
3	18	71	111	200
	75.69	73.23	51.08	
4	69	64	17	150
	56.77	54.92	38.31	
Total	246	238	166	650

Chi-Sq = 0.123 + 0.313 + 1.201 +
          24.779 + 1.429 + 21.420 +
          43.973 + 0.068 + 70.301 +
          2.635 + 1.500 + 11.852 = 179.594
DF = 6, P-Value = 0.000

$\chi^2_{(6,.005)} = 18.55$ Therefore, reject H_0 at the .5% level

b.   The combinations with the largest percentage gap between observed and expected arebetween factory and 11-75 pound packages, and between factory and under 3 pound packages.

14-34 H_0: No association exists between the age of the company and the owner's opinion regarding the effectiveness of digital signatures

H_1: otherwise

Minitab results:

Chi-Square Test: Yes_34, No_34, Uncertain_34

Expected counts are printed below observed counts

	Yes_34	No_34	Uncertai	Total
1	80	68	10	158
	71.27	74.29	12.44	
2	60	90	15	165
	74.43	77.59	12.99	
3	72	63	12	147
	66.31	69.12	11.57	
Total	212	221	37	470

Chi-Sq = 1.070 + 0.533 + 0.478 +
          2.796 + 1.987 + 0.311 +
          0.489 + 0.542 + 0.016 = 8.222
DF = 4, P-Value = 0.084

$\chi^2_{(4,.05)} = 9.49$ Therefore, do not reject H_0 at the 5% level

14-36 H_0: No association exists between reason for moving to Florida and industry type

H_1: otherwise

Minitab results:

Chi-Square Test: Manufact_36, Retail_36, Tourism_36

Expected counts are printed below observed counts

	Manufact	Retail_3	Tourism_	Total
1	53	25	10	88
	42.04	28.31	17.66	
2	67	36	20	123
	58.76	39.56	24.68	
3	30	40	33	103
	49.20	33.13	20.67	
Total	150	101	63	314

Chi-Sq = 2.858 + 0.386 + 3.320 +
　　　　1.156 + 0.321 + 0.887 +
　　　　7.495 + 1.424 + 7.362 = 25.210
DF = 4, P-Value = 0.000

$\chi^2_{(4,.005)}$ = 14.86 Therefore, reject H_0 at the .5% level

14-38 H_0: No association exists between opinions on stricter advertising controls of weight loss products and useage of quick weight reduction product

H_1: otherwise

Minitab results:

Chi-Square Test: Yes_38, No_38

Expected counts are printed below observed counts

	Yes_38	No_38	Total
1	85	40	125
	64.25	60.75	
2	25	64	89
	45.75	43.25	
Total	110	104	214

Chi-Sq = 6.700 + 7.086 +
　　　　9.410 + 9.952 = 33.148
DF = 1, P-Value = 0.000

$\chi^2_{(1,.005)}$ = 7.88 Therefore, reject H_0 at the .5% level

14-40 H_0: No association exists between current customer preferences and preferences two

years ago

H_1: otherwise

Minitab results:

Chi-Square Test: A_40, B_40, C_40, D_40

Expected counts are printed below observed counts

	A_40	B_40	C_40	D_40	Total
1	56	70	28	126	280
	56.00	81.00	42.00	101.00	
2	56	92	56	76	280
	56.00	81.00	42.00	101.00	
Total	112	162	84	202	560

Chi-Sq = 0.000 + 1.494 + 4.667 + 6.188 +0.000 + 1.494 + 4.667 + 6.188 = 24.697

DF = 3, P-Value = 0.000

$\chi^2_{(3,.005)} = 12.84$ Therefore, reject H_0 at the .5% level

14-42   a. H_0: No association exists between class standing and opinions on whether library

hours should be extended

H_1 : otherwise

Here we used PHStat and included only the responses from 340 students who had an opinion about the extension of the library hours.

Observed Frequencies			
	Should Hours be Extended?		
Class Standing	Yes	No	Total
First Year	86	53	139
Sophomores	79	21	100
Juniors	46	15	61
Seniors	29	11	40
Total	240	100	340
Expected Frequencies			
	Should Hours be Extended?		
Class Standing	Yes	No	Total
First Year	98.11764706	40.88235294	139
Sophomores	70.58823529	29.41176471	100
Juniors	43.05882353	17.94117647	61
Seniors	28.23529412	11.76470588	40
Total	240	100	340

Level of Significance	0.05
Number of Rows	4
Number of Columns	2
Degrees of Freedom	3
Critical Value	7.814724703
Chi-Square Test Statistic	9.249892843
p-Value	0.026146475
Reject the null hypothesis	

Expected frequency assumption
is met.

b. Recommendations should include better orientation with the freshmen class in order to better acquaint the students with the library and the hours that the library is open. Also, extending library hours, particularly during heavy usage, would be appropriate.

14-44   Answers will vary.

Chapter 15: Analysis of Variance

15-2   a. $\bar{x}_1 = 73, \bar{x}_2 = 86, \bar{x}_3 = 72, \bar{x}_4 = 72$

n=23, SSW = 228 + 312 + 374 + 428 = 1342

SSG = $5(73 - 75.8696)^2 + 6(86 - 75.8696)^2 + 6(72 - 75.8696)^2 + 6(72 - 75.8696)^2 = 836.6087$

SST = 2178.6087

b. Complete the anova table

One-way ANOVA: Scores_2 versus TA_2

Analysis of Variance for Scores_2

Source	DF	SS	MS	F	P
TA_2	3	836.6	278.9	3.95	0.024
Error	19	1342.0	70.6		
Total	22	2178.6			

```
                                    Individual 95% CIs For Mean
                                    Based on Pooled StDev
Level      N      Mean     StDev    ---------+---------+---------+-------
1          5    73.000     7.550    (---------*---------)
2          6    86.000     7.899                         (-------*--------)
3          6    72.000     8.649    (--------*--------)
4          6    72.000     9.252    (--------*--------)
                                    ---------+---------+---------+-------
Pooled StDev =     8.404               72.0      80.0      88.0
```

$H_0 : \mu_1 = \mu_2 = \mu_3, H_1 : otherwise$

$F_{3,19,.05} = 3.13$, reject H_0 at the 5% level.

15-4   a. $\bar{x}_1 = 17.4, \bar{x}_2 = 16.5, \bar{x}_3 = 17.3$, complete the anova table

One-way ANOVA: Costpm_4 versus CarMaker

Analysis of Variance for Costpm_4

Source	DF	SS	MS	F	P
CarMaker	2	2.43	1.22	0.40	0.676
Error	12	36.10	3.01		
Total	14	38.53			

```
                                    Individual 95% CIs For Mean
                                    Based on Pooled StDev
Level      N      Mean     StDev    -------+---------+---------+---------
1          5    17.400     1.373           (-------------*-------------)
2          5    16.500     2.036    (-------------*-------------)
3          5    17.300     1.731          (-------------*-------------)
                                    -------+---------+---------+---------
Pooled StDev =     1.734              15.6      16.8      18.0
```

b. $H_0 : \mu_1 = \mu_2 = \mu_3, H_1 : otherwise$

$F_{2,12,.05} = 3.89$, do not reject H_0 at the 5% level.

15-6   a. $\bar{x}_1 = 5.35, \bar{x}_2 = 6.65, \bar{x}_3 = 4.85, \bar{x}_4 = 7.95$, complete the anova table

One-way ANOVA: SalesInc_6 versus Region_6

```
Analysis of Variance for SalesInc
Source      DF      SS      MS       F       P
Region_6     3   23.240   7.747   11.80   0.001
Error       12    7.880   0.657
Total       15   31.120
                                Individual 95% CIs For Mean
                                Based on Pooled StDev
Level       N    Mean    StDev   ----+---------+---------+---------+--
1           4   5.3500  1.0878      (-----*-----)
2           4   6.6500  0.6191              (-----*-----)
3           4   4.8500  0.6807   (-----*-----)
4           4   7.9500  0.7724                        (-----*-----)
                                ----+---------+---------+---------+--
Pooled StDev =   0.8103          4.5       6.0       7.5       9.0
```

b. $H_0 : \mu_1 = \mu_2 = \mu_3 = \mu_4, H_1 : otherwise$

$F_{3,12,.01} = 5.95$, reject H$_0$ at the 1% level.

15-8   a. $\bar{x}_1 = 79.4, \bar{x}_2 = 75, \bar{x}_3 = 69.6$, complete the anova table

One-way ANOVA: Score_8 versus Service_8

```
Analysis of Variance for Score_8
Source      DF      SS      MS       F       P
Service_     2   240.9   120.5    1.50   0.263
Error       12   966.4    80.5
Total       14  1207.3
                                Individual 95% CIs For Mean
                                Based on Pooled StDev
Level       N    Mean    StDev   ----+---------+---------+---------+--
1           5  79.400   9.659                 (----------*----------)
2           5  75.000   9.192           (----------*----------)
3           5  69.600   7.987   (----------*----------)
                                ----+---------+---------+---------+--
Pooled StDev =   8.974           64.0      72.0      80.0      88.0
```

b. $H_0 : \mu_1 = \mu_2 = \mu_3, H_1 : otherwise$

$F_{2,12,.05} = 3.89$, do not reject H$_0$ at the 5% level.

15-10   a. $\hat{\mu} = 9.6661$

b. $\hat{G}_1 = 10.9683 - 9.6661 = 1.3022$

$\hat{G}_2 = 10.68 - 9.6661 = 1.0139$

$\hat{G}_3 = 7.35 - 9.6661 = -2.3161$

c. $\hat{\varepsilon}_{32} = 8.28 - 7.35 = .93$

15-12 $H_0 : \mu_1 = \mu_2 = \mu_3$, H_1 : *otherwise*

$R_1 = 61$, $R_2 = 37$, $R_3 = 38$

$$W = \frac{12}{16(17)}\left[(3721/6)+(1396/5)+(1444/5)\right]-3(17)=1.18$$

$\chi^2_{(2,.10)} = 4.61$, therefore, do not reject H$_0$ at the 10% level

Using Minitab:

Kruskal-Wallis Test: SodaSales_1 versus CanColor_1

```
Kruskal-Wallis Test on SodaSale
CanColor    N    Median    Ave Rank       Z
1           6     60.00       10.2      1.08
2           5     52.00        7.4     -0.62
3           5     53.00        7.6     -0.51
Overall    16                  8.5
H = 1.18   DF = 2   P = 0.554
H = 1.19   DF = 2   P = 0.553 (adjusted for ties)
```

15-14 $H_0 : \mu_1 = \mu_2 = \mu_3$, H_1 : *otherwise*

$R_1 = 63.5$, $R_2 = 26$, $R_3 = 81.5$

$$W = \frac{12}{18(19)}\left[(4032.25+676+6642.25)/6\right]-3(19)=9.3772$$

$\chi^2_{(2,.01)} = 9.21$, therefore, reject H$_0$ at the 1% level

Using Minitab:

Kruskal-Wallis Test: Nonconforming_3 versus Supplier_3

```
Kruskal-Wallis Test on Nonconfo
Supplier    N    Median    Ave Rank       Z
1           6     32.00       10.6      0.61
2           6     24.50        4.3     -2.90
3           6     35.00       13.6      2.29
Overall    18                  9.5
H = 9.38   DF = 2   P = 0.009
H = 9.47   DF = 2   P = 0.009 (adjusted for ties)
```

15-16 $H_0 : \mu_1 = \mu_2 = \mu_3$, H_1 : *otherwise*

$R_1 = 66$, $R_2 = 79.5$, $R_3 = 85.5$

$$W = \frac{12}{21(22)}\left[(4356+6320.25+7310.25)/7\right]-3(22)=.7403$$

$\chi^2_{(2,.10)} = 4.61$, therefore, do not reject H$_0$ at the 10% level

15-18 $H_0 : \mu_1 = \mu_2 = \mu_3$, H_1 : *otherwise*

$R_1 = 54.5$, $R_2 = 43.5$, $R_3 = 22$

$$W = \frac{12}{15(16)}\left[(2970.25/6)+(1892.25/4)+(484/5)\right]-3(15)=5.2452$$

$\chi^2_{(2,.10)} = 4.61$, therefore, reject H$_0$ at the 10% level

15-20 a. The null hypothesis tests the equality of the population mean ratings across the classes

b. $H_0 : \mu_1 = \mu_2 = \mu_3, H_1 : otherwise$

$W = .17$

$\chi^2_{(2,10)} = 4.61$, therefore, do not reject H_0 at the 10% level

15-22 a. two-way ANOVA table:

Two-way ANOVA: Yield_22 versus Fertilizer_22, Variety_22

```
Analysis of Variance for Yield_22
Source        DF      SS       MS      F       P
Fertiliz       2    200.7    100.3    4.56    0.062
Variety_       3     62.3     20.8    0.94    0.477
Error          6    132.0     22.0
Total         11    394.9
```

```
                           Individual 95% CI
Fertiliz       Mean    --------+----------+----------+----------+---
1              83.8            (----------*--------)
2              89.3                       (---------*--------)
3              79.3        (--------*---------)
                       --------+----------+----------+----------+---
                            78.0       84.0       90.0       96.0
```

```
                           Individual 95% CI
Variety_       Mean    ---+----------+----------+----------+--------
A              84.3            (--------------*------------)
B              86.3               (--------------*------------)
C              80.3        (--------------*------------)
D              85.3             (--------------*------------)
                       ---+----------+----------+----------+--------
                          75.0       80.0       85.0       90.0
```

b. $H_0 : \mu_1 = \mu_2 = \mu_3 = \mu_4, H_1 : otherwise$

$F_{3,6,.05} = 4.76 > .94$, therefore, do not reject H_0 at the 5% level

c. $H_0 : \mu_1 = \mu_2 = \mu_3, H_1 : otherwise$

$F_{2,6,.05} = 5.14 > 4.56$, therefore, do not reject H_0 at the 5% level

15-24   a. two-way ANOVA table:

Two-way ANOVA: Sales_24 versus Region_24, Color_24

```
Analysis of Variance for Sales_24
Source        DF        SS        MS         F        P
Region_2       3      230.9      77.0      3.22     0.104
Color_24       2       74.0      37.0      1.55     0.287
Error          6      143.3      23.9
Total         11      448.3

                        Individual 95% CI
Region_2   Mean    --------+----------+----------+----------+---
East       53.0                  (----------*-----------)
Midwest    55.7                     (------------*-----------)
South      54.0                   (------------*-----------)
West       44.3    (-------------*-----------)
                   --------+----------+----------+----------+---
                        42.0       48.0       54.0       60.0

                        Individual 95% CI
Color_24   Mean    ------+----------+----------+----------+-----
aRed       48.3     (------------*-----------)
bYellow    53.3           (------------*-----------)
cBlue      53.8           (------------*----------)
                   ------+----------+----------+----------+-----
                       45.0       50.0       55.0       60.0
```

b. $H_0 : \mu_1 = \mu_2 = \mu_3$, $H_1 : otherwise$

$F_{2,6,.05} = 5.14 > 1.55$, therefore, do not reject H_0 at the 5% level

15-26

$$\hat{G}_1 = -3.5$$

$$\hat{B}_1 = 1.25$$

$$\hat{\varepsilon}_{11} = -2.5$$

15-28   a. complete the ANOVA table:

Source of Variation	Sum of Squares	df	Mean square	F Ratio
Agents	268	3	89.3333	1.0255
Houses	1152	9	128.000	1.4694
Error	2352	27	87.1111	
Total	3772	39		

b. $H_0 : \mu_1 = \mu_2 = \mu_3 = \mu_4$, $H_1 : otherwise$ [real estate agents]

$F_{3,27,.05} = 2.96 > 1.0255$, therefore, do not reject H_0 at the 5% level

15-30 Complete the ANOVA table and test the null hypothesis that the population mean scores for audience reactions are the same for all three shows

Source of Variation	Sum of Squares	df	Mean square	F Ratio
Shows	95.2	2	47.6	3.6015
Regions	69.5	3	23.1667	1.7528
Error	79.3	6	13.2167	
Total	244.0	11		

$H_0 : \mu_1 = \mu_2 = \mu_3, H_1 : otherwise$ [shows]

$F_{2,6,.05} = 5.14 > 3.6015$, therefore, do not reject H_0 at the 5% level

15-32 a. ANOVA table:

Source of Variation	Sum of Squares	df	Mean square	F Ratio
Contestant	364.50	21	17.3571	19.2724
Judges	.81	8	.1013	.1124
Interaction	4.94	168	.0294	.0326
Error	1069.94	1188	.9006	
Total	1440.19	1385		

b. H_0: Mean value for all 22 contestants is the same
H_1: Otherwise

$F_{21,1188,.01} \approx 1.88 < 19.2724$, therefore, reject H_0 at the 1% level

H_0: Mean value for all 9 judges is the same
H_1: Otherwise

$F_{8,1188,.05} \approx 1.94 > .1124$, therefore, do not reject H_0 at the 5% level

H_0: No interaction exists between contestants and judges
H_1: Otherwise

$F_{168,1188,.05} \approx 1.22 > .0326$, therefore, do not reject H_0 at the 5% level

15-34 a. ANOVA table:

Source of Variation	Sum of Squares	df	Mean square	F Ratio
Test type	57.5556	2	28.7778	4.7091
Subject	389.0000	3	129.6667	21.2182
Interaction	586.0000	6	97.66667	15.9818
Error	146.6667	24	6.1111	
Total	1179.2223	35		

b. H_0: No interaction exists between contestants and judges
H_1: Otherwise

$F_{6,24,.01} = 3.67 < 15.9818$, therefore, reject H_0 at the 1% level

15-36 a. The implied assumption is that there is no interaction effect between student year and dormitory ratings

  b. Using Minitab:

General Linear Model: Ratings_36 versus Dorm_36, Year_36

```
Factor      Type Levels Values
Dorm_36     fixed     4 A B C D
Year_36     fixed     4 1 2 3 4

Analysis of Variance for Ratings_, using Adjusted SS for Tests
Source       DF    Seq SS    Adj SS    Adj MS      F      P
Dorm_36       3    20.344    20.344     6.781   4.91  0.008
Year_36       3    10.594    10.594     3.531   2.56  0.078
Error        25    34.531    34.531     1.381
Total        31    65.469
```

Source of Variation	Sum of Squares	df	Mean square	F Ratio
Dorm	20.344	3	6.781	4.91
Year	10.594	3	3.531	2.56
Error	34.531	25	1.381	
Total	65.469	31		

  c. H_0: Mean ratings for all 4 dormitories is the same

   H_1: Otherwise

   $F_{3,25,.01} = 4.68 < 4.91$, therefore, reject H_0 at the 1% level

  d. H_0: Mean ratings for all 4 student years is the same

   H_1: Otherwise

   $F_{3,25,.05} = 2.99 > 2.56$, therefore, do not reject H_0 at the 5% level

15-38

Source of Variation	Sum of Squares	df	Mean square	F Ratio
Color	243.250	2	121.625	11.3140
Region	354.000	3	118.000	10.9767
Interaction	189.750	6	31.625	2.9419
Error	129.000	12	10.750	
Total	916.000	23		

  H_0: No interaction exists between region and can color

  H_1: Otherwise

  $F_{6,12,.01} = 4.82 > 2.9419$, therefore, do not reject H_0 at the 1% level

15-40 One-way ANOVA examines the effect of a single factor (having three or more conditions). Two-way ANOVA recognizes situations in which more than one factor may be significant.

15-42

Source of Variation	Sum of Squares	df	Mean square	F Ratio
Between	5156	2	2578.000	21.4458
Within	120802	1005	120.201	
Total	125967	1007		

$F_{2,1005,.01} = 4.61 < 21.4458$, therefore, reject H_0 at the 1% level

15-44   a. Use result from Exercise 50b to find SSG, then compute MSG and finally, find SSW using the fact that $SSW = (n-k)\dfrac{MSG}{F}$

Source of Variation	Sum of Squares	df	Mean square	F Ratio
Between	221.3400	3	73.7800	25.6
Within	374.6640	130	2.8820	
Total	596.0040	133		

b. H_0: Mean salaries are the same for managers in all 4 groups
H_1: Otherwise
$F_{3,130,.01} \approx 3.95 < 25.6$, therefore, reject H_0 at the 1% level

15-46

Source of Variation	Sum of Squares	df	Mean square	F Ratio
Between	11438.3028	2	5719.1514	.7856
Within	109200.000	15	7280.000	
Total	120638.3028	17		

H_0: Mean sales levels are the same for all three periods
H_1: Otherwise
$F_{2,15,.05} = 3.68 > .7856$, therefore, do not reject H_0 at the 5% level

15-48

$H_0 : \mu_1 = \mu_2 = \mu_3 = \mu_4, H_1 : otherwise$

$R_1 = 48.5, \quad R_2 = 55, \quad R_3 = 74, \quad R_4 = 32.5$

$W = \dfrac{12}{20(21)}\left[(2352.25 + 3025 + 5476 + 1056.25)/5\right] - 3(21) = 5.0543$

$\chi^2_{(3,01)} = 6.25$, therefore, do not reject H_0 at the 10% level

15-50 a.
$$SSW = \sum_{j=1}^{K}\sum_{i=1}^{n_i}(x_{ij}-\bar{x}_i)^2$$

$$= \sum_{j=1}^{K}\left[\sum_{i=1}^{n_i}x^2_{ij} - 2n_i\bar{x}^2_i + n_i\bar{x}^2_i\right]$$

$$= \sum_{j=1}^{K}\sum_{i=1}^{n_i}x^2_{ij} - \sum_{i=1}^{K}n_i\bar{x}^2_i$$

b.
$$SSG = \sum_{j=1}^{K}n_i(\bar{x}_i - \bar{x})^2$$

$$= \sum_{i=1}^{K}n_i\bar{x}^2_i - 2\bar{x}\sum_{i=1}^{k}n_i\bar{x}_i + n\bar{x}^2$$

$$= \sum_{i=1}^{K}n_i\bar{x}^2_i - 2n\bar{x}^2 + n\bar{x}^2$$

$$= \sum_{i=1}^{K}n_i\bar{x}^2_i - n\bar{x}^2$$

c.
$$SST = \sum_{i=1}^{K}\sum_{j=1}^{n_i}(x_{ij}-\bar{x}_i)^2$$

$$= \sum_{i=1}^{K}\left[\sum_{i=1}^{n_i}x^2_{ij} - 2\bar{x}\sum_{i=1}^{n_i}x_i + n_i\bar{x}^2_i\right]$$

$$= \sum_{i=1}^{K}\sum_{i=1}^{n_i}(x^2_{ij} - 2n_i\bar{x}\,\bar{x}_i + n_i x^2)$$

$$= \sum_{i=1}^{K}\sum_{j=1}^{n_i}x^2_{ij} - n\bar{x}^2$$

15-52

Source of Variation	Sum of Squares	df	Mean square	F Ratio
Consumers	37571.5	124	302.996	1.3488
Brands	32987.3	2	16493.65	73.4226
Error	55710.7	248	224.6399	
Total	126269.5	374		

H_0: Mean perception levels are the same for all three brands

H_1: Otherwise

$F_{2,248,.01} \approx 4.79 < 73.4226$, therefore, reject H_0 at the 1% level

15-54 a. Using Minitab:

Two-way ANOVA: GPA_54 versus Income_54, SAT_54

```
Analysis of Variance for GPA_54
Source       DF      SS       MS       F        P
Income_5      2   0.0067   0.0033    0.20    0.826
SAT_54        2   0.8267   0.4133   24.80    0.006
Error         4   0.0667   0.0167
Total         8   0.9000
```

Source of Variation	Sum of Squares	df	Mean square	F Ratio
Income	.0067	2	.0033	.2000
SAT Score	.8267	2	.4133	24.8000
Error	.0667	4	.0167	
Total	.9000	8		

b. H_0: Mean gpa's are the same for all three income groups

H_1: Otherwise

$F_{2,4,.05} = 6.94 > .2000$, therefore, do not reject H_0 at the 5% level

H_0: Mean gpa's are the same for all three SAT score groups

H_1: Otherwise

$F_{2,4,.01} = 18.0 < 24.8$, therefore, reject H_0 at the 1% level

15-56 a. $\hat{\mu} = 3.3$

b. $\hat{G}_2 = 0.0$

c. $\hat{B}_2 = .0667$

d. $\hat{\varepsilon}_{22} = .1333$

15-58 ANOVA table:

Source of Variation	Sum of Squares	df	Mean square	F Ratio
Prices	.178	2	.0890	.0944
Countries	4.365	2	2.1825	2.3151
Interaction	1.262	4	.3155	.3347
Error	93.330	99	.9427	
Total	99.135	107		

H_0: Mean quality ratings for all three prices levels is the same

H_1: Otherwise

$F_{2,99,.05} \approx 3.07 > .0944$, therefore, do not reject H_0 at the 5% level

H_0: Mean quality ratings for all three countries is the same

H_1: Otherwise

$F_{2,99,.05} \approx 3.07 > 2.3151$, therefore, do not reject H_0 at the 5% level

H_0: No interaction exists between price and country

H_1: Otherwise

$F_{4,99,.05} \approx 2.45 > .3347$, therefore, do not reject H_0 at the 5% level

15-60 a. ANOVA table:

Source of Variation	Sum of Squares	df	Mean square	F Ratio
Income	.0178	2	.0089	.5333
SAT score	2.2011	2	1.1006	66.0333
Interaction	.1022	4	.0256	1.5333
Error	.1500	9	.0167	
Total	2.4711	17		

b. H_0: Mean gpa's for all three income groups is the same

   H_1: Otherwise

   $F_{2,9,.05} = 4.26 > .5333$, therefore, do not reject H_0 at the 5% level

c. H_0: Mean gpa's for all three SAT score groups is the same

   H_1: Otherwise

   $F_{2,9,.01} = 8.02 < 66.0333$, therefore, reject H_0 at the 1% level

d. H_0: No interaction exists between income and SAT score group

   H_1: Otherwise

   $F_{4,9,.05} = 3.63 > 1.5333$, therefore, do not reject H_0 at the 5% level

Chapter 16: Introduction to Quality

16-2 and 16-4. Various answers.

16-6   a. $\hat{\sigma} = \bar{s} / c_4 = 5.42 / .959 = 5.6517$

b. $CL = \bar{\bar{X}} = 192.6$

$$LCL = \bar{\bar{X}} - A_3\bar{s}, \text{ where } A_3 = \frac{3}{c_4\sqrt{n}} = 192.6 - 1.18(5.42) = 186.2044$$

$$UCL = \bar{\bar{X}} + A_3\bar{s}, \text{ where } A_3 = \frac{3}{c_4\sqrt{n}} = 192.6 + 1.18(5.42) = 198.9956$$

c. $CL = 5.42$
$LCL = .12(5.42) = .6504$
$UCL = 1.88(5.42) = 10.1896$

16-8   a. $\hat{\sigma} = 1.23 / .965 = 1.2746$

b. $CL = 19.86$
$LCL = 19.86 - 1.1(1.23) = 18.507$
$UCL = 19.86 + 1.1(1.23) = 21.213$

c. $CL = 1.23$
$LCL = .18(1.23) = .2214$
$UCL = 1.82(1.23) = 2.2386$

16-10   a. $\bar{\bar{x}} = 4999.4 / 30 = 149.98$

b. $\bar{s} = 179.67 / 30 = 5.989$

c. $\hat{\sigma} = 5.989 / .965 = 6.2062$

b. $CL = 149.98$
$LCL = 149.98 - 1.1(5.989) = 143.3921$
$UCL = 149.98 + 1.1(5.989) = 156.5679$

e. The $\bar{X}$ chart shows a process where the level is under statistical control

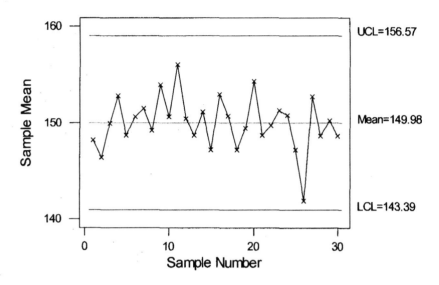

X-bar Chart for Exercise 16-10

f. CL = 5.989
    LCL = .18(5.989) = 1.078
    UCL = 1.82(5.989) = 10.9

g. S-chart

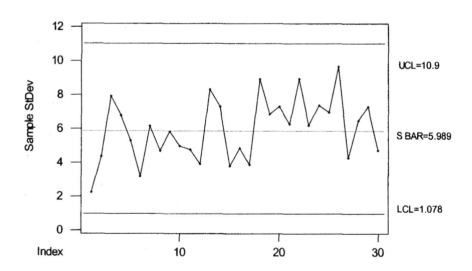

S Chart for 16-10

16-12 a. $192.6 \pm 3(5.6517)$: $(175.6449, 209.5551)$

These values lie within the tolerance limits

b. $C_p = \dfrac{215-170}{6(5.6517)} = 1.327$ The process is not capable since $C_p < 1.33$

c. $C_{pk} = \dfrac{215-192.6}{3(5.6517)} = 1.321$ The process is not capable since $C_{pk} < 1.33$

16-14 a. $19.86 \pm 3(1.2746)$: $(16.0362, 23.6838)$

These limits are beyond the tolerances set by management

b. $C_p = \dfrac{22-18}{6(1.2746)} = .523$ The process is not capable since $C_p < 1.33$

c. $C_{pk} = \dfrac{19.86-18}{3(1.2746)} = .486$ The process is not capable since $C_{pk} < 1.33$

16-16 a. $19.84 \pm 3(2.0903)$: $(13.5691, 26.1109)$

These limits are beyond the tolerances set by management

b. $C_p = \dfrac{24-16}{6(2.0903)} = .638$ The process is not capable since $C_p < 1.33$

c. $C_{pk} = \dfrac{19.84-16}{3(2.0903)} = .612$ The process is not capable since $C_{pk} < 1.33$

16-18 $CL = .016$, $LCL = 0$, $UCL = .016 + 3\sqrt{\dfrac{.016(.984)}{500}} = .0328$

16-20 a. $\bar{p} = 1.02/20 = .051$, $CL = .051$, $LCL = .051 - 3\sqrt{.051(.949)/500} = .0215$

$UCL = .051 + 3\sqrt{.051(.949)/500} = .0805$

b. p-chart

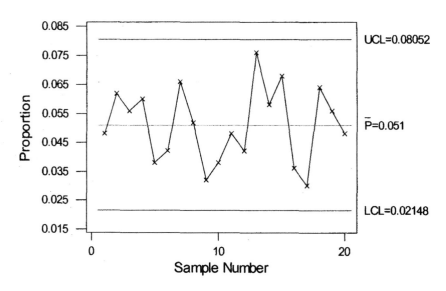

P Chart for Exercise 16-20

No evidence that the process is out of statistical control

16-22 a. $\bar{c} = 112/20 = 5.6$

b. $CL = 5.6, \quad LCL = 0, \quad UCL = 5.6 + 3\sqrt{5.6} = 12.70$

c. C chart

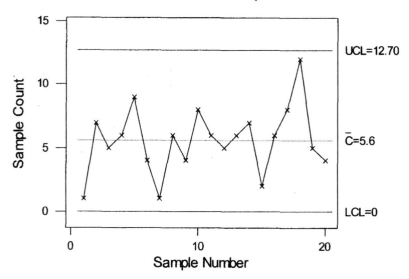

C Chart for Number of Imperfections

No evidence that the process is out of statistical control

16-24 a. $\bar{c} = 208/15 = 13.8667$

b. CL = 13.8667, LCL = $13.8667 - 3\sqrt{13.8667} = 2.6953$

UCL = $13.8667 + 3\sqrt{13.8667} = 25.0381$

c. c-chart

C Chart for Raisins

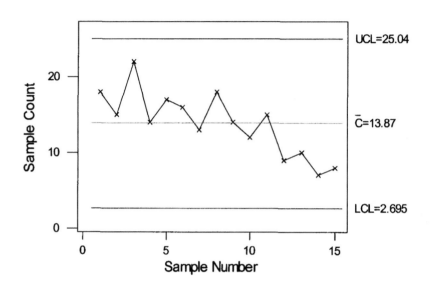

No evidence of a process out of control; however, keep monitoring the process.

16-26 a. Capability process (normal) is meaningless since the process of manufacturing precision bolts is not stable.

b. Capability sixpack (normal) is meaningless since the process of manufacturing precision bolts is not stable.

16-28 a. c-chart for Exercise 16-22

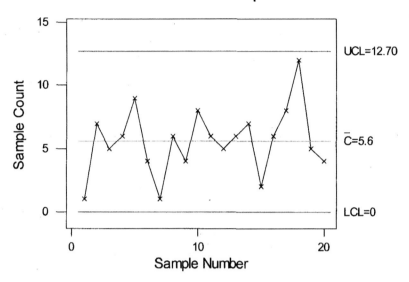

b. c-chart for Exercise 16-23

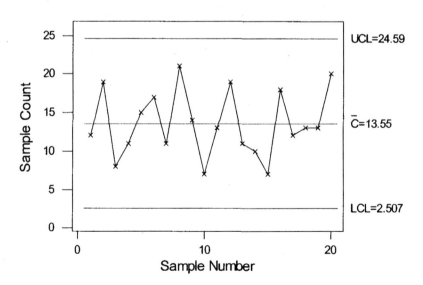

c.   c-chart for Exercise 16-24

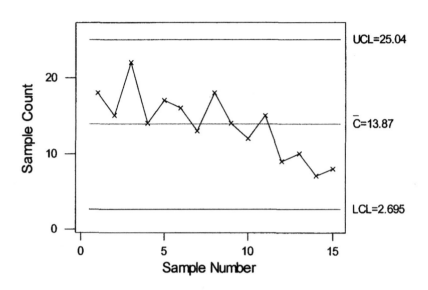

C Chart for Raisins

16-30   There are two types of errors that can be made – 1) identifying a special or assignable cause of variation when there is none and 2) ignoring a special cause by assuming that it is due to natural variability. Control limits that are 'too narrow' will incorrectly flag natural causes of variability as a special cause and the researcher is sent off to find a special cause of variability that does not exist. Control limits that are 'too wide' imply that the researcher is not going off to correct processes that are out of control. The use of the three sigma limits as control limits was set by Shewhart as an appropriate balance between the two types of errors

16-32 a. $\bar{\bar{x}} = 8760.4 / 25 = 350.416$
       b. $\bar{s} = 140.05 / 25 = 5.602$
       c. $\hat{\sigma} = 5.602 / .965 = 5.8052$
       d. CL = 350.416
           LCL = $350.416 - 1.1(5.602) = 344.2538$
           UCL = $350.416 + 1.1(5.602) = 356.5782$

e. The X-bar chart provides no evidence that the process is out of control.

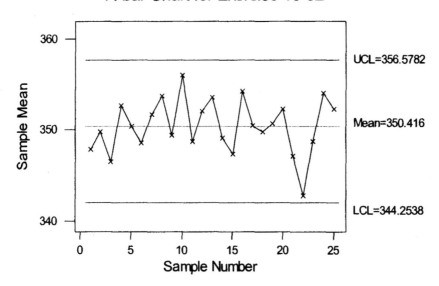

f. CL=5.602
    LCL = .18(5.602) = 1.0084
    UCL = 1.82(5.602) = 10.1956
g. s-chart

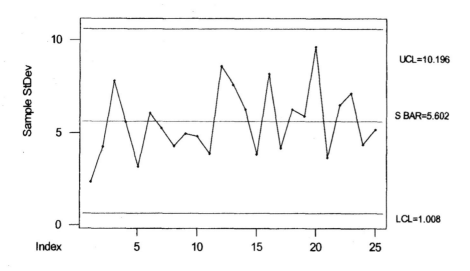

No pattern analysis rules are violated. Process is in control.

h.   i) $350.416 \pm 3(5.8052)$: $(333.0004, 367.8316)$

 ii) $C_p = \dfrac{375 - 325}{6(5.8052)} = 1.435$

Therefore, the process is capable

 iii) $C_{pk} = \dfrac{375 - 350.416}{3(5.8052)} = 1.412$

Therefore, the process is capable

16-34 a. $\bar{c} = 270/18 = 15$

b. CL $= 15$

LCL $= 15 - 3\sqrt{15} = 3.381$

UCL $= 15 + 3\sqrt{15} = 26.619$

c., d. C chart shows no evidence of a process that is out of statistical control.

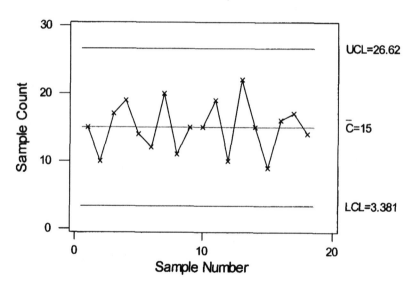

16-36 a. Common cause – affects all workers within the process

b. Common cause – affects all workers within the process

c. Assignable cause

d. Assignable cause

e. Assignable cause

16-38   a. Machine 1 – X bar – s chart:

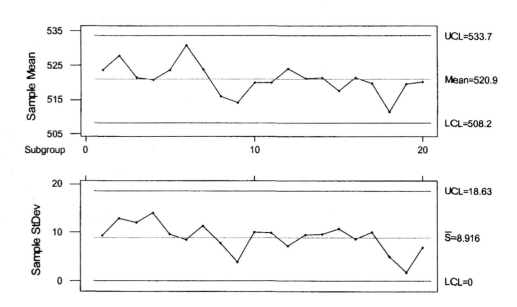

Machine 1 shows no evidence of being 'out of statistical control'

b. Machine 2 – X bar – s chart:

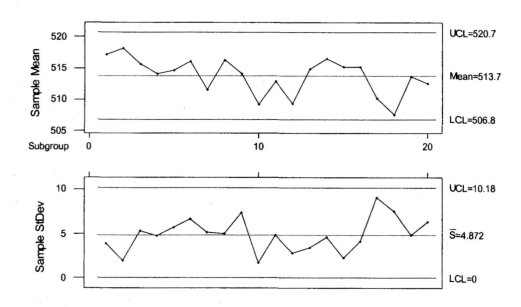

Likewise, Machine 2 shows no evidence of being 'out of statistical control'

c. Machine 1 – capability analysis shows that Cp =0.44 and Cpk=0.14. Machine 1 is not capable of meeting specifications.

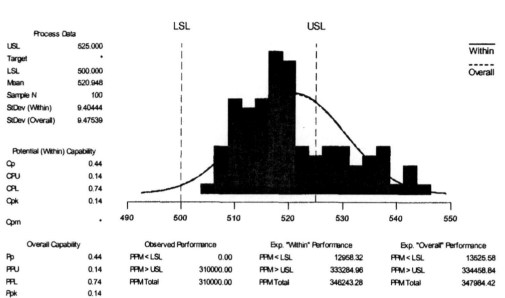

Process Capability Analysis for Machine 1

d. Machine 2 – capability analysis shows that Cp =0.80 and Cpk=0.72. Machine 2 is not capable of meeting specifications.

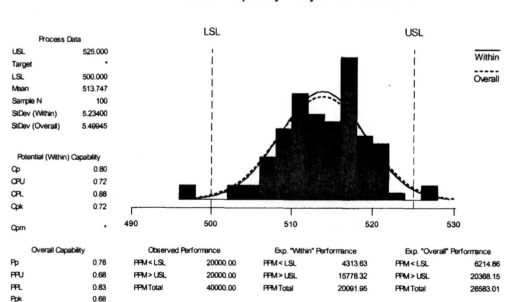

Process Capability Analysis for Machine 2

e. Neither machine is capable of meeting specifications. Both of the machines produce a product with greater variability than the specification limits call for. Note that Machine 1 has greater variability than Machine 2.

16-40   X bar chart for TOC data:

Xbar/S Chart for Leak Rates

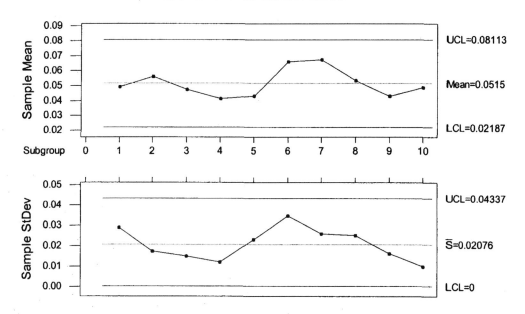

All data points are within the control limits. No pattern analysis rule has been violated.

Chapter 17: Time Series Analysis and Forecasting

17-2

    a. e.g., $I_2 = 100(35.875/35) = 102.5$

    b. e.g., $I_1 = 100(35/34.375) = 101.82$

Week_17-2	Price	Base_Week1	Base_Week4
1	35	100.00	101.82
2	35.875	102.50	104.36
3	34.75	99.29	101.09
4	34.375	98.21	100.00
5	35	100.00	101.82
6	34.875	99.64	101.45
7	35	100.00	101.82
8	34.75	99.29	101.09
9	34.75	99.29	101.09
10	35.25	100.71	102.55
11	38.75	110.71	112.73
12	37.125	106.07	108.00

17-4   a. Unweighted average index

Year	Average	Index of Average
1	11.8	100.00
2	12.43	105.37
3	12.93	109.60
4	13.30	112.71
5	13.63	115.54
6	13.83	117.23

    b. Laspeyres index

Year	$\sum q_{oi}p_{1i}$	Laspeyres Index
1	1120.4	100.00
2	1174.30	104.81
3	1237.90	110.49
4	1256.40	112.14
5	1296.40	115.71
6	1316.10	117.47

17-6   A price index for energy is helpful in that it allows us to say something about price movements over time for a group of commodities, namely, energy prices. A weighted index of prices allows one to compare the cost of a group of products across periods.

17-8   Runs test on Inventory to Sales Ratio
Runs Test: Ratio
```
Ratio    K =      1.4450
The observed number of runs =    7
    The expected number of runs =    7.0000
    6 Observations above K     6 below
 * N Small -- The following approximation may be invalid
              The test is significant at   1.0000
              Cannot reject at alpha = 0.05
```

17-10   Runs test on Gold Price
Runs Test: Price_17-10
```
Price_17    K =     392.0000
    The observed number of runs =    5
    The expected number of runs =    8.0000
    7 Observations above K     7 below
 * N Small -- The following approximation may be invalid
              The test is significant at   0.0951
```

17-12   a. Runs test on Earnings per share
Runs Test: Earnings
```
Earnings    K =      30.7000
    The observed number of runs =    7
    The expected number of runs =    15.0000
    14 Observations above K    14 below
              The test is significant at   0.0021
```

b. From the time series plot below, cyclical behavior tends to dominate with upward trend for the most recent 7 years.

Annual earnings per share
Exercise 17-12

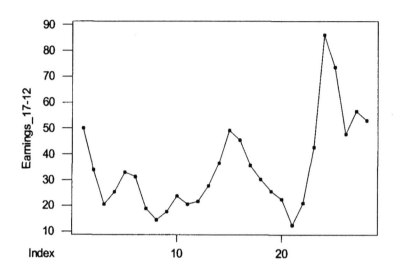

17-14   a. Time series plot – Quarterly Sales

Quarterly Sales
Six years of data

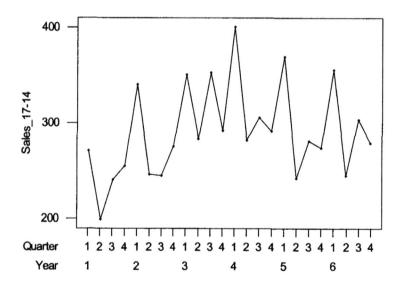

The data exhibits seasonality and a quadratic trend

b.

Period	4 Period MA	$100\dfrac{X_t}{X_t^*}$	Seas. Factor	Adj. Series
1-1			122.110	221.930
2			87.483	227.474
3	250.000	96.000	96.129	249.664
4	264.625	96.363	94.278	270.477
2-1	271.125	125.772		279.255
2	274.250	89.699		281.199
3	278.000	88.130		254.566
4	283.875	96.874		291.691
3-1	302.000	116.225		287.445
2	317.625	89.099		323.493
3	326.000	108.282		367.214
4	332.125	87.919		309.723
4-1	326.125	122.959		328.391
2	320.125	88.091		322.350
3	316.125	96.797		318.322
4	307.250	94.711		308.663
5-1	299.125	123.694		303.004
2	293.875	82.348		276.626
3	290.000	96.897		292.315
4	288.625	94.933		290.631
6-1	291.875	121.970		291.539
2	295.375	82.945		280.056
3				316.241
4				295.934

17-16 Housing Starts – Annual, per thousand population, U.S.

Starts	5ptMA17-16
1	*
2	*
3	7.76
4	7.66
5	7.80
6	7.56
7	7.30
8	7.10
9	6.94
10	6.82
11	7.62
12	8.58
13	9.02
14	8.84
15	8.52
16	7.96
17	7.52
18	7.40
19	7.70
20	7.76
21	7.28
22	6.38
23	*
24	*

Private Housing Starts - U.S. (per thous. population)

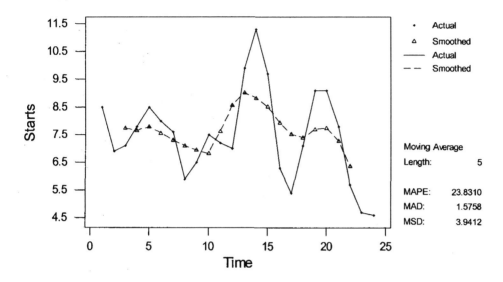

Strong cyclical behavior is evident in the smoothed series

17-18 $X^*_{t+1} - X^*_t = \dfrac{1}{2m+1}\sum_{j=-m}^{m} X_{t+j+1} - \dfrac{1}{2m+1}\sum_{j=-m}^{m} X_{t+j} = \dfrac{1}{2m+1}(X_{t+m+1} - X_{t-m})$

➔ $X^*_{t+1} = X^*_t + \dfrac{X_{t+m+1} - X_{t-m}}{2m+1}$

Using this formula, one may avoid summing $2m+1$ terms when calculating each moving average value

17-20 a. $X^*_t = \dfrac{X^*_{t-.5} + X^*_{t+.5}}{2} = \dfrac{\sum_{j=-(s/2)+1}^{s/2}(X_{t+j-1} + X_{t+j})}{2s}$

$= \dfrac{X_{t-(s/2)} + 2(X_{t-(s/2)+1} + \cdots + X_{t+(s/2)-1}) + X_{t+(s/2)}}{2s}$

b. $X^*_{t+1} = \dfrac{X_{t-(s/2)} + 2(X_{t-(s/2)+1} + \cdots + X_{t+(s/2)-1}) + X_{t+(s/2)}}{2s} + X^*_t - X^*_t$

$= X^*_t + \dfrac{X_{t+(s/2)+1} + X_{t+(s/2)} - X_{t-(s/2)+1} - X_{t-(s/2)}}{2s}$

17-22   In Minitab input Smoothing constant of .6 (alpha of .4). Set initial smoothed value – use average of first '1' observations

Single Exponential Smoothing

```
Data        Ratio
Length      12.0000
NMissing    0
```

```
Smoothing Constant
Alpha: 0.6
```

```
Accuracy Measures
MAPE: 3.54254
MAD:  0.05135
MSD:  0.00439
```

Row	Time	Ratio	SMOO1	FITS1	Error
1	1	1.41	1.41000	1.41000	0.000000
2	2	1.45	1.43400	1.41000	0.040000
3	3	1.57	1.51560	1.43400	0.136000
4	4	1.48	1.49424	1.51560	-0.035600
5	5	1.46	1.47370	1.49424	-0.034240
6	6	1.44	1.45348	1.47370	-0.033696
7	7	1.43	1.43939	1.45348	-0.023478
8	8	1.45	1.44576	1.43939	0.010609
9	9	1.43	1.43630	1.44576	-0.015757
10	10	1.52	1.48652	1.43630	0.083697
11	11	1.37	1.41661	1.48652	-0.116521
12	12	1.33	1.36464	1.41661	-0.086608

Row	Period	Forecast	Lower	Upper
1	13	1.36464	1.23883	1.49045
2	14	1.36464	1.23883	1.49045
3	15	1.36464	1.23883	1.49045
4	16	1.36464	1.23883	1.49045

Single Exponential Smoothing

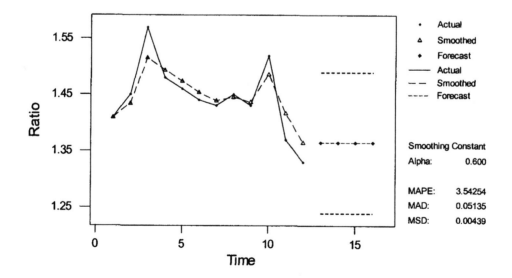

17-24 Use smoothing constant of .5 (alpha of .5) with an Options... of set intial
smoothed value at the average of the first '1' observations.

Single Exponential Smoothing
```
Data        Starts
Length      24.0000
NMissing    0

Smoothing Constant
Alpha: 0.5

Accuracy Measures
MAPE: 18.1090
MAD:   1.2352
MSD:   2.6282
```

Row	Time	Starts	SMOO3	FITS3	Error
1	1	8.5	8.50000	8.50000	0.00000
2	2	6.9	7.70000	8.50000	-1.60000
3	3	7.1	7.40000	7.70000	-0.60000
4	4	7.8	7.60000	7.40000	0.40000
5	5	8.5	8.05000	7.60000	0.90000
6	6	8.0	8.02500	8.05000	-0.05000
7	7	7.6	7.81250	8.02500	-0.42500
8	8	5.9	6.85625	7.81250	-1.91250
9	9	6.5	6.67812	6.85625	-0.35625
10	10	7.5	7.08906	6.67812	0.82188
11	11	7.2	7.14453	7.08906	0.11094
12	12	7.0	7.07227	7.14453	-0.14453
13	13	9.9	8.48613	7.07227	2.82773
14	14	11.3	9.89307	8.48613	2.81387
15	15	9.7	9.79653	9.89307	-0.19307
16	16	6.3	8.04827	9.79653	-3.49653
17	17	5.4	6.72413	8.04827	-2.64827
18	18	7.1	6.91207	6.72413	0.37587
19	19	9.1	8.00603	6.91207	2.18793
20	20	9.1	8.55302	8.00603	1.09397
21	21	7.8	8.17651	8.55302	-0.75302
22	22	5.7	6.93825	8.17651	-2.47651
23	23	4.7	5.81913	6.93825	-2.23825
24	24	4.6	5.20956	5.81913	-1.21913

Row	Period	Forecast	Lower	Upper
1	25	5.20956	2.18328	8.23585
2	26	5.20956	2.18328	8.23585
3	27	5.20956	2.18328	8.2358

Single Exponential Smoothing

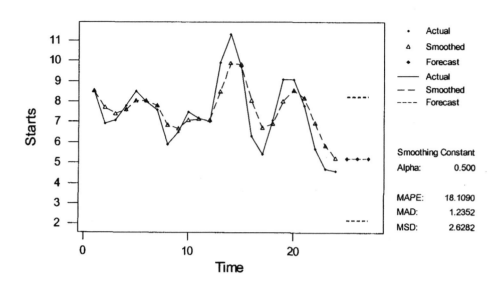

17-26 a. $\hat{X}_t = \hat{X}_{t-1+1} = \hat{X}_{t-1}$; $e_t = X_t - \hat{X}_t = X_t - \hat{X}_{t-1}$

   b. $\hat{X}_t = \alpha \hat{X}_{t-1} + (1-\alpha)X_t$; $\hat{X}_{t-1} = \dfrac{\hat{X}_t - (1-\alpha)X_t}{\alpha}$

   $e_t = X_t - \hat{X}_{t-1} = \dfrac{\hat{X}_t - (1-\alpha)X_t}{\alpha}$

   $\hat{X}_t = X_t - \alpha e_t$

17-28 Simple exponential smoothing is appropriate only when a data series is stationary – no consistent trend and non-seasonal. The technique attempts to forecast the level of the time series. Under these circumstances, the estimates will not be absurd, but they will differ from the observed values, as will all estimates.

17-30 Use level of .7 (alpha of .3) and trend of .6 (beta = .4)
Double Exponential Smoothing

Data	Earnings_17-
Length	24.0000
NMissing	0

Smoothing Constants
Alpha (level): 0.7
Gamma (trend): 0.6

Accuracy Measures
MAPE: 0.575278
MAD: 0.062174
MSD: 0.009089

Row	Time	Earnings_17-30	Smooth	Predict	Error
1	1	10.58	10.5761	10.5670	0.012967
2	2	10.67	10.6520	10.6100	0.059961
3	3	10.48	10.5493	10.7111	-0.231124
4	4	10.59	10.5664	10.5114	0.078622
5	5	10.67	10.6374	10.5615	0.108525
6	6	10.74	10.7214	10.6781	0.061915
7	7	10.74	10.7544	10.7881	-0.048072
8	8	10.80	10.8003	10.8009	-0.000878
9	9	10.84	10.8419	10.8464	-0.006351
10	10	10.87	10.8746	10.8853	-0.015325
11	11	10.81	10.8405	10.9116	-0.101581
12	12	10.93	10.9014	10.8348	0.095206
13	13	10.94	10.9387	10.9357	0.004256
14	14	10.96	10.9644	10.9748	-0.014817
15	15	11.05	11.0333	10.9943	0.055685
16	16	10.83	10.9070	11.0866	-0.256553
17	17	11.05	10.9907	10.8525	0.197528
18	18	11.02	11.0198	11.0192	0.000791
19	19	11.06	11.0566	11.0486	0.011437
20	20	11.11	11.1041	11.0902	0.019828
21	21	11.15	11.1488	11.1460	0.004017
22	22	11.19	11.1907	11.1924	-0.002413
23	23	11.22	11.2240	11.2333	-0.013329
24	24	11.17	11.1973	11.2610	-0.091005

Row	Period	Forecast	Lower	Upper
1	25	11.1961	11.0438	11.3484
2	26	11.1949	11.0026	11.3872
3	27	11.1937	10.9579	11.4294

17-32

Double Exponential Smoothing

```
Data        ProfitMargin
Length      11.0000
NMissing    0
Smoothing Constants
Alpha (level): 0.4
Gamma (trend): 0.4
```

```
Accuracy Measures
MAPE: 11.6395
MAD:   0.8225
MSD:   0.9428
```

Row	Time	ProfitMargin_17-32	Smooth	Predict	Error
1	1	8.4	8.04545	7.80909	0.59091
2	2	7.4	7.78618	8.04364	-0.64364
3	3	7.4	7.56883	7.68138	-0.28138
4	4	7.2	7.33140	7.41901	-0.21901
5	5	6.3	6.80793	7.14654	-0.84654
6	6	7.9	7.05257	6.48762	1.41238
7	7	7.7	7.25495	6.95824	0.74176
8	8	7.1	7.20758	7.27930	-0.17930
9	9	8.5	7.72195	7.20324	1.29676
10	10	7.0	7.55506	7.92509	-0.92509
11	11	5.7	6.84611	7.61019	-1.91019

Row	Period	Forecast	Lower	Upper
1	12	6.59561	4.58061	8.61062
2	13	6.34512	4.15832	8.53191

17-34 $\hat{X}_n = 304.1145,\ \ T_n = 2.6105$

Forecast for eight quarters:

Year	1	2	3	4
7	367.8818	257.6526	310.1514	290.0101
8	380.4057	266.3499	320.5333	299.6372

17-36   The first-order autoregressive model is

Regression Analysis: TradeVol_17-36 versus TradeVol_lag1

```
The regression equation is
TradeVol_17-36 = 18.5 - 0.032 TradeVol_lag1
11 cases used 1 cases contain missing values
Predictor       Coef     SE Coef        T        P
Constant       18.515      5.609     3.30    0.009
TradeVol      -0.0317      0.2910    -0.11    0.916
```

$$\hat{y}_t = 18.515 - .032 y_{t-1} + a_t$$

$$\hat{y}_{13} = 18.515 - .032(20.5) = 17.86$$

$$\hat{y}_{14} = 18.515 - .032(17.86) = 17.94$$

$$\hat{y}_{15} = 18.515 - .032(17.94) = 17.94$$

17-38
4th order model:
Regression Analysis: Earnings versus epslag1, epslag2, epslag3, epslag4
```
The regression equation is
Earnings = 14.7 + 1.22 epslag1 - 0.938 epslag2 + 0.632 epslag3 - 0.348 epslag4
24 cases used 4 cases contain missing values
Predictor       Coef     SE Coef         T        P
Constant      14.684       7.370      1.99    0.061
epslag1       1.2234       0.2270      5.39    0.000
epslag2      -0.9379       0.3832     -2.45    0.024
epslag3       0.6319       0.4051      1.56    0.135
epslag4      -0.3479       0.3032     -1.15    0.265

S = 11.93      R-Sq = 66.3%      R-Sq(adj) = 59.1%
```
$z - statistic$ for $\phi_4 = -1.147$, Fail to reject H_0 at the 10% level

3rd order model:
Regression Analysis: Earnings versus epslag1, epslag2, epslag3
```
The regression equation is
Earnings = 10.2 + 1.13 epslag1 - 0.657 epslag2 + 0.246 epslag3
25 cases used 3 cases contain missing values
Predictor       Coef     SE Coef         T        P
Constant      10.183       6.112      1.67    0.111
epslag1       1.1349       0.2097      5.41    0.000
epslag2      -0.6574       0.2895     -2.27    0.034
epslag3       0.2460       0.2093      1.18    0.253

S = 11.74      R-Sq = 64.3%      R-Sq(adj) = 59.2%
```
$z - statistic$ for $\phi_3 = 1.175$, Fail to reject H_0 at the 10% level

2nd order model:
Regression Analysis: Earnings versus epslag1, epslag2
```
The regression equation is
Earnings = 13.7 + 1.05 epslag1 - 0.438 epslag2
26 cases used 2 cases contain missing values
Predictor       Coef     SE Coef         T        P
Constant      13.717       5.314      2.58    0.017
epslag1       1.0486       0.1839      5.70    0.000
epslag2      -0.4382       0.1870     -2.34    0.028

S = 11.68      R-Sq = 62.2%      R-Sq(adj) = 58.9%
```
$z - statistic$ for $\phi_2 = -2.344$, Reject H_0 at the 10% level

Regression Analysis: Earnings versus epslag1
```
The regression equation is
Earnings = 9.65 + 0.721 epslag1
27 cases used 1 cases contain missing values
Predictor       Coef     SE Coef         T        P
Constant       9.646       5.387      1.79    0.085
epslag1        0.7211       0.1403      5.14    0.000

S = 12.71      R-Sq = 51.4%      R-Sq(adj) = 49.4%
```

Use 2nd order model for forecasts:

$\hat{y}_{29} = 44.628, \hat{y}_{30} = 37.274, \hat{y}_{31} = 33.270, \hat{y}_{32} = 32.291, \hat{y}_{33} = 33.018$

17-40 a. $\hat{\phi}_2 / s_2 = -1.874$. Fail to reject H_0 at the 5% level.

$\hat{\phi}_1 / s_1 = 9.103$. Reject H_0 at the 5% level. Therefore, select the first order model

b. $\hat{X}_{31} = 193.27 + .883(1289) = 1331.457$

$\hat{X}_{32} = 1368.946$, $\hat{X}_{33} = 1402.049$

17-42 For $h = 1$: $\hat{X}_{n+1} = X_n$

For $h = 2$: $\hat{X}_{n+2} = \hat{X}_{n+1} = X_n$

Thus, for h: $\hat{X}_{n+h} = \hat{X}_{n+h-1} = \cdots = X_n$

17-44 a. Index with month 1 as the base

e.g., $I_2 = 100(10.67 / 10.58) = 100.85$

b. Index with month 15 as the base

e.g., $I_2 = 100(10.67 / 11.05) = 96.56$

Earnings_17-44	Base_Mo1	Base_Mo15
10.58	100.00	95.75
10.67	100.85	96.56
10.48	99.05	94.84
10.59	100.09	95.84
10.67	100.85	96.56
10.74	101.51	97.19
10.74	101.51	97.19
10.8	102.08	97.74
10.84	102.46	98.10
10.87	102.74	98.37
10.81	102.17	97.83
10.93	103.31	98.91
10.94	103.40	99.00
10.96	103.59	99.19
11.05	104.44	100.00
10.83	102.36	98.01
11.05	104.44	100.00
11.02	104.16	99.73
11.06	104.54	100.09
11.11	105.01	100.54
11.15	105.39	100.90
11.19	105.77	101.27
11.22	106.05	101.54
11.17	105.58	101.09

17-46 Values of a time series can be made up of trend, seasonal, cyclical and random components. For example, total retail sales in the U.S. tend to have a seasonal component with much larger retail sales in the November/December months than others due to gift buying for the holiday season. Strong trend components tend to exist in total personal income in the U.S. since the factors that influence income change slowly over time. Unemployment rates in the U.S. show strong cyclical behavior due to the ups and downs of the business cycle.

17-48 This will very likely not be a successful strategy since the manager could use the trend and seasonal patterns that exist in the monthly data to generate more accurate forecasts.

17-50 a.

Runs Test: IPIndex_50
```
IPIndex_
K =      88.5000
    The observed number of runs =    6
    The expected number of runs =    8.0000
    7 Observations above K     7 below
  * N Small -- The following approximation may be invalid
                The test is significant at   0.2658
                Cannot reject at alpha = 0.05
```

   b. The time series plot shows evidence of strong trend and some cyclical behavior

Industrial Production
U.S. - Index

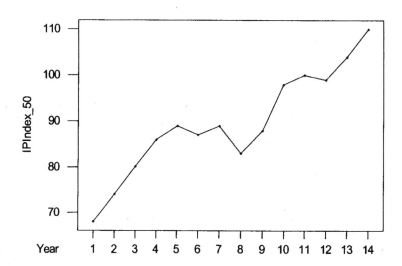

c.

Year	IPIndex	3pt MA
1	68	*
2	74	74.000
3	80	80.000
4	86	85.000
5	89	87.333
6	87	88.333
7	89	86.333
8	83	86.667
9	88	89.667
10	98	95.333
11	100	99.000
12	99	101.000
13	104	104.333
14	110	*

U.S. Index of Industrial Production

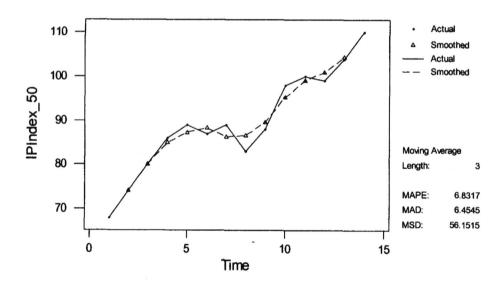

The 3 point centered Moving Average exhibits both trend and cyclical behavior.

17-52   a.

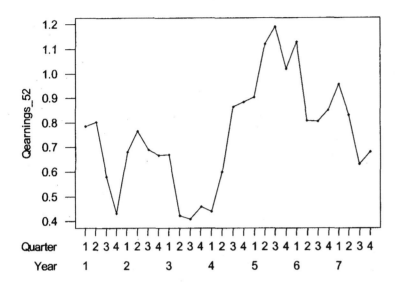

Quarterly earnings per share

No evidence of a strong seasonal pattern

b. Seasonally adjusted data

Period	4 Period MA	$100 \dfrac{X_t}{X_t^*}$	Seas. Factor	Adj. Series
1-1			89.385	.879
2			61.016	1.095
3	.783	110.217	140.489	.614
4	.786	102.770	109.110	.740
2-1	.788	101.744		.897
2	.791	87.730		1.098
3	.763	116.046		.630
4	.704	114.367		.738
3-1	.675	85.730		.648
2	.684	61.887		.693
3	.671	134.800		.644
4	.650	130.873		.780
4-1	.676	63.657		.481
2	.716	57.133		.670
3	.761	147.272		.797
4	.798	120.031		.878
5-1	.813	83.615		.761
2	.806	57.072		.754
3	.801	148.611		.847
4	.809	102.596		.761
6-1	.785	97.549		.857
2	.739	59.540		.721
3	.705	144.784		.726
4	.715	88.112		.577
7-1	.749	92.154		.772
2	.769	78.049		.983
3				.804
4				.623

17-54.

Single Exponential Smoothing

```
Data        Sales_51
Length      24.0000
NMissing    0

Smoothing Constant
Alpha: 0.5

Accuracy Measures
MAPE:     18.1
MAD:     123.6
MSD:   26144.1
```

Row	Time	Sales_51	SMOO11	FITS11	Error
1	1	853	853.000	853.000	0.000
2	2	693	773.000	853.000	-160.000
3	3	715	744.000	773.000	-58.000
4	4	785	764.500	744.000	41.000
5	5	851	807.750	764.500	86.500
6	6	797	802.375	807.750	-10.750
7	7	758	780.188	802.375	-44.375
8	8	593	686.594	780.188	-187.188
9	9	650	668.297	686.594	-36.594
10	10	751	709.648	668.297	82.703
11	11	723	716.324	709.648	13.352
12	12	702	709.162	716.324	-14.324
13	13	991	850.081	709.162	281.838
14	14	1129	989.541	850.081	278.919
15	15	972	980.770	989.541	-17.541
16	16	631	805.885	980.770	-349.770
17	17	538	671.943	805.885	-267.885
18	18	708	689.971	671.943	36.057
19	19	907	798.486	689.971	217.029
20	20	912	855.243	798.486	113.514
21	21	777	816.121	855.243	-78.243
22	22	569	692.561	816.121	-247.121
23	23	473	582.780	692.561	-219.561
24	24	459	520.890	582.780	-123.780

Row	Period	Forecast	Lower	Upper
1	25	520.890	218.107	823.674
2	26	520.890	218.107	823.674
3	27	520.890	218.107	823.674

All forecasts are 520.89

17-56

Winters' multiplicative model

Data   Qearnings_52
Length   28.0000
NMissing   0

Smoothing Constants
Alpha (level):   0.6
Gamma (trend):   0.4
Delta (seasonal): 0.8

Accuracy Measures
MAPE: 20.4021
MAD: 0.1418
MSD: 0.0352

Row	Time	Qearnings_52	Smooth	Predict	Error
1	1	0.786	1.03109	0.89414	-0.108139
2	2	0.802	0.79540	0.63915	0.162850
3	3	0.579	0.70911	0.59635	-0.017353
4	4	0.430	0.56405	0.45150	-0.021498
5	5	0.680	0.47301	0.34607	0.333934
6	6	0.766	0.58562	0.53547	0.230535
7	7	0.690	0.59984	0.60445	0.085554
8	8	0.668	0.62732	0.65137	0.016635
9	9	0.670	0.86630	0.90303	-0.233027
10	10	0.423	0.75907	0.73997	-0.316975
11	11	0.409	0.45957	0.38002	0.028982
12	12	0.460	0.36786	0.30066	0.159336
13	13	0.440	0.46461	0.43066	0.009338
14	14	0.600	0.39216	0.36366	0.236344
15	15	0.863	0.53019	0.55979	0.303210
16	16	0.885	0.75725	0.86176	0.023244
17	17	0.904	0.91593	1.03107	-0.127073
18	18	1.120	0.98002	1.06690	0.053102
19	19	1.190	1.13366	1.23645	-0.046450
20	20	1.020	1.10041	1.18385	-0.163855
21	21	1.130	1.07790	1.12170	0.008299
22	22	0.807	1.22652	1.27637	-0.469374
23	23	0.805	0.99828	0.93527	-0.130266
24	24	0.851	0.75195	0.66924	0.181764
25	25	0.958	0.81395	0.77307	0.184933
26	26	0.830	0.81513	0.81836	0.011639
27	27	0.630	0.92814	0.93491	-0.304908
28	28	0.680	0.74525	0.67944	0.000559

Row	Period	Forecast	Lower	Upper
1	29	0.637574	0.290271	0.98488
2	30	0.494291	0.028335	0.96025
3	31	0.423883	-0.169589	1.01735
4	32	0.417169	-0.308021	1.14236

Chapter 18: Additional Topics in Sampling

18-2 and 18-4   Answers should refer to each of the steps outlined in Figure 18.1 Steps in a sampling study

18-6 and 18-8   Answers should deal with issues such as (a) the identification of the correct population, (b) selection (Nonresponse) bias, (c) response bias

18-10 and 18-12   Within Minitab, go to Calc → Make Patterned Data… in order to generate a simple set of numbers of size 'n'. Then use Calc → Random Data… Sample from Columns… in order to generate a simple random sample of size 'n'.

18-14 $\bar{x} = 9.7, s = 6.2$

$$\hat{\sigma}_{\bar{x}} = \sqrt{\frac{(s)^2}{n} \frac{N-n}{N}} = \sqrt{\frac{(6.2)^2}{50} \frac{139}{189}} = .7519$$

$9.7 \pm 1.96\,(.7519)$ $(8.2262, 11.1738)$

18-16 $\hat{\sigma}_{\bar{x}} = \sqrt{\frac{(5.32)^2}{40} \frac{85}{125}} = .6936$

$7.28 \pm 2.58\,(.6936)$ $(5.4904, 9.0696)$

18-18 $\hat{\sigma}_{\bar{x}}^2 = \frac{(s)^2}{n} \frac{N-n}{N} = \frac{s^2}{n}\left[1 - \frac{n}{N}\right] = s^2\left[\frac{1}{n} - \frac{1}{N}\right]$

18-20 95% confidence interval:

$N\bar{x} - Z_{\alpha/2}N\hat{\sigma}_{\bar{x}} < N\mu < N\bar{x} + Z_{\alpha/2}N\hat{\sigma}_{\bar{x}}$

where $N\bar{x} = (820)(127.43) = 104,492.6$

$$N\hat{\sigma}_{\bar{x}} = \sqrt{\frac{s^2}{n} N(N-n)} = \sqrt{\frac{(43.27)^2}{60} 820(820-60)} = 4,409.8619$$

$104,492.6 \pm 1.96(4409.8619)$

$95,849.2706 < N\mu < 113,135.9294$

18-22 $\bar{x} = 143/35 = 4.0857$

90% confidence interval:

$N\bar{x} - Z_{\alpha/2}N\hat{\sigma}_{\bar{x}} < N\mu < N\bar{x} + Z_{\alpha/2}N\hat{\sigma}_{\bar{x}}$

where $N\bar{x} = (120)(4.0857) = 490.2857$

$$N\hat{\sigma}_{\bar{x}} = \sqrt{\frac{s^2}{n} N(N-n)} = \sqrt{\frac{(3.1)^2}{35} 120(120-35)} = 52.9210$$

$490.2857 \pm 1.645(52.9210)$

$403.2307 < N\mu < 577.3407$

18-24 $p = 56/100 = .56$

$$\sigma_p = \sqrt{[p(1-p)/(n-1)][(N-n)/N]}$$
$$= \sqrt{[(.56)(.44)/99][(420-100)/420]} = .0435$$

90% confidence interval: $.56 \pm 1.645(.0435)$: .4884 up to .6316

18-26 $p = 31/80 = .3875$

$$\sigma_p = \sqrt{[p(1-p)/(n-1)][(N-n)/N]}$$
$$= \sqrt{[(.3875)(.6125)/(79)][(420-80)/420]} = .0493$$

90% confidence interval: $.3875 \pm 1.645(.0493)$: .3064 up to .4686

$128.688 < Np < 196.812$ or between 129 and 197 students intend to take the final.

18-28   a. $\bar{x}_3 = 43.3$, $\hat{\sigma}^2_{\bar{x}_3} = \dfrac{s^2}{n} \dfrac{N-n}{N} = \dfrac{(12.3)^2}{50} \dfrac{208-50}{208} = 2.2984$

90% confidence interval: $43.3 \pm 1.645\sqrt{2.2984}$: 40.806 up to 45.794

b. $\bar{x}_{st} = \dfrac{1}{N}\displaystyle\sum_{j=1}^{k} N_j \bar{x}_j = \dfrac{152(27.6)+127(39.2)+208(43.3)}{487} = 37.3306$

c. $\hat{\sigma}^2_{\bar{x}_1} = \dfrac{(7.1)^2}{40} \dfrac{152-40}{152} = .9286$

$\hat{\sigma}^2_{\bar{x}_2} = \dfrac{(9.9)^2}{40} \dfrac{127-40}{127} = 1.6785$

$\hat{\sigma}^2_{\bar{x}_{st}} = \dfrac{(152)^2(.9286)+(127)^2(1.6785)+(208)^2(2.2984)}{(487)^2} = .6239$

90% confidence interval: $37.3306 \pm 1.645\sqrt{.6239}$: 36.0313 up to 38.6299

95% confidence interval: $37.3306 \pm 1.96\sqrt{.6239}$: 35.7825 up to 38.8787

18-30   a. $\hat{\sigma}^2_{\bar{x}_1} = \dfrac{s^2}{n} \dfrac{N-n}{N} = \dfrac{(1.04)^2}{50} \dfrac{632-50}{632} = .0199$; $3.12 \pm 1.96\sqrt{.0199}$:

2.8435 up to 3.3965

b. $\hat{\sigma}^2_{\bar{x}_2} = \dfrac{(.86)^2}{50} \dfrac{529-50}{529} = .0134$; $3.37 \pm 1.96\sqrt{.0134}$: 3.1431 up to 3.5969

c. $\hat{\sigma}^2_{\bar{x}_{st}} = \dfrac{(632)^2(.0199)+(529)^2(.0134)}{(1161)^2} = .0087$; $\bar{x}_{st} = 3.2339$

$3.2339 \pm 1.96\sqrt{.0087}$: 3.0513 up to 3.4166

18-32 a. $N\overline{x}_{st} = 237(120) + 198(150) + 131(180) = 81720$

b. $\hat{\sigma}^2_{\overline{x}_1} = \dfrac{s^2}{n}\dfrac{N-n}{N} = \dfrac{93^2}{40}\dfrac{120-40}{120} = 144.15$, $\hat{\sigma}^2_{\overline{x}_2} = \dfrac{64^2}{45}\dfrac{150-45}{150} = 63.7156$,

$\hat{\sigma}^2_{\overline{x}_3} = \dfrac{47^2}{50}\dfrac{180-50}{180} = 31.9078$

$\hat{\sigma}^2_{\overline{x}_{st}} = \dfrac{(120)^2(144.15)+(150)^2(63.71556)+(180)^2(31.9078)}{(450)^2} = 22.4354$

95% confidence interval: $181.6(450) \pm 1.96\sqrt{22.4354}\,(450)$:
$77,542.3153 < N\mu < 85,897.6847$

18-34 a. $p_{st} = [100\dfrac{6}{25} + 50\dfrac{14}{25}]/150 = .3467$

b. $\hat{\sigma}^2_{p_1} = \dfrac{p_1(1-p_1)}{n_1-1}\dfrac{N_1-n_1}{N_1} = \dfrac{.24(.76)}{25-1}\dfrac{100-25}{100} = .0057$

$\hat{\sigma}^2_{p_2} = \dfrac{.56(.44)}{25-1}\dfrac{50-25}{50} = .0051$, $\hat{\sigma}^2_{st} = \dfrac{(100)^2(.0057)+(50)^2(.0051)}{(150)^2} = .0031$

90% confidence interval: $.3467 \pm 1.645\sqrt{.0031}$: $.2550$ up to $.4383$

95% confidence interval: $.3467 \pm 1.96\sqrt{.0031}$: $.2375$ up to $.4559$

18-36 a. $n_3 = \dfrac{208}{487}130 = 55.52(56)$

b. $n_3 = \left[\dfrac{208(12.3)}{152(7.1)+127(9.9)+208(12.3)}\right]130 = 67.95(68)$

18-38 a. $n_1 = \dfrac{632}{1161}100 = 54.43(55)$

b. $n_1 = \left[\dfrac{632(1.04)}{632(1.04)+529(.86)}\right]100 = 59.09(60)$

18-40 a. $n_2 = \dfrac{1031}{1395}100 = 73.91(74)$

b. $n_2 = \left[\dfrac{1031(219.9)}{364(87.3)+1031(219.9)}\right]100 = 87.71(88)$

18-42 How large n?

$n = \dfrac{N\sigma^2}{(N-1)\sigma_{\overline{x}}^2 + \sigma^2} = \dfrac{(400)(10,000)^2}{(399)(1215.8055)^2 + (10,000)^2} = 57.988$,

take 58 observations

18-44 $\sigma_p = \dfrac{.04}{1.645} = .0243$

$n = \dfrac{417(.25)}{416(.0243)^2 + .25} = 210.33(211)$

18-46 $\sigma_{\bar{x}} = \dfrac{500}{1.96} = 255.1020$

$\sum N_j \sigma^2{}_j = 1150(4000)^2 + 2120(6000)^2 + 930(800000)^2 = 15424 \times 10^7$

$n = \dfrac{15424 \times 10^7}{4200(255.1020)^2 + 15424 \times 10^7 / 4200} = 497.47(498)$

$\sum N_j \sigma_j = 1150(4000) + 2120(6000) + 930(8000) = 24760000$

$n = \dfrac{(24760000)^2 / 4200}{4200(255.1020)^2 + 15424 \times 10^7 / 4200} = 470.78(471)$

18-48   a. $\bar{x}_c = \dfrac{69(83) + 75(64) + \cdots + 71(98)}{497} = 91.6761$

b.

$\hat{\sigma}^2_{\bar{x}_c} = \dfrac{(52-8)}{52(8)(61.125)^2} \dfrac{(69)^2(83 - 91.67605634)^2 + \cdots + (71)^2(98 - 91.67605634)^2}{8-1}$

$= 66.409$

99% confidence interval: $91.6761 \pm 2.58 \sqrt{66.4090}$

70.6920 up to 112.6602

18-50   a. $p_c = \dfrac{24 + \cdots + 34}{497} = .4507$

b. $\hat{\sigma}^2{}_{p_c} = \dfrac{52-8}{52(8)(62.125)^2} \dfrac{(69)^2 \left(\dfrac{24}{69} - .4507 \right)^2 + \cdots + (71)^2 \left(\dfrac{34}{71} - .4507 \right)^2}{8-1} = .0013$

95% confidence interval: $.4507 \pm 1.96 \sqrt{.0013}$: .38 up to .5214

18-52 $\sigma_{\bar{x}} = \dfrac{5000}{1.645} = 3039.5$

$n = \dfrac{720(37600)^2}{719(3039)^2 + (37600)^2} = 126.34(127)$

Additional sample observations needed is 127-20 = 107

18-54 $\sigma_{\bar{x}} = \dfrac{20}{1.96} = 10.2$

$n = \dfrac{(100(105) + 180(162) + 200(183))^2 / 480}{480(10.2)^2 + (100(105)^2 + 180(162)^2 + 200(183)^2) / 480} = 159.35(160)$

Additional sample observations needed: $160 - 30 = 130$

18-56   Discussion question – various answers

18-58   a. $\bar{x} = \dfrac{747}{10} = 74.7$

$s = 11.44$

$\hat{\sigma}^2_{\bar{x}} = \dfrac{(11.44)^2}{10} \dfrac{90 - 10}{90} = 11.633$

90% confidence interval: $74.7 \pm 1.645 \sqrt{11.633}$: 69.089 up to 80.311

b. The interval would be wider; the z-score would increase to 1.96

18-60 a. $p = \dfrac{38}{61} = .623$

$\hat{\sigma}^2_{p} = \dfrac{.623(.377)}{61} \dfrac{100 - 61}{100} = .0015$

90% confidence interval: $.623 \pm 1.645 \sqrt{.0015}$: .559 up to .687

b.   If the sample information is not randomly selected, the resulting conclusions may be biased

18-62 a. $\bar{x}_{st} = 11.5845$

$\hat{\sigma}^2_{\bar{x}_1} = .7321$

$\hat{\sigma}^2_{\bar{x}_2} = 1.9053$

$\hat{\sigma}^2_{\bar{x}_3} = 1.7508$

$\hat{\sigma}^2_{\bar{x}_{st}} = \dfrac{(352)^2(.7321) + (287)^2(1.9053) + (331)^2(1.7508)}{(970)^2} = .4671$

99% confidence interval for managers in subdivision 1:

$9.2 \pm 2.575 \sqrt{.7321}$: 6.997 up to 11.403

b.   99% confidence interval for all managers:

$11.5845 \pm 2.575 \sqrt{.4671}$: 9.8247 up to 13.3444

18-64 $p_1 = \dfrac{9}{20} = .45, \; p_2 = \dfrac{15}{20} = .75$

$p_{st} = .63, \; \hat{\sigma}^2_{p_1} = \dfrac{p_1(1-p_1)}{n_1 - 1} \dfrac{N_1 - n_1}{N_1} = \dfrac{.45(.55)}{20 - 1} \dfrac{120 - 20}{120} = .0109$

$\hat{\sigma}^2_{p_2} = \dfrac{p_1(1-p_1)}{n_1 - 1} \dfrac{N_1 - n_1}{N_1} = \dfrac{.75(.25)}{20 - 1} \dfrac{180 - 20}{180} = .0088$

$\hat{\sigma}^2_{st} = \dfrac{(120)^2(.0109) + (180)^2(.0088)}{(300)^2} = .0049$

90% confidence interval is:

$.63 \pm 1.645\sqrt{.0049}$ or 0.5147 up to 0.7453

18-66   a. $n_1 = \dfrac{120}{300} 40 = 16$

b. $n_1 = \left[\dfrac{120(.98)}{120(.98) + 180(.56)} \right] 40 = 21.54(22)$

18-68 $\sigma_{\bar{x}} = \dfrac{2000}{1.645} = 1215.8$

$n = \dfrac{328(12000)^2}{327(1215.8)^2 + (12000)^2} = 75.28(76)$

18-70   a. $\overline{X}_C = 62.7607; \;$ and $\hat{\sigma}^2_C = 23.1736$

95% confidence interval: $62.7607 \pm 1.96\sqrt{23.1736}$: 53.3255 up to 72.1959

b. $p_c = .55, \quad \hat{\sigma}^2_c = .0038$

95% confidence interval: $.55 \pm 1.96\sqrt{.0038}$: .4292 up to .6708

Chapter 19: Statistical Decision Theory

19-2   D is dominated by C. Therefore, D is inadmissible.

19-4   a. Note – D is dominated by C. Hence D is inadmissible
       Maximin criterion would select production process C:

Actions	States of Nature			
Prod. Process	Low Demand	Moderate Demand	High Demand	Min Payoff
A	100,000	350,000	900,000	100,000
B	150,000	400,000	700,000	150,000
C	250,000	400,000	600,000	250,000

b. Minimax regret criterion would select production process A:

Actions	States of Nature			
Prod. Process	Low Demand	Moderate Demand	High Demand	Max Regret
A	150,000	50,000	0	150,000
B	100,000	0	200,000	200,000
C	0	0	300,000	300,000

19-6

Actions	States of Nature			
Prod. Process	Low Demand	Moderate Demand	High Demand	Min Payoff
A	70,000	120,000	200,000	70,000
B	80,000	120,000	180,000	80,000
C	100,000	125,000	160,000	100,000
D*	100,000	120,000	150,000	Inadmissible
E	60,000	115,000	220,000	60,000

*inadmissible
Therefore, production process C would be chosen using the Maximin Criterion

Actions	Regrets or Opportunity Loss Table			
Prod. Process	Low Demand	Moderate Demand	High Demand	Max Regret
A	30,000	5,000	20,000	30,000
B	20,000	5,000	40,000	40,000
C	0	0	60,000	60,000
D*	0	5,000	70,000	Inadmissible
E	40,000	10,000	0	40,000

*inadmissible

Therefore, production process A would be chosen using the Minimax Regret Criterion

19-8 Assume a situation with two states of nature and two actions. Let both actions be admissible. The payoff Matrix is:

Action	S1	S2
A1	M_{11}	M_{12}
A2	M_{21}	M_{22}

Then action A1 will be chosen by both the Maximin and the Minimax Regret Criteria if for: $M_{11} > M_{21}$ and $M_{12} < M_{22}$ and $(M_{11} - M_{21}) > (M_{22} - M_{12})$

19-10 a. Payoff table for students' decision-making problem

Actions	Offered Better Position	Not Offered Better Position
Interview	4500	-500
Don't Interview	0	0

b. EMV(Interview) = .05(4500) + .95(-500) = -250
EMV(Don't Interview) = 0
Therefore, the optimal action: Don't Interview

19-12 a. EMV(Certificate of Deposit) = 1200
EMV(Low risk stock fund) = .2(4300) + .5(1200) + .3(-600) = 1280
EMV(High risk stock fund) = .2(6600) + .5(800) + .3(-1500) = 1270
Therefore, the optimal action: Low risk stock fund

b. Decision tree

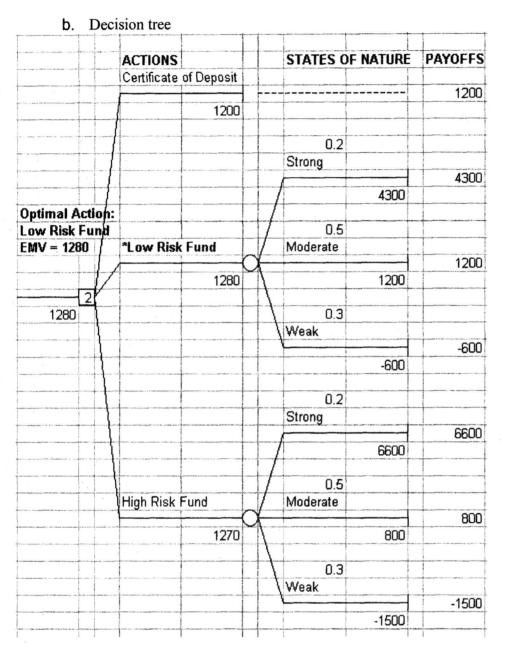

ACTIONS

Certificate of Deposit

1200

1200

0.2
Strong

4300

4300

Optimal Action:
Low Risk Fund
EMV = 1280

0.5
Moderate

*Low Risk Fund

1280

1200

2

1280

1200

0.3
Weak

-600

-600

0.2
Strong

6600

6600

0.5
Moderate

High Risk Fund

800

1270

800

0.3
Weak

-1500

-1500

STATES OF NATURE   PAYOFFS

19-14 a. i) false ii) true iii) true
     b. No

19-16 a. EMV(New) = .4(130,000) + .4(60,000) + .2(-10,000) ≈ 74,000
EMV(Old) = .4(30,000) + .4(70,000) + .2(90,000) = 58,000
Therefore, the optimal action: New center
b. Decision tree

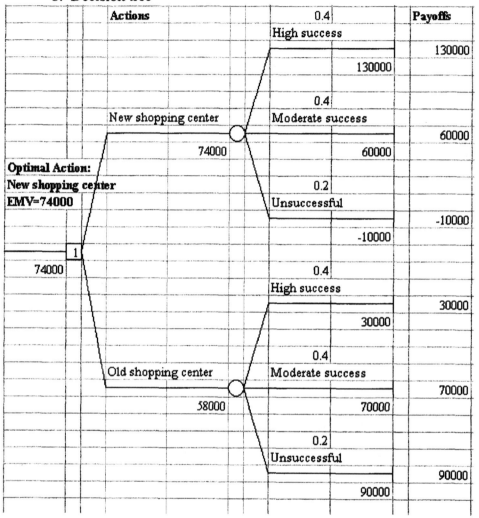

19-18 a. EMV(A) = 30,000 + 350,000p + 900,000(.7 – p) = 660,000 – 550,000p
EMV(B) = 45,000 + 400,000p + 700,000(.7 – p) = 535,000 – 300,000p
EMV(C) = 75,000 + 400,000p + 600,000(.7 – p) = 495,000 – 200,000p
EMV(D) = 75,000 + 400,000p + 550,000(.7 – p) = 460,000 – 150,000p
EMV(A) = 660 – 550p > 535 – 300p = EMV(B) when p < .5
EMV(A) = 660 – 550p > 495 –200p = EMV(C) when p < .471
EMV(A) = 660 – 550p > 460 – 150p = EMVA(D) when p < .5
For p < .471, the EMV criterion chooses action A

b. EMV(A) = 170,000 + .3a > 415,000 = EMV(B) > EMV(C) > EMV(D) when a
> 816,667

19-20 a. EMV(check) = .8(20,000 – 1,000) + .2(20,000 – 1,000 – 2,000) = 18,600

EMV(not check) = .8(20,000) + .2(12,000) = 18,400

Therefore, the optimal action: Check the process

b. Decision tree

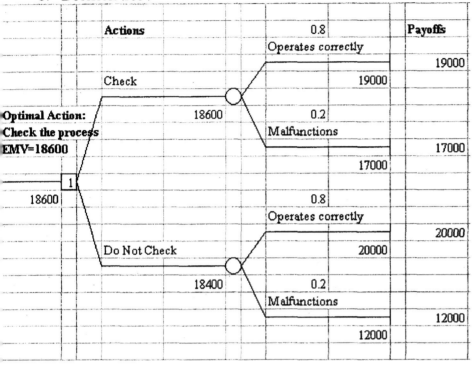

b. EMV(check) = 19,000p + 17,000(1 – p) > 20,000p + 12,000(1 – p) when p <
5/6

19-22 a. payoff table for a car rental agency

Extra Ordering	6	7	8	9	10
0	0	-10	-20	-30	-40
1	-20	20	10	0	-10
2	-40	0	40	30	20
3	-60	-20	20	60	50
4	-80	-40	0	40	80

b. Per the EMV criterion, the optimal action is to order 2 extra cars:

Extra Orders	6	7	8	9	10	EMV
0	0(.1)	-10(.3)	-20(.3)	-30(.2)	-40(.1)	-19
1	-20(.1)	20(.3)	10(.3)	0(.2)	-10(.1)	6
2	-40(.1)	0(.3)	40(.3)	30(.2)	20(.1)	16
3	-60(.1)	-20(.3)	20(.3)	60(.2)	50(.1)	11
4	-80(.1)	-40(.3)	0(.3)	40(.2)	80(.1)	-4

19-24 a. Action A1 is taken if $M_{11}p + M_{12}(1 - p) > M_{21}p + (1 - p)M_{22}$ or $p(M_{11} - M_{21}) > (1 - p)(M_{22} - M_{12})$

b. Action A1 inadmissible implies that A1 will be chosen only if $p > 1$. In short, for part a. to be true, both payoffs of A1 cannot be less than the corresponding payoffs of A2.

19-26 a. Optimal action per the EMV criterion is action A (see answer to 19-13)

b. $P(L \mid P) = \dfrac{(.5)(.3)}{(.5)(.3)+(.3)(.4)+(.1)(.3)} = \dfrac{.15}{.3} = .5$

$P(M \mid P) = \dfrac{(.4)(.3)}{(.5)(.3)+(.3)(.4)+(.1)(.3)} = \dfrac{.12}{.3} = .4$

$P(H \mid P) = \dfrac{(.1)(.3)}{(.5)(.3)+(.3)(.4)+(.1)(.3)} = \dfrac{.03}{.3} = .1$

c. EMV(A) = .5(100,000)+.4(350,000)+.1(900,000) = 280,000
EMV(B) = .5(150,000)+.4(400,000)+.1(700,000) = 305,000
EMV(C) = .5(250,000)+.4(400,000)+.1(600,000) = 345,000
Therefore, the optimal action: C

d. $P(L \mid F) = \dfrac{(.3)(.3)}{(.3)(.3)+(.4)(.4)+(.2)(.3)} = \dfrac{.09}{.31} = .2903$

$P(M \mid F) = \dfrac{(.4)(.4)}{(.3)(.3)+(.4)(.4)+(.2)(.3)} = \dfrac{.16}{.31} = .5161$

$P(H \mid F) = \dfrac{(.2)(.3)}{(.3)(.3)+(.4)(.4)+(.2)(.3)} = \dfrac{.06}{.31} = .1935$

e. EMV(A) = .2903(100,000)+.5161(350,000)+.1935 (900,000) = 383,815
EMV(B) = .2903(150,000)+.5161(400,000)+.1935(700,000) = 385,435
EMV(C) = .2903(250,000)+.5161(400,000)+.1935(600,000) = 395,115
Therefore, the optimal action: C

f. $P(L \mid G) = \dfrac{(.2)(.3)}{(.2)(.3)+(.3)(.4)+(.7)(.3)} = \dfrac{.06}{.39} = .1538$

$P(M \mid G) = \dfrac{(.3)(.4)}{(.2)(.3)+(.3)(.4)+(.7)(.3)} = \dfrac{.12}{.39} = .3077$

$P(H \mid G) = \dfrac{(.7)(.3)}{(.2)(.3)+(.3)(.4)+(.7)(.3)} = \dfrac{.21}{.39} = .5385$

g. EMV(A) = .1538(100,000)+.3077(350,000)+.5385(900,000) = 607,692
EMV(B) = .1538(150,000)+.3077(400,000)+.5385(700,000) = 523,077
EMV(C) = .1538(250,000)+.3077(400,000)+.5385(600,000) = 484,615
Therefore, the optimal action: A

19-28 a. $P(E \mid P) = \dfrac{(.8)(.6)}{(.8)(.6)+(.1)(.4)} = \dfrac{.48}{.52} = .9231$

P(not E|P) = 1 – P(E|P) = 1 - .9231 = .0769

b. EMV(S) = .9231(50,000)+.0769(50,000) = 50,000
EMV(R) = .9231(125,000)+.0769(-10,000) = 114,615
Therefore, optimal action: retain

c. $P(E|N) = \dfrac{(.2)(.6)}{(.2)(.6)+(.9)(.4)} = \dfrac{.12}{.48} = .25$, P(not E|N) = .75

d. EMV(S) = .25(50,000)+.75(50,000) = 50,000
EMV(R) = .25(125,000)+.75(-10,000) = 23,750
Therefore, optimal action: sell

19-30 a. P(2 | 10%) = .01, P(1 | 10%) = .18, P(0 | 10%) = .81
b. P(2 | 30%) = .09, P(1 | 30%) = .42, P(0 | 30%) = .49
c. Probability of the states of 10% defective and 30% defective given:

# defective	10% defect	30% defect
2 defective	.308	.692
1 defective	.632	.368
0 defective	.869	.131

EMV of actions	check	Do not check
2 defective	17,616*	14,464
1 defective	18,264*	17,056
0 defective	18,737	18,952*

*optimal action given the circumstance

19-32 a. Perfect information is defined as the case where the decision maker is able to gain information to tell with certainty which state will occur
b. The optimal action: Low risk stock fund (see question 19-12)
EVPI = .2(6600 – 4300) + .5(0) + .3(1200 – (-600)) = 1000

19-34 Given that the optimal action is: New center
EVPI = .4(0) + .4(70,000 – 60,000) + .2(90,000 – (-10,000)) = 24,000

19-36 The expected value of sample information is $\sum_{i=1}^{M} P(A_i)V_i$ where

$P(A_i) = \sum_{j=1}^{H} P(A_i \mid s_j)$. For perfect information,

$P(A_i \mid s_j) = 0 \ for \ i \neq j \ and \ P(A_i \mid s_j) = 1 \ for \ i = j, thus \ P(A_i) = P(s_i)$

19-38 VSI = .3(345,000 – 280,000) + .31(395115 – 383815) + .39(0) = 23003

19-40 Given that the optimal action: retain the patent (see question 19-28)
EVSI = .42(0) + .52(50,000 – 23,750) = 13,650

19-42 a. EVSI = .11(-600 – (-910)) + .89(0) ≈ 34.1

b. EVSI = .013(-600 – (-1540)) + .194(-600 – (-825)) + .793(0) = 55.87

c. The difference = 21.77

d. None

e. 24.75

19-44 a.

Payoff	-10000	30000	60000	70000	90000	13000
Utility	0	35	60	70	85	100

b. EU(New) = .4(100) + .4(60) + .2(0) = 64
EU(Old) = .4(35) + .4(70) + .2(85) = 59
Therefore, the optimal action: New center

19-46   94000p – 16000(1-p) = 0 ➔ p = 16 / 110

Payoff	-160000	0	94000
Utility	0	160 / 110	100

$$\text{Slope(-16000,0)} = \frac{160/110}{16000} = .00009$$

$$\text{Slope(0,94000)} = \frac{100 - 160/110}{94000} = .00105$$

Therefore, the contractor has a preference for risk

19-48 a. P(S1) = .3(.6) = .18, P(S2) = .42, P(S3) = .12, P(S4) = .28
    b. EMV(A1) = 460, EMV(A2) = 330, EMV(A3) = 0, EMV(A4) = 510
        Therefore, the optimal action: A4
    c. Draw the decision tree

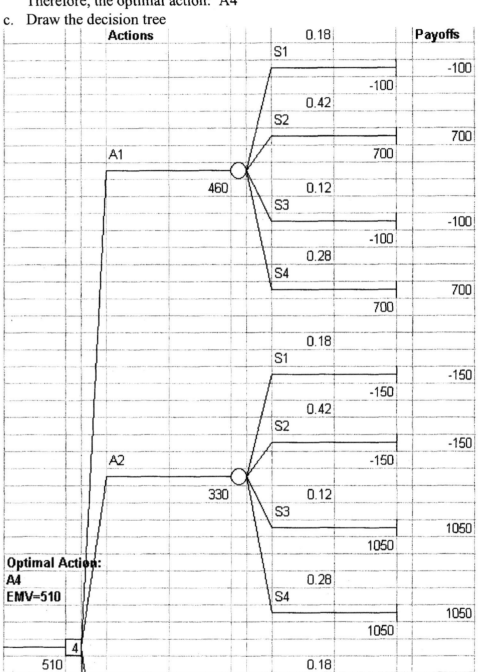

(Continued on next page)

TreePlan (Continued for 19-48):

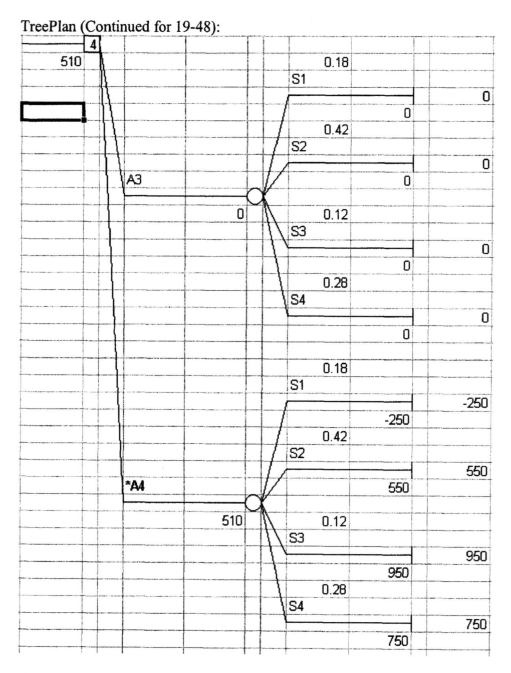

d.   EVPI = .18(250) + .42(150) + .12(100) + .28(300) = 204
e.   79